Spies in the Empire

Other titles of interest:

Lee Jackson *A Dictionary of Victorian London* (2006)
Michael Diamond *Lesser Breeds* (2006)
Thomas Holmes *London's Underworld* (2005)
Blanchard Jerrold *London: A Pilgrimage* (2005)
Ian St John *Disraeli and the Art of Victorian Politics* (2005)
Michael Diamond *Victorian Sensation* (2004)

Spies in the Empire

Victorian Military Intelligence

Stephen Wade

ANTHEM PRESS

LONDON · NEW YORK · DELHI

Anthem Press
An imprint of Wimbledon Publishing Company
www.anthempress.com

This edition first published in UK and USA 2007
by ANTHEM PRESS
75-76 Blackfriars Road, London SE1 8HA, UK
or PO Box 9779, London SW19 7ZG, UK
and
244 Madison Ave. #116, New York, NY 10016, USA

British Library Cataloguing in Publication Data
A Catalogue record for this book is available from the British Library.

Library of Congress Cataloguing in Publication Data
Wade, Stephen, 1948 –
Spies in the Empire: Victorian Military Intelligence / Stephen Wade.
p. cm. includes bibliographical references.
ISBN 978-1-84331-262-8 (Pbk)
1. Military Intelligence - Great Britain - History - 19th Century.
2. Intelligence Service - Great Britain - History - 19th Century.
I. Title. II. Title: Victorian Military Intelligence.
UB251.G7W34 2007
355.3'432094109034 - dc22
2007026386

ISBN-10: 1 84331 262 X (Pbk)
ISBN-13: 978 1 84331 262 8 (Pbk)

1 3 5 7 9 10 8 6 4 2

Printed in the EU

Contents

Notes on Illustrations

1. Frontispiece of *Narrative of a Journey to Khiva, Moscow and St. Petersburg* by Captain James Abbott. One of the very first narrative texts of the Great Game.
2. Summud Khaun – Abott's steward. He was valuable as a linguist and guide on the Khiva expedition.
3. Captain Thomas Montgomerie, who raised the pundit corps.
4. Nain Singh – a principal pundit who worked with Montgomerie.
5. General James Walker, Surveyor-General of India.
6. William Howard Russell of *The Times*. His despatches from the Crimea are classics of war reportage.
7. Lord Raglan. Criticised for orders leading to the 'Charge of the Light Brigade.'
8. The Sobraon Barracks, Lincoln: a survival to remind England of one of the most significant battles of the First Sikh War of 1845-6.
9. The Return of the Spies. In Russell's diary of his Indian journey, this picture shows the military native spies back at camp, working with the Quartermaster General.
10. From the same memoirs, 'Good news in dispatches' shows General Mansfield and Lord Clyde studying intelligence notes.
11. The Dalhousie Barrack, Fort William, Calcutta.
12. Sir Garnet Wolseley. Won fame in the Ashanti War of 1873-4.
13. Picture of Lord Chelmsford from *The Illustrated London News,* 1879. At the time, news of the disaster of Isandlhwana had not reached the press.
14. Gonville Bromhead, one of the heroes of Rorke's Drift.
15. Wolseley in *Punch* just before Tel-El-Kebir. Here he is 'The Modern Caesar'.
16. Gordon as sketched in his journals in the first edition.
17. Gordon in his robes when he acquired the name 'Chinese Gordon'.
18. Rex Wingate – Kitchener's Chief of Intelligence.
19. Rudolf Slatin – intelligence second-in-command in Egypt – in chains being shown Gordon's head.
20. Lord Kitchener on 'Democrat' in *Vanity Fair* magazine, 1910.
21. Kitchener saves Conder's life in Palestine, from the first biography of the master tactician.
22. The Khoord Khyber, Afghanistan, from *The Illustrated London News* 1879.
23. G W Steevens, spy, military theorist and journalist.
24. Sir William Robertson at the time of the Great War.
25. Robertson at the Army Manoeuvres, 1913.
26. Robertson at the time he worked in the new Intelligence Branch of 1902.
27. 'The Death of two Japanese Spies', a sensational story from *The British Workman* magazine 1907.
28. Rufus Isaacs, later Lord Chief Justice, involved in spy trials.
29. Mata Hari, spy destined to be shot.
30. Gustav Steinhauer, the Kaiser's Master Spy, from his memoirs.
31. Dublin Castle – British stronghold and Jenkinson's base against the Fenians.

Acknowledgements

I am indebted to the Royal Geographical Society for the permissions to reproduce images on the pundits. Also, I am thankful to the National Portrait Gallery for the images illustrated and described in the text.

Preface

Since the scope of the present history is quite vast, the task of collating massive amounts of information from several conflicts that broke out in the nineteenth century has been an enormous one. I have needed help in all kinds of areas, as I can only be an enthusiast in an area in which specialists have done groundbreaking work.

Writing this book proved to reinforce my view prior to the undertaking that the whole subject of the history of military intelligence in all its forms is one that defies definition, but I have at least tried to impose some patterns on the varied and often chaotic growth of the profession. Of course, plenty of spies have stood in front of the firing squads long before they had time to write any memoirs; other people, often from within the more administration-based sources, have had plenty to write. Others did write but from the historian's point of view, they wrote in too piecemeal a fashion. Happily for me and for others who will approach this elusive subject, we have the memoirs of Field Marshall Sir William Robertson, *From Private to Field-Marshall*, published in 1921. 'Wully' Robertson did indeed want to recall his life in the Intelligence Branch, and in detail.

There have had to be omissions – the most notable is the subject of maritime intelligence; though I have touched on this, I have introduced the topic albeit marginally in the penultimate chapter.

There are also the wider social historical dimensions of espionage: this aspect becomes apparent only when something impinges on the national consciousness and the repercussions are usually dire and often terrifying. Such would be the paranoia about German 'spies' in the Great War and for years before the actual outbreak of that war in Europe. Related to this is the cultural mediation of the spy – in Conan Doyle's *Sherlock Holmes*, it was Holmes who tackled the spies; William Le Queux transformed spies into attractive heroes, and Joseph Conrad in *The Secret Agent* (1907) transformed the entire business of Anarchists quite disturbing in the tranquil world of the new commuters who read their improving periodicals on the bus into the city.

I am grateful to Steve Watham who gave a great deal of his time and knowledge to the enterprise. Various librarians were also very helpful, and the staff at picture libraries all helped me find what I wanted to add to the narrative. Particularly useful was the special collection from private libraries at the University of Hull and some other individual contacts who delved into some byways of military history for me.

My editor, Paolo Cabrelli, has to be thanked, along with other people whose learned specialisms in related areas helped me to a great extent. Although there are far too many names that can be mentioned in this context, but everyone working in this discipline owes a debt to Christopher Andrew and Richard Deacon, whose books ventured into this notoriously difficult aspect of Victorian history. I genuinely appreciate the help extended to me by Mike Pollard while working with the research materials for the final chapter. I am also thankful to Luigi di Dio for actively participating in searching out picture permissions. Laura Carter did some of the line drawings from contemporary and very obscure sources.

I have tried to bring together much disparate information, in an effort to integrate the stories of numerous people involved in all the expressions of that activity we loosely call 'spying'. I am aware that terminology also has to be flexible to a certain extent. For instance, one of my illustrations is of a look out point at Courbevoie. In other words it implies reconnaissance; on the other hand, the question which often loomed at large was where do we place Baden-Powell and the distinctive separate conceptions of what he called 'scouting'? Such shifting definitions may have been problematical, but in the end I chose to amalgamate all the words referring to activities that may be understood within the spectrum of 'military intelligence'.

Finally, the timescale. Actually, my chapters go beyond Queen Victoria's death in 1901 and I conclude with the situation with regard to German spy-scares on the domestic front in the years up to and including the Great War. These developments, along with the establishment of MI5, seemed to create a natural point of conclusion, before the complexities of the twentieth century and the revolutions in espionage that inevitably took place. This implies that I am particularly interested in the work undertaken in the era in which a gentleman was not entirely comfortable with the term 'spy', and those officers who did take the role seriously did so with a gradually receding code of honour. In some ways, the Boer War of 1899–1902 put paid to all that.

1

Introduction

The scope of this book is immense, covering the individual adventurers of the 1840s who ventured into the mountains and borders of northern India, to the life and achievements of Vernon Kell and the beginnings of MI5. But the project has been assisted by the excellent work done on the Great Game - the intelligence interplay between Russia and Britain throughout the greater part of the nineteenth century - notably by the doyen of that subject, Peter Hopkirk. Nevertheless, there is much more to the subject than the Great Game.

In the history of military intelligence, 80 years embraces several major areas of interest and these provide the basis of the following chapters:

(1) The gradual emergence of the intelligence arm of the military structure of the Empire.
(2) The influential individuals who played a major role in the professionalization of intelligence.
(3) The failure of intelligence in several important campaigns, and the lessons learned.
(4) Foreign policy and the men who brought about reforms.

Underlying all this, however, there is the undeniable hue of romance colouring the subject. In fact, the old male romance of the late Victorian novelists William Le Queux, Rider Haggard and Conan Doyle have all played their part in this. But at the centre of the arena is the mix of the romance of 'spying' and the straightforward military duties we would term 'intelligence'. This means that the word *espionage* in the context of the Victorian imperial quest covers several elements, all a part of the scene. The sources of military information available during this period include activities as diverse as map-making and surveying; amateur scholars supplying cultural information; linguists and travellers who learned about the enemy, though in a desultory manner; personnel within the army, for a long period the ranks of the engineers; political officers on missions and most fundamental of all, native ranks and civilians such as the 'pundits' employed by the administrators of the Raj.

In practical terms it meant that military intelligence for this 70 years was diverse, piecemeal, chaotic and massively amateur. What was needed was some method of classification and systematic implementation of knowledge. What happened until the last few decades of the century was very much a pragmatic process; ad hoc information was gained in any way possible. Of course, there were several reasons for this slow and haphazard scale of change: the sheer vastness of the Empire – the pink on the map – constituted the main feature. In a world map included in a geography textbook published in 1908, the Empire's pink stands out – bold and prominent: the Dominion of Canada, British Guiana, nine African possessions, India, Australasia and another 40 islands or smaller places. The central geographical location of the following history – India – is explained in this way:

Our Indian Empire
Our Indian empire comprises the central and by far the most important of the three great peninsulas of Southern Asia, together with large

territories on the eastern side of the Bay of Bengal. The total area of these vast dominions, most of which are under direct British rule, and the rest subject to British control, is upwards of 1, 800, 000 square miles, or more than thirty times as large as England and Wales, while the population is (according to the Census of 1901) 294, 417, 000.[1]

From the early years of Victoria's reign there had been a flowering of all manner of academic disciplines with the intention of listing, filing and describing the nature of the diverse range of peoples within this Empire. It was amateur, random and passionate. Very little in its aims had any link whatsoever with military intelligence. But as the century wore on, the high command gradually realized the usefulness of this vast store of knowledge.

Knowledge of language, culture and history was one thing worth attention, but at the basis of the whole enterprise – primarily before the arguably major turning point of the Crimean War – was seldom related to direct information about the opposing armies in a war. In many ways, Britain learned the value of such activities from the Prussians and the French. It seems incredible to note now that the systems of Napoleon in this respect were hardly noticed or studied. Napoleon's method was to have a string of local and regional agents who, in turn, paid a set sum of money to their own agents. In that way, the obvious advantages of having native speakers of the language of the enemy was gained, and also local knowledge of topography, customs and political affairs was already in place to be exploited when the time came. As Edward Whitcomb has explained in the case of Napoleon's information on Russia: 'Bignon was appointed in December 1810 to obtain information on Russia. It was not until August 1811 that he was given 3, 000 francs per month for espionage, and not until December 1811 that he was specifically instructed to establish a hierarchy or cell system'.[2] In other words, Napoleon was well aware of the need to make the diplomatic sources not only more reliable but better organized.

Yet, in spite of the general history involved, the preliminary considerations necessary for this historical survey must begin with the impact of the subject on the individual imagination. In an interview with *The Times* in April 2006, Peter Hopkirk stressed the importance of Rudyard Kipling's novel, *Kim* in this respect. *Kim* was published in 1901, when the Great Mutiny of 1857 was still in the memory but far enough to be reconsidered. Hopkirk explains the influence of the book in this way: 'I used to dream of being sent on some secret mission by Kim's spymaster, Colonel Creighton... Unfortunately, by the time I was old enough the British had left India'. It is the imaginative pull of the Great Game that persists. The history around it also persists, as Hopkirk said in the same interview: 'It's extraordinary to see how history is repeating itself... Some of the players are different, but the Game goes on. Perhaps my books should be read as cautionary tales. Had the Soviet Union learned from the lessons of history, it would never have invaded Afghanistan'.[3]

The mention of Russia is what completes the picture for the historian of the Victorian Great Game. The principal area of interest in this history has to be the three-edged combat zone of Russia, Afghanistan and British India, but as in the case of all wars, other states and communities were drawn in. It is almost impossible now to imagine the sheer courage and sense of adventure in a political officer such as Captain James Abbott, a man who travelled from Herat to Moscow. His account of this journey, published in 1842, is one of the foundation texts of the military intelligence of that century. However, there is more to the origins of the subject in the Indian subcontinent than just individuals, such as the administrators, their family members and political officers – all these will be taken into account in the main section of this book.

The individual imagination – powerful in the case of the lone adventurers – was always subject to the distortions of media representation later on, and so we have an inheritance of falsification, a view of the spying within the Raj that has generated myths and legends such as we find in the character and career of Sir Richard Burton. His image, as depicted in the brooding melancholic photograph of him in a long cape – taken around 1855 – exemplifies this need to see the political officers, as especially Byronic figures, somehow doomed to be loners in both a physical and a spiritual wilderness. Burton and his personal qualities will recur throughout this history, not only in himself but in his nature as a template for that figure of mystery and intrigue. His biographer, Byron Farwell, crystallizes this strange fusion of the eccentric and the rigidly professional trait in his personality: 'He learned "mantih", or eastern logic, in order to train his mind to think as an oriental. He mixed with *Jat* camel-men, studying their language and way of life'. But he was capable of another cast of mind entirely: 'Always fascinated by gold, he took up alchemy and tried his hand at producing gold from baser metals'.[4]

There is also a theoretical dimension to this enquiry. The vastly influential classic work – *On War* by Carl von Clausewitz – was published in 1830, just before his death. But the influence came much later; as Louise Wilmott has noted:

> For some thirty years after his death in 1831, his ideas made little impact. More popular with the general staffs of European armies were contemporaries like Jomini who emphasised formal manoeuvres and rules of conduct, and who forsook the ambiguity and complexity which Clausewitz insisted were an integral part of war. This situation only began to change in the 1860s and 1870s.[5]

The reasons why military theory of an adventurous and intellectual turn did not have an impact on the British Army are not hard to find. Even after the triumphs of the war against Napoleon, little changed in the organization of the structural nature of the army. In many ways, the concise statements made by Clausewitz on 'information' were exactly what the first intelligence groups were to find out and understand: 'A Great part of information obtained in war is contradictory, a still greater part is false, and by far the greatest part is of a doubtful character'.[6]

Basically, at the beginning of the period covered here, military intelligence meant unearthing information by the traditional means: scouts, basic geography, questioning locals and most of all, making sure that there were capable linguists in the regiment. At the heart of the whole enterprise was the officer class, and to understand the achievements of the political officers, it is essential to comprehend the means by which the officer class communicated, bonded and nurtured that special *esprit de corps* that would pay dividends in battles. One interesting method of gaining an insight into this mindset is to look at the publications of the regiments. For instance, *The Journal of the Household Brigade* of 1871 provides something profoundly important about the army's sense of identity at the time of the Franco-Prussian War in Europe. The Journal covers sports reports, lists of brigade masters of hounds, 'the chase and the turf', steeplechasing, pigeon-shooting, theatricals, yachting, balls and concerts. Nothing could exemplify the spawning-ground of the political officer as well as this: notice that the list of activities represented the enormous gap of time that had to be filled when an officer went on leave, away from the front line of active service. But it was training in disguise: the sport and other personal developmental activities helped in forming an attitude. After having equipped himself with all the habits of endurance, hard work, teamwork and invention, in India he would go shooting for weeks, and in between the sport there was 'information' and of course, improvement of spoken Hindi, perhaps.

These officers were to cluster around the more charismatic figures in the Empire, men such as John Nicholson - hero of the Mutiny - and Henry Lawrence, who had a group of protégés for whom he had a special regard and whose careers he has nurtured. Charles Allen had defined this 'band of brothers' very clearly:

Such close friendships, between lonely men who lived many miles from each other, finding open expression only in the event of the death of one of their company, were very much the order of the day. This was a brotherhood of young men who shared a vocation: they saw themselves very much as a band of brothers, Paladins at the court of their master and mentor, Henry Lawrence.[7]

It is no accident that the date of 1873 is an important one for the history of military intelligence. As Sir George Aston wrote in his memoirs: 'After 1870 the whole of Europe sat at the feet of the Germans as the most efficient soldiers in the world'. A whole tranche of army reforms in Britain followed that key date, and as Aston notes:

Once started, the idea that the British army was maintained, partly at all events, for waging war began to take root, with the obvious corollary that the more that it knew about foreign armies the better. The result was the establishment of an Intelligence Branch (under the adjutant-general of the forces) on a separate basis on the first of April, 1873.[8]

The military intelligence existing in the Victorian period has been overlooked in much military history in recent years. It is not an easy matter to explain this. Even John Keegan's book – *Intelligence in War: Knowledge of the Enemy from Napoleon to Al-Qaeda* – avoids the British situation in this period and discusses Stonewall Jackson instead. It is tempting to say that the story of the secret services in the years between Victoria's accession in 1837 and the establishment of the Intelligence Branch at Queen Anne's Gate in 1871 is so piecemeal that historians have observed no distinctive narrative.

It cannot be denied that from the early nineteenth century, when police informers and *agents provocateurs* were profitably employed by Lord Sidmouth to root out radicals in the working class movements, to the Crimean War in 1853-6, all varieties of intelligence-gathering were rather ad hoc and rarely well-organized. The foundation of the police force in 1830 by Sir Robert Peel was viewed by many as the first step towards a totalitarian regime in Britain, but no one in the establishment had objected when some of Feargus O'Connor's 'Physical Force' Chartists were spied upon and monitored as they drilled on Woodhouse Moor in Leeds.

Throughout the century there was an overlap between 'military intelligence' in the strict sense of the term and all foreign affairs. There was also a blurring of distinctions when it came to be understood what the separate roles of the police were, as opposed to the army personnel, when the Fenians and Anarchists began to infiltrate London from the 1850s onwards. In fact, in much popular writing, police spies were seen as the lowest of the low, often depicted melodramatically as if they were products of the worst excesses of the French Revolution.

But the fact remains that from Waterloo to the Crimea, intelligence available to military commanders was often nothing more than hearsay reported by travellers or even newspaper articles. Wellington was asked in 1851 about the Kaffir War, and he replied that he had 'never had any information on the causes of the war...or the objects of the government in carrying it on...' The Duke relied on newspaper reports during the period of his last years as Commander-in-Chief, 1842-52.

Another reason why the subject has not been explored for some time is that the army tended to rely on the reports of English gentlemen who travelled in the dangerous regions where border disputes and potential invasions were always likely. The obvious example is Afghanistan, in the period from c. 1830 to the end of the century. Most of the intelligence work when the Russians were seriously engaged in making incursions into India by way of Khiva and Bokhara was done by bold individuals, either private citizens or young officers who worked hard to build a good reputation.

In many instances, commanders of British forces would be learning desperately important information as they moved their forces around, hoping that the right characters would be on hand, or that sheer courage and reputation would see them through. One of the direst learning experiences was to be in the Zulu campaigns of 1879, when certain examples of the superiority of the intelligence gained by some of the Zulu *Impis* embarrassed the British forces, with their reputation for efficiency.

A typical example of the kind of wayward character who tended to figure prominently in intelligence-gathering at the time was Charles Masson – a wanderer and scholar who actually travelled on foot across vast areas of Central Asia, and was only discovered after many years of random information scouring by Captain Claude Wade, the political agent in Ludhiana. Masson was in reality a deserter from the East India Company called James Lewis. While Lt Alexander Burnes had been cultivating the friendship of Dost Mohammed in Kabul to maintain a buffer state against Russian designs on northern India, Masson/Lewis was preoccupied at the same time. When the British government wrote to Dost Mohammed in a tone of haughty disapproval, with no real promises made about backing or supporting him in military terms, it emerged that Burnes's spying and intelligence-gathering had been in vain: the Russians had been in touch with Dost from the very beginning and alliances had already been made between the two parties. Masson blamed Burnes for this debacle.

The affair highlights the failures and dangers of the methods at work at that time: it was desultory and pragmatic. If information was needed, a young officer would be sent to sort it out. The officers in question usually had command of several languages, had diplomatic skills and preferably, had a talent for making rough maps and accurate sketches as they moved along through the potentially hostile people and terrain.

When some kind of system did appear on the table for discussion, it came from a man who was a mere retired Major from the Bombay Sappers and Miners. This was Thomas Best Jervis. He had a passion for maps and worked energetically to persuade the War Office that cartography should be more highly prized. In 1837 he was made the Surveyor-General of India and was supposed to succeed Colonel Everest, but he became tired of waiting for the said opportunity and returned home. There he followed all kinds of practical geography and wrote to Lord Aberdeen to insist that cartography would have helped immeasurably in recent foreign skirmishes.

It was the outbreak of the Crimean War that made heads turn and since then everyone started taking Jervis's advice seriously. Lord Raglan, in command of the expedition, was known to comment on his lack of any knowledge of the theatre of war he was about to enter. Amazingly, Jervis obtained a detailed map of the Crimea – from a contact in Belgium who found him a map made by the Russian General Staff. Jervis was going to be listened to after that.

In 1855, the War Office eventually created a specific department for cartography and statistics. The Topographical and Statistical Department (T&S) was to be the first real step towards proper military intelligence within the military establishment.

It has to be asked, however, what kind of intelligence was going to be needed as the Empire expanded and British forces were continually packing up and setting off for distant shores? Clearly, accurate maps were useful, and so was general information about the cultures of the societies who would be hosting our military presence. But what about actual military policy – with some kind of system – in that respect? In this case, Britain had learned a hard lesson, and that was from the Prussian Wilhelm Stieber. When he came to the Great Exhibition in 1851, Stieber was seen by many as a 'freelancer' and that instead of being dedicated to the Prussian services, he was in the pay of Russia. It became clear that Stieber had succeeded in operating as a double agent in many European cities, and when he finally surfaced in Russia after some years of absence, he eventually became the man who did most to initiate the feared *Ochrana* – the Russian secret police in the Tsarist Empire.

It had to be considered: if other powers could do this kind of covert work, why not Britain? Indeed, we were to learn that aspect of the Great Game, in such figures as Major Henri le Caron, otherwise known as Thomas Beach from Colchester. Yet, it took 20 years from the creation of the T&S to the first formation of the Intelligence Branch. By that time, it was beginning to dawn on the leaders of the armed forces that military intelligence was a much more complex process than had previously been thought. As John Keegan points out in his book – *Intelligence in War: Knowledge of the Enemy from Napoleon to Al-Qaeda* – the process involves acquisition, delivery, acceptance, interpretation and implementation. When the Thukela garrison in the Zulu War Eshowe Campaign of 1879 was ready to move, the commanding officers who controlled the then British Empire realized with a sense of shock and alarm that the Zulus were aware of their intentions. The journal of Lt Hamilton at that time notes that some Zulu spies were captured who even disclosed to Colonel Pearson all kinds of startling information, including the fact that the British force was surrounded by 35, 000 men.

Obviously, the Zulus had a full understanding of the five stages of intelligence: they had acquired knowledge of the garrison, delivered that information to the *Impi* generals, accepted the facts to be true by dint of observation, interpreted the facts and details in the light of what could be seen and counted, and finally implemented their strategy in response by gathering three *Impis* at the right place.

Of course, in 1873, the Intelligence Branch had a massive brief and a whole third of the earth to handle as its province, rather than a stretch of Natal. It seems odd now to read that the first staffing arrangements for the new Branch involved, for instance, two officers and a clerk to cover the Russian Empire. The base they operated from comprised a house in Adelphi Terrace and a shambling old coach-house and stables tucked away in Whitehall.

The aims of the new Branch were expressed this way: 'The preparation of information relating to the military defence of the Empire and the strategical considerations of schemes of defence; the collection and distribution of all information relating to the military geography, resources and armed forces of foreign countries and the British colonies and possessions; the compilation of maps and the translations of documents'.

The two officers and the clerk must have contemplated the map of Russia with a sense of awe and confusion.

By the end of the century, however, when London itself and even the person of the Queen were targets of the enemies, there had been an expansion of the responsibilities covered by the Branch, and a sure liaison with the Metropolitan Police. When Sir William Melville – a top policeman in 1896 – set to work in defending the capital city, he did so in tandem with the army. This was the man who first recruited the infamous Sidney Reilly, and subsequently ushered in the next 'Age of the Spy'.

At the beginning of Victoria's reign, the nature and composition of the armies who preserved the Empire is of particular interest with regard to military intelligence. There were two armies of course, when it came to India, the 'Jewel in the Crown' where most anxieties lay in terms of Russian expansionism. There was a force of a quarter of a million men serving the East India Company, and the 100, 000 members of the British Army per se with headquarters at the Horse Guards in London. This duality was resolved after the Sepoy Mutiny of 1857 when the direct rule of India was transferred to the British government from the Company. The British Army comprised 32 regiments and engineers. The sappers were, it seems, a floating concept. They were so indefinable in the sense of what duties they performed that at most stages of a campaign, they were seen as the home of whatever intelligence personnel could be identified with in a particular setting.

As Jan Morris has pointed out the fact that in most aspects the British Army had not changed attitudes and conduct since Waterloo was never going to help the receptivity needed for anything innovative that could be introduced. New ideas were not apparent in the attire, nor on the parade ground and not even in marksmanship. Basically, ritual was at the heart of the army and that had served well as a way of integrating men of all kinds and backgrounds, so why change the whole war machine? It was going to take a major war to highlight the need for proper, respected and effective military intelligence.

The final piece in the mosaic here is the place of the Foreign Secretary and of the general practice of diplomacy and intrigue. How the interests of administrators and military men could clash and cause havoc was observed in the Dost Mohammed affair. This was when Lord Auckland, in Simla, had not understood the relationship between the British buffer zone, the Sikh leader, Ranjit Singh and the various aspirants to the government of Afghanistan. Nonetheless, at a more general level much depended on the Foreign Secretary at home.

The most celebrated example is Lord Palmerston. In the Athenian incident of 1850, when a trader was trying to force some compensation from the Greek government, Palmerston sent a gunboat to sort it out, and his words of explanation were important in understanding how military intelligence and diplomatic intrigue were to become so complicated: 'A British subject, in whatever land he may be, shall feel confident that the watchful eye and the strong arm of England will protect him against injustice and wrong'.

Palmerston's statement would prove very difficult to enforce in the distant and dangerous borderland of the Kizilkum desert and the Emirate of Bokhara, where British agents had been tortured and killed in the 1830s. But Palmerston showed what needed to be done in the role of relating foreign affairs to popular knowledge and support at home – he was skilled in media relations and he knew how to take the pulse of popular feeling about world affairs.

After the fiasco of the Crimea, the importance of the relationship between the implementation of foreign policy and the work done by the War Office on promoting military intelligence was to become increasingly the centre stage in imperial politics. In hindsight and with the sophistication that comes with the more complex technological warfare, recent analyses of some of the major battles of the nineteenth century have expended pages of indignant commentary on military incompetence. A publication of 1903 has this comment on a Boer War confrontation: 'In spite of much British bravery, the combat of Lang's Nek was an unquestionable and severe defeat. But many noble deeds were performed'. In recent times, Saul David rightly comments on another imperial battle, '...the British commander, Lord Chelmsford, had made the cardinal error of not according their (the Zulus) capabilities proper respect'.[9] In other words, in an age in which military intelligence is highly regarded and has become an academic and strategic discipline, the wars of the Victorian era, with their amateurish reliance on dash and valour, seem ludicrously simple and defeats are all too easily understood.

However, quite frequently in British history, the significant advances in intelligence were made in a gentlemanly, inventive way, by individuals. It took a long time for individual men of genius to actually find the right kind of discourse for the subject of 'spying' but when they did, it was with a workable mixture of delight and military briskness, as in Baden-Powell's account – *My Adventures as a Spy (1916)* – published in an Edwardian compendium of spy stories. Baden-Powell writes lucidly of the three categories of spies as he saw it: (i) strategical and diplomatic agents; (ii) tactical, military or naval agents, and (iii) field spies. By 1910, the whole subject was open to discussion and established as a part of the scene. Yet this man of extensive knowledge and experience could also 'spin a good yarn' as was the tradition of the gentleman-spy, from Abbott to Francis Younghusband, a major player in chapter three.

There is also a need to consider the changes in the Russian Army throughout this period. After all, the political officers such as Francis Younghusband ventured into the Russian camps and talked with their officers, and this kind of interplay went on throughout the Great Game. The Russian Bear which was always loitering on the borderlands, at times came into Afghanistan. Therefore, in order to understand the advance of military intelligence, it was essential to know something about the Russian presence and the nature of their armed forces. After their disastrous Crimean experience, their army was reformed and the composition and background of the Russian officer class was radically changed. Russia was also, naturally, similarly challenged by the formidable geography and people of the India–Afghanistan frontier, and had to slowly build up buffer states before it could trek into Khiva and Bokhara; the similarities with the British problems in tackling the terrain of northern India, and in trying to understand the politics of the tribal cultures are evident when we look at their strategies at this time.

In conclusion, it is hoped that this history will provide a survey of the Victorian period to match the admirable account of the Elizabethan secret services by Alan Haynes, *The Elizabethan Secret Services* (1992). Victorian Britain may not have had a mastermind to watch Sir Francis Walsingham, but it did have a large number of courageous (often foolhardy) individual officers who, in carrying on with the long tradition of the gentleman soldier/scholar, made a more streamlined military intelligence establishment possible. Perhaps, the most astonishing aspect of the pattern of development in the years between Queen Victoria's accession and the Great War was the gradual realization that a mass of knowledge gathered and not applied tends to create more problems than it solves. The Victorian period might not have had the small and more visible population of the Elizabethan scene, and there might not have been a puppet-master to compare with Walsingham, but there was more than enough intrigue on the frontiers of the Empire to keep the intelligence-gatherers occupied in between their shooting expeditions and their Arabic lessons.

Notes and References:

[1] George Philip, *Advanced Classbook of Modern Geography*, London, 1908, p. 353.

[2] Edward A Whitcomb, 'The Duties and Functions of Napoleon's External Agents,' in *History* Vol. 57 no. 190, June 1972, pp. 189–204.

[3] Peter Hopkirk in *The Times*, Sept. 10, 2005.

[4] see Byron Farwell, *Richard Burton*, Harrap, London, 1955.

[5] Louise Wilmot (ed.) *Clausewitz on War*, Wordsworth editions, London, 1997, p. xix.

[6] Ibid., p. 64.

[7] Charles Allen, *Soldier Sahibs*, Abacus, London, 2001, p. 47.

[8] Sir George Aston, *Secret Service*, Faber, London, 1930, p. 19.

[9] Saul David, *Military Blunders*, Robinson, London, 1998, p. 251.

2

The Beginnings: Enlightenment Information

In the 1830s in Britain, society was consolidating its quest for applying knowledge of all kinds to the world beyond its shores. The eighteenth century Enlightenment was beginning to percolate into practical knowledge and the gentleman scholar was increasingly showing an interest in applying knowledge instead of merely gathering facts and filling notebooks with description and analysis. Yet paradoxically, the new towns of the Industrial Revolution still reflected the persistence of marginal and pseudo-scientific occupations such as astrologers, 'wise women' and the so-called 'cunning folk'. The sharpest contrast was perhaps when the ordinary working people were visiting cunning folk to enquire about illness or future work, science was giving forensic science the Marsh Test to identify arsenic traces in suspected poisoning cases.

The Society for the Diffusion of Useful Knowledge reflects this interest in moving away from folk tales and superstition to practical knowledge in its 1828 publication, *The British Almanac*. As Roy Porter notes: 'From that hour it was piously declared, the empire of astrology was at an end'.[1] Every new profession and many of the old ones was starting the long process of modernizing attitudes and attempting to gather knowledge of all kinds. The Royal Geographical Society was founded in 1830 and their importance for future military intelligence can be observed in their relationship to David Livingstone; although his interests were missionary rather than military, is it notable that when he began his trek to find Lake Ngami in 1849, he had to cross the Kalahari desert. His achievement, however, typified what was increasingly going on in the ranks of the political officers in the Raj. As Niall Ferguson puts it: 'The expeditions to Ngami were the first of a succession of almost superhuman journeys that were to enthral the mid-Victorian imagination'.[2]

Gathering knowledge, as a pursuit in itself, was to affect every area of life. When the high command finally recognized the value of having a database of geographical information, the practice of intelligence was transformed. However, in a strange and haphazard manner, the collection of information, even by men working within the East India Company or the British Army itself, was rarely collected and used in any purposeful way. As research by Douglas M Peers has shown, scholars within the army treated their information-gathering as something marginal and incidental to their everyday military work. Peers believes that 'Military officers and surgeons played a critical role in the collection, analysis and dissemination of knowledge in colonial India. Yet the little attention to date [2005] that has been directed at scholars with military backgrounds has treated their army service as incidental to, rather than formative of, their contributions to knowledge of India'.[3]

We are considering a gentlemanly army of scholar-officers here; travel gave them the incentive they craved to play a small part in the new utilitarian world of information. Peers makes the point that many had a primary interest simply in cultural topics, but areas such as linguistic study would naturally prove to be invaluable as the army began to see the need for proper training when political work was undertaken. Before this was acknowledged, men like Abbott who began their long journeys into the dangerous frontiers in the mountains had somehow taught themselves other languages and it could prove a perilous amateur endeavour – as Abbott notes in his journey to Khiva; in the course of that epic journey he had to try to get by with some Arabic, Persian and Hindi.

Naturally, these gentlemen officers would record, in writings and with drawings, their travels to all corners of the Indian subcontinent and indeed elsewhere in the Empire. But as Peers notes that this information was of mixed value to the army establishment: 'Such local depictions ranged from the banal and anecdotal to detailed and systematic descriptions of local topography and resources'.[4] Arguably, the most significant achievement of these men was the creation of their own information networks. On an everyday level it would work in this way: an officer would be posted from one place to another, perhaps from Africa to the Indian frontier; he might be asked to switch handling confrontations from Zulu peoples to Sikhs and Pathans. The climate, the culture, the languages and military structures would all be different. But the network would be working all the time, in many ways, from journals to newspapers and private letters. Officers would spend months together when they were at home on leave (periods of a year were sometimes spent at home). In the case of India, these men were partly smitten with the 'romance' of the East, of Orientalism, and there was always an element of seeing that world through rose-coloured spectacles. But the hard experience of the Mutiny and of the earlier Sikh Wars would put that right.

This communication network, on which so much of the valuable intelligence was to happen, found consolidation in the establishment of clubs and societies across India. As Peers explains: 'By the third decade of the nineteenth century, officers in India had their own trade periodicals and book clubs... The membership roll of the Bengal Club, founded in 1828, is replete with military officers: its founding president was General Combermere, commander-in-chief in India'.[5] After this came the Madras Club in 1831, the Byculla Club in 1833 and the Western India Turf Club in 1837. Some officers within this context made a significant contribution to the baseline knowledge of the culture in which the wars of the Raj were fought. Such a man was Robert Orme, who worked for the East India Company, and his chronicle of military actions in India, led to his appointment as the official historiographer of the Company. Orme's accounts of conflicts led to a series of supposed insights (largely generalizations) which would influence major figures in the course of the Raj's history. Comments such as this typify his writing: 'The Hindus have from time to time immemorial been as addicted to commerce, as they are averse to war. They have therefore always been immensely rich and have always been incapable of defending their wealth'.[6]

What is of genuine interest in the history of military intelligence, however, is the more structured education provided by the two armies, British and 'John Company'– the latter better known as the East India Company. Each had its own education centre for officers in England: Addiscombe for the Company and Sandhurst for the British Army. They both extended the curriculum of the public schools, but what was of vital interest was the inclusion of geography, cartography and languages. A typical Addiscombe syllabus included plan drawing, topographical and military drawing, landscape drawing, a smattering of the Indian lingua franca, Hindi (as Hindi and Urdu are similar – a broad knowledge of the spoken language would be essential) and classical languages continued to feature in the syllabus. It was quite simple to see that many of these skills were to prove essential particularly to the young political officers who were on the verge of being given assignments among the tribal communities in Kashmir or Baluchistan.

This makes a sharp contrast with the nature of the Russian officers during the reign of Nicholas I. Throughout his reign, the majority of the officers were poorly educated, and in spite of the increased number of officer cadets being put through the system, the cream of the army officers were channelled into an elite force. As one historian noted: 'This was a highly unsatisfactory way of staffing the army, and it seems probable that the ignorant and poorly trained officers were one reason for the defeat in the Crimea'.[7]

As the Great Game began to accelerate, subsequently after the hard lessons of the Crimean War in the 1850s, the two major players – Britain and Russia – were undergoing radical reforms in their armies, but in the area of intelligence, both were moving slowly and tentatively. It was, as always in the British military history, down to the individuals of rare talent to change things.

The powerful men in India were the district officers, and a look at the work done by the charismatic Lawrence brothers' shows how all this knowledge was applied. What they wanted in their agents, or political officers, was, as David Gilmour writes:

Young men who could mix freely with the people and do prompt justice in their shirt sleeves rather than propound laws to the discontent of all honest men. He certainly had a talent for attracting the daring and the self-confident. [8]

Men like Henry Lawrence would send his young officers on long and dangerous missions, usually demanding that they perfected the art of disguise. Inevitably, this was always a risky business. An English gentleman had to learn not only how to talk like a native, but to dress and move like one. Perhaps, the most difficult aspect of this was to develop the attitudes, tone and responses of a particular cultural or religious viewpoint. As to the down-to-earth mundane knowledge of military or martial affairs, the officers did acquire an incredible amount of information regarding the equipment and practicalities of war. As Abbott proudly wrote during his trek to Khiva in the 1840s, explaining the details about local swords: 'In fact I have given much attention to the subject and am convinced that in this country nothing is known of the real excellence of the sabre. The grain of the Isfahan blade is infinitely coarser than the Damascus blade'.[9]

From those dual standpoints: Russia with a vast army slowly penetrating the buffer states north of Afghanistan on the one hand, and British political officers riding north with guides and provisions on the other, it comes as no surprise to appreciate the appeal of the intelligence operations as mediated by Kipling and others. Not only would these young officers need to know their Orientalism: they would start to acquaint themselves with Russian military habits and practices as well. What was to take a very long time was the establishment of a good support system for these intelligence men. But right through to the end of the Great Game, to the expeditions of Francis Younghusband in Tibet in the first years of the twentieth century, the tradition of the lone officer with perhaps one subordinate and one native guide were to continue. Kipling's depiction of Colonel Creighton gives us one of the best insights into this type of man:

> All we ethnological men are jealous as jackdaws of one another's discoveries. They're of no interest to anyone but ourselves, of course, but you know what book-collectors are....[10]

He uses the front of the scholar, stressing the nature of knowledge per se: its application seems to be related to something secondary. But of course, the main argument is that he indicates the life of a loner: the 'jealousy' he speaks of hints at the camaraderie of the young officers, and that was, in many important ways, the bedrock of military intelligence, rather than paperwork and administration.

The beginnings of the Intelligence Branch were to be found in this attitude of the love of knowledge for its own sake, the inheritance of the Enlightenment when scholars and gentlemen began to gather information, to observe nature closely, to understand languages and so on. William Jones had written his major studies of Indo-European language, using the knowledge of Sanskrit, at the turn of the century; codes and encryption had been advanced during the Napoleonic wars. Now, it was the turn of the map-makers and surveyors. After all, nobody was into advanced planning in a theatre of war in terms of paper; little was changing the rigidity of all aspects of the army at this time. Even changes in the uniform took decades to establish and the purchase of promotion was still in practice when the first steps towards an organized Intelligence Branch were taken.

In 1838, Thomas Best Jervis, still a Lieutenant after 17 years of service, was involved in a major row with George Everest. It was all due to Everest's conviction that Jervis's attempt at continuing the mapping of India had not been up to scratch. Unfortunately for Everest, a letter from the Royal Society signed by 38 fellows (including Michael Faraday) did not agree with the great cartographer. Everest was well aware that the massive enterprise of measuring the earth's surface, begun by Col. William Lambton in 1802, had been in his hands and that his successor in surveying and map-making would have to be someone special.

The row soon blew over by December 1838, and Jervis, got promoted to the rank of a Major. *The Bombay Times* dated 19 December recorded that Jervis was to 'take rank, by Brevet, of major'. This was destined to be a great help to him when it came to his lobbying of the War Office to make cartography an integral part of the imperial military structure.

Thomas Best Jervis was fundamentally a scholar. Throughout his very busy life he wrote on topics such as *A Description of the State, Surveys and Prospects of the Various Surveys and other Scientific Enterprises Instituted by the East India Company*, (1838); *The Origin of the Present*

State of the Surveys in India, (1840) and *India in relation to Great Britain*, (1853). Making maps was his passion, even down to such precise and minute productions like his Map of Circassia and the Russian Territories – a very useful document at a time when Tsar Nicholas I had plans to invade the British buffer states across northern India. Nicholas had had constant problems with the Circassians – who eventually turned out to be good allies of Britain in the future. This proves that Jervis was not always simply following dry studious pursuits: he had an eye to practical geopolitics as well.

When he was the Collector for South Konkan he crusaded with the task of giving India 'useful knowledge' and it was at that time that the great Orientalist – Lancelot Wilkinson – an acquaintance of Jervis, signed a petition put forward by Jervis to improve vernacular education.

He was also a 'joiner', a party man and a sharp man to have on the committee. Apart from writing for the *Journal of the Royal Geographical Society* (something Capt. Alexander Burnes of Kabul fame also did), Jervis joined societies and became a guiding force in their process of administration. In that way he made some powerful acquaintances. He was made a Fellow of the Royal Astronomical Society, the Royal Geographical Society and the Royal Asiatic and Royal Society. Along with so many middle class Victorian gentlemen, he had his pet obsessions too: one was the abolition of duelling, and he joined a society working for that purpose.

The best description we have of Jervis is from his son, who wrote that his father had 'an open countenance, bespeaking genuine candour, and illuminated by far-sighted, limpid, grayish-blue Saxon eyes'. He also observed in his father a 'loving soul of the most expansive nature'. When he set to work on a campaign to change society, it was the familiar Victorian type, the 'Meliorist' – the man imbued with the new scientific spirit who believed that man was perfectible, and that knowledge would enable him to become better, both morally as well as intellectually. In order to possess some definite practical attainments, Jervis set about pressing the authorities to listen to his ideas on a number of topics, including emigrant ships, the cultivation of silkworms and the education of the poor in India.

It was in 1846 that he began to outline his reforms and proposals for military cartography, and he wrote to Lord Aberdeen, explaining that the War Office needed someone to improve the geographical information available to expeditionary forces. That someone was, of course, Thomas Best Jervis.

The war in the Crimea proved Jervis's point. The commanders had no idea of the terrain they were encroaching. The setbacks in the early phase of that conflict gave Jervis the ideal pretext for an audience including the Secretary of State for War – Lord Newcastle. Amazingly, but typical of the attitude to intelligence at the time, Newcastle could not be persuaded to form any official corps, but permitted Jervis the task of doing the work himself.

How could he possibly let time drift now and wait for further military failures to prompt action? He certainly did not. He went to work with alacrity and created a map of the Crimea in ten sheets. Most impressive was his composition of the marine and terrain contours in different colours. When he put forward his material, he also expressed a criticism of the Crimea campaign: he stated that Britain had 'sheer ignorance and contempt of an enemy by no means contemptible'.

The dedication and hard work paid off. On 2 February 1855, Newcastle's successor, Lord Panmure, finally made the foundation of an intelligence department official. It was to be called the Topographical and Statistical Department. Jervis was to take command, and then, unbelievably after waiting for quite sometime to become a Major. However, Jervis was now promoted to the rank of Lieutenant Colonel. Although destined to be short-lived and limited to cartography most of the time, the T&S did at least, serve the function of becoming a resource-bank for the pre-knowledge that was so essential when a force of men had to be sent to previously politically stable states or territories.

Sir George Aston provides a realistic account of the mindset behind the establishment of the 'T&S':

> The history of its origin is illuminating in connection with the origin of the 'stupid John Bull' legends. Between the Battle of Waterloo and the Crimean War very little interest was taken by the British public in the efficiency of its army, with the usual result. The whole military system broke down as it was put to the test. The scandals of the Crimean campaign led to the establishment of a 'Topographical and Statistical Department'.[11]

As Aston notes: 'Its principal activities seem to have been devoted to studying the topography of foreign countries'. He comments that actual direct military information-gathering was still not a part of the scene.

Jervis died in 1857, and the Crimean War had run its course. The historian, Christopher Andrew, notes that by the mid-1860s, 'The T&S was being given such trivial tasks as preparing illustrations for army dress regulations'. Clearly, someone in the high office had merely thought that the T&S was a useful place to find talented draughtsmen who could turn their hand to anything involving visual information.

Once again, the department was in danger of becoming that bugbear of the Victorian military establishment – an amateur outfit with no clear definition or aims.

The situation needed a man of considerable presence and determination to keep the T&S going, and the right man came along: Captain (later Major General) Sir Charles Wilson. That did not happen until 1870 and at that time he was constructively critical of the work done, including the perception that the foreign map collection was only fairly minimal and much more work had to be done.

Notes and References:

[1]   Roy Porter, *The Enlightenment*, Penguin, London, p. 151.
[2]   Niall Ferguson, *Empire*, Penguin, London, p. 127.
[3]   Douglas M Peers, 'Colonial Knowledge and the Military of India 1780-1860' in *Journal of Imperial and Commonwealth History*, Vol. 33 no. 2 May 2005, pp. 157-180, p. 157.
[4]   Ibid., p. 174.
[5]   Ibid., p. 163.
[6]   Ibid., p. 166.
[7]   See Peter Waldron, *The End of Imperial Russia*, Palgrave, London, 1997, pp. 139-147.
[8]   David Gilmour, *The Ruling Caste*, John Murray, London, 2005, pp. 188-189.
[9]   James Abbott, *Narrative of a Journey to Khiva*, London, 1843, p. 50.
[10]   Rudyard Kipling, *Kim*, Penguin, London, 1901, p. 113.
[11]   Sir George Aston, as above (see note 8, Indroduction) p. 17.

3

Heroes of the Great Game: The Russia/India Axis

Before looking at the Great Game in India, something must be said by way of contrast so that Britain's attitude to espionage may be better understood. The contrast is between what was happening in London compared with the work of one of the founding fathers of military intelligence – Wilhelm Stieber. To know what he achieved in Prussia and elsewhere is to understand how Britain lagged behind for so long.

Stieber was the head of intelligence for Otto von Bismarck, founder of a united Germany in 1870. He was born in 1818 in Saxony and began his career as a lawyer in Berlin. At a time when the *agent provocateur* was the favoured instrument of the state in prising out radicals and revolutionaries into view, Stieber operated as a police spy, with a front of being pro-radicals (and this was in the years before the Year of Revolutions, 1848, when radicals were to take to the barricades). First established as an undercover agent, Stieber then graduated to a position of more power after saving the life of King Friedrich Wilhelm IV: he was appointed the Chief of police.

Where Stieber becomes really interesting however – and partly in the context of the Great Game – is when he begins to work for Russia. He made plenty of enemies in Germany and became something of a freelance, going on to St Petersburg and starting to work for the Russian Foreign Office. When the Tsarist 'Third Section' of secret police was formed, Stieber was given the role of administrating the foreign network of spies. In 1858, he started to influence the Russian community in London, working on potential double agents and assassins, and instated what we would now call 'counter intelligence'. When he returned to Prussia he was instrumental in many of the most prominent actions of Realpolitik in the forthcoming war between France and Germany in 1870. When King Wilhelm entered Paris at the height of Prussian success, an incredible number of 300 Prussian spies were present in the French capital to offer him a warm welcome. Stieber had played a prominent part in the rise of Bismarck and in the consolidation of his power. As John Hughes-Wilson has written: Stieber was '...the first national intelligence chief to use agents to monitor and control the press, the banks, business and industry. His collection of comprehensive military intelligence ensured Prussia's victory on the battlefield'.[1]

In contrast to the above developments, it was important to take note of what Britain was doing during the same period. In the 1860s the Raj was not only trying to recover from the Great Mutiny of 1857 by rebuilding their political stronghold, the colonial rulers were also simultaneously fighting innumerable small wars that had sprung up in all corners of the Empire. However, round about the same time Britain was also learning the utility of employing spies. In the 1850s, the new police detectives understood that they would have to put in a lot of effort for tracking the Fenians who were unleashing terror in London by bombing the city. But as an actual intelligence focus within the heart of Empire, the reliance was largely on the senior officers and their networks of younger officers in the field, and on the trunk roads north across the Indian subcontinent. What was not being implemented was the 'secret police' mentality and ruthlessness of Stieber.

The main reason for this lack of logistics at the heart of military things at the time of the Crimean War and the treks of the Great Gamers was the massive scale of operations. While Kabul is over 600 miles from Delhi, its distance from Karachi on the Indian Ocean to Calcutta across the Indian subcontinent is around 1, 500 miles. These bare facts alone perhaps explain why the surveys came first: the work of Everest and the surveyors, then the pundits who advanced geographical and cultural knowledge were doing the 'groundwork' in the metaphorical as well as in the literal sense. Only with fundamental knowledge of geography and topography could the adventures begin.

The phrase 'The Great Game' invokes gentlemanly adventure and male romance; the notion that a confrontation of two major world powers in a vast theatre of espionage and reconnaissance could generate Kipling's novel *Kim* as a central document in a myth would have seemed ludicrous to the men who explored the far reaches of northern India, Persia and Tibet in the nineteenth century. But that is the basis of the term and the literature going with it as a self-contained microcosm in which officers, guides, interpreters, map-makers and native pundits roamed across a vast stretch of Asia in order to ascertain any kind of knowledge that might contribute to the military intelligence so essential to London and St Petersburg.

In terms of the sheer proportion of books and articles relating to military intelligence in the nineteenth century, those relating to the British Raj have always dominated. The wars in Africa attracted exceptional men, such as Baden-Powell in the Matabele wars; the Fenian activities in Canada created their charismatic figures, but the Raj in the years 1840–1900 provide military historians with too many narratives of discovery to cope with.

The basis of the whole business was the certainty in Whitehall that Russia had designs on extending power to India via Afghanistan. Although that meant a confrontation with a whole range of tribal and national groups and allies, in intimidating terrain, the fears were well founded. But we have to ask why such intelligence-gathering as was achieved by generations of young British officers and colonial staff was so diverse, so apparently random and lacking in a central logistical base until 1873. In some ways, the kinds of enterprises undertaken in this context could be bizarre and eccentric, such as the brief given to the great explorer Sir Richard Burton, when, as a young officer, he was sent by Sir Charles Napier to visit souks and bazaars. One of the main motives behind this assignment was to unravel the documentary interest in sexual behaviour. He discovered just to what extent British officers visited brothels and the whole affair was glossed over, resulting in Burton's transfer elsewhere.

To understand exactly what the 'Game' was all about, we need to grasp the nature of the Russian ambitions towards India. The core of the Russian expansionist plan was to gradually invade and absorb nations contiguous to its heartland. They had thus become accustomed to coping with all kinds of ethnic diversity and were adept at taking in these new subjects of the Tsar. After all, in Britain's eyes, the Russian Empire comprised a huge composite block, unlike the British Empire which was spread across the world in clusters. Until the mid-nineteenth century the Russian Empire stretched from Prussia in Europe across to the Kazakhs and by the end of the same century Russia expanded her Empire further by annexing areas of the Uzbekh territory, Konkad and Karakum together with the Pamirs.

What most irritated Britain was the Russian desire to occupy the key locations of Bokhara and Khiva. And eventually, these places did become a part of the Russian domains. Linked to Turkestan, these two *khanates* were situated dangerously close to British India, and therefore, the fear of a Russian Army finding its way through into the Punjab always lurked at large in the British mind. The British Army and the army of the East India Company had coped fairly well with regard to controlling the massive Indian territory and the related states for over a century until the outbreak of the Indian Mutiny of 1857, which proved to be a notable warning to the complacency within the Raj. But Russia was going even further afield in the mid-century: Nikolai Muravev - Governor of Eastern Siberia - sent various expeditions into the Far East in the 1850s and by 1859, they managed to take control of Vladivostok. Britain's unwavering confidence of holding on to India without having to face much opposition was severely shaken by the Mutiny, of course, and the 30 years of Great Game activities preceding that event had been largely directed by a rising paranoia about Russia 'on their patch'.

Naturally, it was also a question of the defence of British India, not merely a fear of expansion. Conolly (eventually murdered in 1842 by the Khan of Bokhara) had shown that it was quite possible for a Russian Army to march into India by the infamous Khyber Pass, or even through Persia and Herat. Captain Abbot had explored the latter possibility also. What these journeys and their evidence of Russian potential demonstrated above all else was the absolute necessity of having in-depth knowledge of the states involved: their structures, ambitions, temperament, bellicosity and most of all perhaps, their susceptibility to bribes and blandishments.

The Russian threat had been most cogently described and argued in a publication of 1829 with the title, *On the Practicability of an Invasion of British India*. This was written by Colonel George de Lacy Evans, and he estimated that it would only take the Russians three months to move from the Caspian to the Oxus, that is from Turkey to the first main river-border on entry to India: the route taken by Alexander the Great in 331 BC. According to Lawrence James's book - *Raj: The Making of British India* - in 1836 there were only 17, 000 British troops in India, and of these 1, 400 were invalids. Common sense dictated that a revolt would be hard to contain. The Duke of Wellington understood the central problem - the nature of the native/indigenous troops – the sepoys. If the British had been thoughtful and considerate from the very beginning regarding the organization of their Empire in military terms, they would have surely rendered support and showed their respect towards the sepoys all along.

There were various perceptions of how the Great Game would progress at that crucially important point c. 1840. Some considered that there would be a sudden escalation into warfare: open conflicts caused by a Russian Army on the move into a zone perilously close to the Raj borderland. Others, largely the officers on the spot such as Abbot, Conolly and later Sykes and Burnaby, were certain that the Game was destined to become a relentlessly steady and uncertain series of moves, like a game of chess. Whatever the course of events, one fact was certain: key buffer states would always be prime targets, notably Persia and Turkestan, and in India, the region of Sind. A typical manoeuvre in the intelligence machinations in this context was the Russian attempt to persuade the Shah in the 1830s to make a move on Herat. In the 1830s, Russia not only worked hard to influence the Shah, but also made significant forays in Kabul with the aim of capturing the Afghan city. The theories of Lacy Evans, in this context, therefore seemed to contain much truth.

Because intelligence in the mid-century, from the Crimean War to the turning point of the early 1870s was piecemeal and ad hoc, it is difficult to see exactly what was going on. But there are three definite areas of interest in a general history of spies and spying in the Victorian Age: the individual officers and the interplay with Russian movements; the work on the pundits and Captain Thomas Montgomerie and the senior officers as well as administrators who gathered 'soldier sahibs' around them to form operational units that were ready to move to any part of India whenever an assignment came about.

The doyen of Great Game studies, Peter Hopkirk, selects Lieutenant Arthur Conolly as the typical Great Game player. Conolly had been on the road for more than a year when he finally arrived in a village on the North West Frontier in 1831. He was only 23 years old at the time. Apart from this, Conolly, in a letter to a friend had first coined the phrase 'Great Game'. One of the most significant contributions of Conolly was monitoring the Russian Army closely. But in order to take that enterprise to its conclusion, he had to cross the feared Karakum desert, and that challenge exemplified the nature of the 'Great Gamer'. The defining feature of that person was disguise. The officer sent on an intelligence mission had to detach himself from his European identity so much so that he had to move, speak and think like a native wherever he was stationed. For this reason, many British officers became authorities on the most obscure cultural habits and traditions of numerous tribal states and kingdoms across the continent.

The Officers on Missions:
From Abbot to Younghusband

To find a specific journey for military intelligence purposes to use as a representative one is difficult. Most briefs given to the young men who undertook these missions were pragmatic and often done in reaction to an immediate military necessity. But, there is a basic feature here which needs to be understood. The men who figured in the central narrative of the Great Game were mostly officers who clustered around charismatic men in the Raj's military structure, notably known as 'Henry Lawrence's Young Men'. Apart from comprising Lawrence and other political officers who joined a little later and served in the special elite force on the North West Frontier in the next generation, the category also included the junior officers of the Bengal Army.

Henry Lawrence was one of the five brothers who went out to serve in India. He became most celebrated for his heroic death in the Mutiny, dying at the siege of the Residency at Lucknow. When his brother John heard the news of Henry's death, he wrote: 'My brother Henry was wounded... he died like a good soldier in discharge of his duty; he has not left an abler or a better soldier behind him; his loss just now will be a national calamity'. Henry had gathered the best young officers around him and in a letter to a friend he paid tribute to these intelligence gatherers: 'I was very fortunate with my assistants, all of whom were my friends, and almost every one was introduced into the Punjab through me... Men such as you will seldom see anywhere, but when collected under one administration were worth double and treble the number taken at haphazard'.[2]

It appears that the battle of Sobraon in the First Sikh War of 1846 was the occasion for the assembling of the 'young men' and Lawrence. Some of the most prominent officers, destined to distinguish themselves in intelligence work, were on the battlefield: William Hodson, Herbert Edwardes and Harry Lumsden. As for any intelligence work in that battle, however, it fades into insignificance when we recall that it was at Sobraon that General Sir Hugh Gough's force advanced on a Sikh artillery position, with the Tenth Lincolnshires on the left taking the prominent role, advancing in silence, walking through artillery fire. The British then charged the position and got hold of the area.

Lawrence was always on the lookout for recruits who could be sent for the northern missions. He carried a notebook in which he jotted down the names mentioned during the course of the conversations. At one point, he was also discharged with the duty to begin administration work in Lahore. In order to do so, he started gathering his political agents. One description of Lawrence emphasizes his knowledge of character: 'The colonel surpasses the brothers by having all their decision, all their experience, but with a refined sensitive nature... He surpasses all men I have seen as a perfect knower of men'.[3]

But intelligence work in the field in India was still a shaky item as late as 1880 when at the battle of Maiwand near Kandahar Brigadier General Burrows brigade was decimated by Ayub Khan's artillery and the young Robert Baden-Powell – a man with ambitions to become a top intelligence man – was sent to write a report on what went wrong. He stressed poor reconnaissance and acted in a way that many of the political officers would have done – wanting to be noticed and giving an exciting brief to perform. Baden-Powell became known to Colonel St John, the Chief political officer. That action must have been replayed in a thousand different situations in the history of the Raj: intelligence being something gathered piecemeal, in diverse places, and each event being unique, so that what was needed was a process of collation. Few men had the foresight and perception to observe that during the time of campaigns.

It was clear from the beginning and from de Lacy's book that Afghanistan and the borders were to be the focus for the trial of Britain's imperial design. The military senior ranks and the General Staff therefore, realized that knowledge had to be gained and logged. The young men began to go on their journeys, risking their lives at all times in the perilous far reaches of the continent. The struggle for the mastery of Central Asia was to be, as the Russians dubbed it – a 'tournament of shadows' – and the shadows would be made by lonely men with a dream of adventure, doggedly riding over wastelands and mountains to move unseen among all the participants in the Game, large and small.

Summarizing every mission in this chronicle would take a lifetime, but certain individuals claim the attention and the first has to be Lieutenant Alexander Burnes, known as 'Bokhara Burnes'. After his visit to the Sikh ruler Ranjit Singh in 1831, Burnes proposed a trip to Kabul to negotiate with Dost Mohammed, and then to cross the Hindu Kush mountains to Bokhara. The notion was to collect military information on the Russians and on Afghanistan. At that time Kabul was the focus, as so often in history, of political rivalry and there were claimants to power in various quarters. But the primary fear in Britain was whether or not any Russian delegates had been stationed in Kabul. The Governor General supported Burnes's seemingly very ambitious plan and he took an English doctor – James Gerard – with him, along with two guides. One of the two, Ali, was a former surveyor with the East India Company and the other, Lal, was a linguist. Everything about Burnes's expedition is informative regarding the perceived aims of intelligence at the time. A priority was simply writing a journal so that all the details were recorded: this secretarial duty was given to Lal. The need to be 'native' and avoid suspicion made languages essential and, like Richard Burton who is perhaps the best-known multilingual officer in the Raj's history, Burnes would have had to learn Hindi and Arabic from books and from conversation, picking up survival vocabulary at first and then learning to speak only when necessary, allowing guides to take on most of the conversation as they wandered into places where local dialects or a lingua franca would prevail.

However, even with all these precautions, it was still practically impossible to be undetected. Therefore, the aim was basically not to be noticed. As soon as the party approached the Khyber Pass, they realized that it would be better for them to try out another route since Burnes who was also travelling with them possessed both letters of introduction as well as his passport – the disclosure of which would lead to the easy identification of the entire party. They went a long way round, going to Jalalabad; it took six weeks to go from the Indus to Kabul where he would eventually meet Dost Mohammed – the man who had wrenched the kingdom of Kabul from his brothers by successfully displacing Shah Shujah and had been ruling the kingdom for six years at the time of Burnes arrival. The crux of the matter was that Britain saw the need to take a lead in diplomacy with Dost, as the Russians would most certainly try to do the same. Burnes was a groundbreaker in this respect. As Dost despised Ranjit Singh – who shared cordial relations with the

British – Burnes had to learn to be a diplomat as well as a soldier. He was becoming a skilled intelligence man through sheer hard necessity.

What Burnes and other officers on these missions actually did was to raise questions that had multiple answers; much of their behaviour when in personal contact with important figures in the domains they entered depended on smart survival skills and clever lying. Burnes in Bokhara had prepared the way by writing a letter packed with compliments and praise to the Grand Vizier and when this gained him an audience with the great man, it was a delicate situation. What Burnes had to be aware of comprised several layers of knowledge such as facts about where the non-Muslims were allowed to go, and more importantly, what to say and how to speak when asked awkward questions. No one had trained or prepared Burnes for such close-up 'spycraft'. He had to think on his feet and if there was any doubt, then he had to create some kind of a safe middle ground of half-truth and diversion to avoid being committed to follow up any statement made.

In this case, Burnes was compared to all other foreigners and infidels; naturally he came to be compared with the Russian envoys, and to make matters worse, the Bokharans were a slave-dependent society and Burnes, as all future agents were to find out, had to adapt his thinking and his emotions to such cultural factors, or he would have made grave errors. But most important of all in these dangerous endeavours was the point that genuine friends could be made. The Grand Vizier certainly became friendly; the potentates in such isolated places wanted to know about the distant world in Europe and Burnes was a skilful storyteller.

What the senior officers wanted, however, was military information, and what strikes the modern reader about this is that the reports written for their superiors by the political officers were naturally going to be interpretations and theories of strategy based on observation and various conversations. In other words, they were most likely to be erroneous and were invariably subjective;

Burnes's report was entirely typical. His main aim had been to find out about the Russian activities in the high borderlands and to ascertain the attitudes of the buffer states. As he returned to India there was a crisis in Constantinople, as Mohammed Ali – the then ruler of Egypt – had marched on Constantinople and also a Russian fleet had moored there. This led to an impasse and a delicate situation for the Foreign Office. Never was knowledge of Russian aims and objectives more pressing.

Burnes conjectured that the cities of Herat and Kabul must not be allowed to be taken over by Russia; the route from there to India was through the Hindu Kush and Burnes knew that an army could succeed in negotiating that terrain. He estimated that a Russian Army could defeat Afghans in their home base: something we know with the hindsight of history was entirely wrong-headed. But Burnes did see the importance of holding on to Kabul. What he had realized was that the longitudinal string of locations from Teheran across to the River Indus was the key to control; if the Russains had Persia and then moved along that line, occupying Meshed, Balkh, Herat before Kabul, they could, if they consolidated at each point, work towards controlling the regions around Kabul and eventually isolate the Afghans. South of that line were the deserts of Kerman and Helmund. Below that, leading to the Punjab, was a route through Baluchistan – the route Alexander the Great had taken. However, in view of the existing Russian territories, the southern route did not appear to be feasible since the route was not only extensive but also lacked proper facilities for sustaining an army.

With these thoughts and conjectures, Burnes presented his military report. British agents had also been directed to some of the other *khanates* south of the Caspian Sea and Russia was becoming aware of this; they knew about Burnes also, and they knew that there was a potential action by Britain in the lesser states to play a part in preventing Russian expansion. When Burnes was asked to go to Kabul on his next trip, St Petersburg had decided to act. Nicholas I

– the Tsar from 1825 to 1855 – had witnessed the expansion of his Empire to such an extent that it was financially strong; he had reached a point in which trade with China was thriving; the number of working class people to maintain the daily labour of keep the Empire had trebled. But what the Raj administration did not perhaps fully appreciate was that Tsar Nicholas had a priority and that was not really expanding beyond Persia: he wanted to expunge Turkey from the land of Europe. His reign had seen problems with Hungarian and Polish nationalism and a focus on India was not yet a central concern.

Burnes did return to Kabul and there he met Dost Mohammed. As Nicholas was informed that Afghanistan deserved some attention – he had an officer called Vitkevich who was sent in response for a cry for help from Dost – who was also playing the Game in keeping British interests sweet and apparently welcome. Dost wanted substantial help from Britain before Vitkevich arrived. In this context, we now find that another category of agent also formed a part of the scene. The East India Company, at this point in somewhat of a decline, had its own team of political agents in the field where there was a need for one. Confusion, duplicity and mixed fortunes dogged Burnes, and this situation was no different, because the Company agent (called a 'news writer') had deserted. This was none other than a highly condemned man named Masson. Captain Wade of the British Army found out about Masson and had his death penalty annulled. Masson soon came across as someone who extremely disapproved of Burnes and his missions. In fact, as a case study in Raj intelligence work, the Burnes–Masson mission at Kabul emerged as a highly informative one.

Basically, Burnes was caught between the two rulers in search of further power: since Ranjit Singh, an enemy of Dost, already enjoyed complete British support, Britain aspiring to maintain a good rapport with both Ranjit and Dost, tried to appease the latter by reassuring him (Dost) that he mattered to them. In the middle of this was Burnes. What happened subsequently was that Lord Auckland – the then

Governor General – wrote a letter to Dost which created massive problems for Burnes and for all sorts of intelligence work. Auckland's tone was a threat: Dost would be punished if he allied himself with the Russians. It followed that Dost's ambitions to run Peshawar could never happen. It must have seemed to the court in Kabul that the British were acting like a schoolmaster in a bad mood, stating in plain terms exactly what would and would not happen.

The intelligence case study now turns to the issue of the individual, working in a military context, being uninvolved in the general diplomacy of a region in the Raj. Burnes was the man on the spot who had to face Dost – not Auckland. What this reveals is the nature of work in the field, so to speak, at any location in the Empire: there might be a threefold layering of activity, all impinging on intelligence work but not working together: diplomacy, general spying by native personnel and Company men and finally, the young officers like Burnes with a specific brief to fulfil.

Dost Mohammed – if he had not until then thought seriously about a deal with the Russians – was thinking seriously now: Captain Vitkevich was in Kabul and unaware of what Auckland had done, but Burnes welcomed him and dined with him at Christmas, 1837. Vitkevich won the day, of course: Burnes eventually left, with a sense of failure. Vitkevich had given Russia a foothold of diplomacy in the fortress – the Bala Hissar – in Kabul. Masson, all set to criticize Burnes, spent all his time and energy minutely making note of the officer's faults.

The Burnes case is instructive in showing clearly the clash between individuals on intelligence missions and the complex machinations of the Raj administration. It also highlights the limitations of the intelligence network because Rawlinson – the agent in Persia – had not known and given notice of, the Russian advance into Afghanistan. As was the case in so many instances, the lone spy was the unknowing victim of this many layered process of dealing with a succession of rulers in the buffer states.

If we now divert our attention to the situation 40 years later, the focus shifts from Kabul to Khiva, and the outstanding character in intelligence work in the Great Game was then, for many, Frederick Burnaby. Khiva is located between Merv in the south of Turkestan and the Aral Sea, about 230 miles west of Bokhara. At the time when the Russians had just started an expedition from Orenburg in the Urals, Khiva, came across to the Russians as the first town of considerable size that could be worth seizing. If the Russians were to send an army into Turkestan, it would have been like passing through a formidable country stretching over for 800 miles before they could have witnessed the walls of Khiva. The place was notoriously barbaric: when the Hungarian linguist Arminius Vambery went there in 1863 in disguise, he saw human heads rolled from old sacks and old men having their eyes prised out of their sockets. It was known as 'the secret city'. Three years before Fred Burnaby published his book – A *Ride to Khiva* (1876) – a Russian force under General Kauffmann had occupied the town.

Captain Burnaby of the Blues (The Royal Horse Guards) was an adventurer who had already seen much of the world when he took on the task of travelling from Orenburg to Merv. He knew that the Russians were then prominent in the whole area and that he was ostensibly following their main army. Almost 20 years had passed since the end of the Crimean War and Russia had not only regrouped, but had effected major reforms in the army, notably a new attitude towards the officer class. Many new officers were, by the 1870s, not aristocratic but in English terminology belonged to the 'lower middle class'. The emancipation of the serfs had taken place in 1861 and the Russian Empire was being re-energized by a very different outlook to that in Burnes's time. Burnaby, therefore, considered this development as his primary brief to enquire into the nature of the Russian presence. He did far more than that: his book is a disquisition on Russian character and habits, with a military strategy built into the argument.

In 1864, the Russian Chancellor - Gortchakoff - wrote a memorandum for all the European powers, to make Russia's situation vis-à-vis Central Asia clear. His forces had just taken the town of Chemkent in Turkestan and he wrote that as Russia had consolidated their control on the border states, they had no ambitions to extend their interests into India. But this meant nothing really: only short time after the memorandum, General Tchernayeff besieged Tashkent and finally captured it in July 1865. The British attitude towards Russia at the time of Burnaby's ride was mixed and ambivalent. Die-hard Tories like Burnaby wanted a tough line on the 'Russian Bear' and his book not only appraises the Russian temperament but he wanted more than the diplomacy of Gladstone, who, after coming to power in 1868 had sent an envoy to agree on keeping Afghanistan as a buffer, neutral and comforting to both powers in its independence. The statesmen agreed that Russian activity and imperial designs should have a limit at the River Oxus, but there was no agreement reached on the North West Frontier. Therefore, after several decades of wrangling and paranoia about the Afghans, nothing changed on that front.

Burnaby's mission consequently had the central aim of finding out just to what extent Russia had advanced into Turkestan. He cast scorn on the idea expressed by some in Britain that there were benefits in Russia and India being neighbours. He wrote:

> People in this country who advocate the two empires touching are not perhaps aware that our Indian army would then have to be increased to three times its present strength, and in spite of that precaution, there would be less security for ourselves.[4]

Amazingly, Burnaby planned his journey for winter. His leave of absence from his regiment could only begin in December, and this reminds us that officers engaged in intelligence in the Raj tended to make their contributions in their own time: on official leave for several months, they would often prefer a trek into unknown regions rather than a trip home. After all, many of them had no family back home. The way he prepared for the trip, throughout November, is informative on the attitudes behind such intelligence planning. He bought a huge sleeping bag made of sail cloth and took two guns: one for protecting himself from the wolves and the other (a service revolver) for defending himself against all his human enemies. Essential items such as quinine and cooking materials added to the weight of his burden. But the most intriguing feature of this trip, as in all Great Game journeys, was the very fact that liaison with the Russian high command was sought. This was still an era in which officers and gentlemen would converse, be civil and indeed cooperate with actions taken by the enemy. Hence, the word *Game* came into being. Consequently, Burnaby tried to talk to the Russian War Minister – Milutin – but instead, he realized that there had been a breach of etiquette, and that Milutin was perturbed: 'I now first learned that General Milutin... was personally opposed to the idea of an English officer travelling in Central Asia, particularly in that part which lies between the boundaries of British India and Russia... a Russian traveller, a Mr Pachino, had not been well treated by the authorities in India. This gentleman had not been permitted to enter Afghanistan and in consequence General Milutin did not see why he should allow an Englishman to do what was denied to a Russian subject'.[5]

By the 1870s, we have to conclude from this, the Great Game had become a strange concept: on the one hand the military aristocracy still perceived the manoeuvres on both side in attempting to gain intelligence to be a gentlemanly affair, while on the other hand, with pragmatic diplomacy in mind, there was a new Machiavellian ruthlessness emerging.

But Burnaby developed a report on military affairs of a practical nature which he incorporated into his book. For instance, at one point he notes about Kirghiz horses: 'We are apt to think very highly of English horses and deservedly, so far as pace is concerned; but if it came to a question of endurance, I much doubt whether our large and well-fed horses could compete with the little half-starved Kirghiz animals. This is a subject which must be borne in mind in the event of future complications in the East'.[6] More seriously, he assessed the Russian officer class and their attitudes to expansion and open conflicts with Britain. The fact was that the officers were often in isolated border areas, with little to do but patrol and observe; they could go hunting to enliven their time on duty, but Burnaby saw that there was more than this. He noted:

> You cannot be with Russian officers in Central Asia for half an hour without remarking how they long for a war. It is very natural; and the wonder to my mind is why Russia has not extended herself still farther... and as the only public opinion that is said to exist in the Tsar's empire is represented by the military class, which in a few years will absorb all the male population of the nation, we ought to be thoroughly prepared and ready for an emergency.[7]

Reading Burnaby's book, the reader is staggered by the apparent availability of statistics; he quotes facts and figures that, if accurate, would have been very valuable to all kinds of people, however, since he himself was not quite sure about the level of accuracy, he preferred not to divulge any information regarding his sources. He writes that if Russian reserves were called out they could put 1, 300, 000 men in the field and that there were 33, 893 Turkomen males who could conceivably be one army in active service for Russia. But Burnaby writes that these are 'Russian data' and then admits that there is no way of ascertaining their accuracy. This once again leads us to believe that the agents on the Great Game missions relied on hearsay, chance conversations and any ostensibly 'official' data that might have been gained – possibly just from the newspapers.

The lackadaisical attitudes to the journeys of the officers on these missions were staggering. When Burnaby was planning his trip, he quite sensibly went to see the Military Attaché at the British Embassy in Orenburg; Burnaby comments: '... there was no-one at home save the Military Attaché and he was so engaged in having a lesson that he had no time to see me'.[8] The only advice he was given was that the Russians would never believe that a British officer would travel to a place like Khiva for mere diversion and interest. It seemed astounding that decades after the work done by Abbott and Burnes, attitudes had not changed and that policy still relied for its workings on amateurs and officers on vacation.

In 1877 Burnaby published a second book, *On Horseback through Asia Minor*, and here, although the pattern of enquiry and reportage was the same as in his first book, he added considerable detail in his appendices which showed very clearly what the value of his work was going to be: more perhaps in the factual basis of his writing than in his growing Russophobia. For instance, he gave a detailed account of the routes traversing Asia Minor, covering the rivers Euphrates and Tigris. It appeared that, as the nineteenth century wore on, the command at the Staff College gradually realized the importance of all the pathfinding work done by men like Burnaby, the mass of facts was seen as something to re-evaluate. Burnaby's notes include just the kind of practical data that would be valued by future military movement and gambits, such as his account of a path from Angora to Sivas: 'The road by Angora by Tokat to Sivas is the shortest. It is best provided with provisions... the route from Caesarea to Diarbekir leads eastwards along Melas till that river joins the Euphrates below Malatia. The river is then crossed by a ferry-boat...' He was, in fact, doing the kind of work done by the Indian pundits, in concentrating on the topography and the fine details of transport. But Burnaby also dipped into geopolitics as we would now call it, writing copious notes on 'The military importance of Syria' for instance, in which he concludes that 'If Syria is easy to attack- she is equally difficult to conquer. Her territory is mountainous. A small army could defend itself for a long time against a large force. In Mesopotamia and in Egypt a single battle won would be sufficient to reduce the entire country. In Syria it would only enable the foe to occupy a more advanced position'.

Burnaby was six feet four inches tall and weighed 15 stones; he was destined to die in action, speared to death in the Sudan in 1885, aged 42. As Peter Hopkirk has noted, when London learned of Burnaby's death, 'the nation was plunged into a frenzy of grief'. A poet called Burrows-Smith wrote a poetic tribute to the hero with the following lines:

> Again he leads his daring band with noble mien, And with them makes one gallant stand For England's Queen.

James Tissot painted Burnaby reclining on a sofa, (now in the National Portrait Gallery) languidly holding a cigarette and wearing his smartest mess uniform; that became the abiding image of the man as a heroic Victorian. The words beneath the image are: 'Frederick Gustavus Burnaby, 1842-85. Soldier, traveller, politician and balloonist. Memorable for his famous 'A Ride to Khiva' in 1875-6. Killed in action in the Sudan'.

Burnaby's A Ride to Khiva had made him a celebrity – something that did not happen to the officers around Henry Lawrence. He was invited to dine at Windsor and the media wanted him to lecture the world on the Russian 'menace'. But there is a final irony about the expedition. This was evident when he fell into conversation with a Russian colonel about his mission, the content of the dialogue was 'Anyhow, I have seen Khiva'.

'Khiva, that is nothing', the colonel replied deprecatingly, 'Why, one of your colleagues, Major Wood, an officer in the Engineers, was here last summer; he could have gone to Khiva any day he liked...'[9]

Burnaby's books received mixed responses and the common criticism was expressed most neatly by The Spectator, with the point that 'It has been outrageously puffed by party writers and absurdly praised by people in society' and the book was summed up in the same piece as 'an indictment of Russia and a panegyric upon the pashas in general'.[10]

Burnaby's adventures apart from reminding the historians about the Great Game also revealed the necessity of segregating intelligence work, which was regarded more as an official brief from those activities that were taken on as unofficial initiatives. Burnaby falls into the latter category, and a comparison of the Burnes and Burnaby expeditions help to enlighten matters in the context of the Victorian ethos at the time. By the time Burnaby's books got published, the Russian question was not so far from an open conflict and the Crimean War was still fairly fresh in the minds of his readers and military colleagues. He was, therefore, aware that he was making a contribution to a national paranoia about the Slavic imperial drive. The propaganda about pan-Slavism was well entrenched in the worlds of literature and art. But for men like Burnes and Abbott, the focus was all on Afghanistan and about control of the key communication channel between Russia and India.

Strangely, little was to change in this pattern of individual prowess and courage, done by outstanding officers in various regiments, up to the time of the end of the Great Game in the early years of the twentieth century. With that in mind, the attention must now shift towards Sir Francis Younghusband and what he represents. By the end of the century, the spying – taking place as part of the Great Game – was being defined and mythologized after Kipling's novel, *Kim*, published in 1901. By then, the male adventure genre in popular fiction had begun to include the spy as a type, and with the Dreyfus affair in France in which army officer Alfred Dreyfus was found guilty of selling secrets to the Germans (1899), the business of espionage was becoming fascinating to the general public in a new way, reflecting an idea of warfare that asked questions about morality as well as politics. In this less clear-cut and ideologically explained world, Younghusband came to represent the ethos of the Great Game in decline.

In 1903, the Russian threat was still looming at large and this time it was Tibet that became the focus of attention. Lord Curzon – then Viceroy of India – refused to take any further chances as he was absolutely sure of the fact that a Russian threat existed in reality. He said he was 'a firm believer in the existence of a secret understanding, if not a secret treaty, between Russia and China about Tibet'. The British force which went up into the Himalayas was led by Younghusband – a man whose military career begun in 1881 when he was accepted by the Royal Military Academy at Woolwich. Younghusband was born at Muree on the North West Frontier on 31 May 1863. Within less than a year of Younghusband's acceptance into the Academy – the Tsar of Russia, Alexander II – was assassinated and at the time, the young officer was taken into the King's Dragoon Guards. He was posted to India, where his brother George was already on active service.

Younghusband made several expeditions in the Far East, notably to Manchuria and to the extreme edge of the Russian Empire. But we have to wonder at the very offhand and leisurely nature of the Anglo-Russian military behaviour at that time. Younghusband over the years had tramped through numerous hostile countries, including a trek through Manchuria to Kirin, where he witnessed factories producing field guns and rifles; but when his party reached the Sea of Japan and saw Russian troop activities, everything became very friendly and relaxed. At Novokievsk, he dined with the Russian officers, after being escorted by a Cossack guide to the meeting place. There, the Russians were quite open with information; when Younghusband and others walked around the port, no one was suspicious of them. In fact, quite surprisingly Younghusband took notes, including some statistics on the manpower at the border in terms of both the cavalry and the artillery.

By venturing into China, Younghusband realized that he was breaking new ground, and from his studies and reports he nurtured the idea that there was a serious threat to Manchuria from Russia – something that would indeed be verified in 1900 when that actually happened. After the death of General Gordon at Khartoum there had been some misgivings about the way Britain was dealing with the Imperial domain, but Lord Salisbury's government was all for maintaining the Empire, and so any information forthcoming from the outer reaches (and so it would enhance the hold on India) was always welcome. Apart from Younghusband, one named Colonel Bell was active in China during that time and eventually the two prominent personalities decided to meet. It was after meeting Bell that Younghusband set out on his most dangerous and ambitious adventure to date: a ride from Pekin to Srinagar – in other words, he traversed through the entire breadth of China.

It was on this incredible journey that he met the notorious Russian agent – Nikolai Notovich – the figure Kipling had used to base his spy in *Kim*. When Younghusband reached Srinagar in October 1887, he had been in China for a year and a half. He had become the expert on China and was in great demand as a lecturer in reputed places, including an invitation to speak at the Royal Geographical Society in 1888. At the peak of his Great Game experience, Younghusband met another Great Gamer – perhaps the most celebrated. This was the enigmatic Ney Elias. They met on a train and began to talk. But the man whom Younghusband called – 'the best traveller there has ever been in Central Asia'– managed to evade anything too revealing and got off the train at the first opportunity.

At the other edge of the Russian Empire, bordering on Persia, Percy Sykes was Great Gaming. He also met Ney Elias as he was travelling through Persia. Elias's family was from Bristol; they were originally Jewish but had been acculturated in Britain. Elias took up service for the government and became an expert on the passes located in northern India, which is why Sykes and Younghusband knew of him and held him in awe: he had explored 40 Himalayan passes, in fact. But Sykes, besides meeting and learning from Elias, did something else that was strikingly unusual in the annals of the Great Game: he became a close friend of the Governor of Kerman – Prince Farman Farma. Their close friendship was to prove the most prominent aspect of Sykes's forays into the Russian borderlands. Sykes learned the value of alliances and cultural interchange in the world of military intelligence. He went hunting with Farman quite often and as a result his hunting skills improved to a great extent and became a real asset in the years that followed. The tendency for young officers who entered intelligence to go hunting in far-off reaches of India instead of being categorized as ordinary soldiers on the parade ground and at social parties became a real virtue for men like Sykes.

After passing out from Sandhurst, Sykes was initially commissioned in the Sixteenth Lancers. Very soon he was sent to India where he did all the usual/routine activities of the young officers who had enough leisure, until 1892 when he was sent on his first intelligence mission. Both Sykes and Lieutenant Coningham were sent to Odessa to meet Colonel Stewart, the Consul, and were given the brief of travelling into the Russia – Persia borderlands to check on the rumour that a massive military movement was unfolding in the land of the Pamirs on the northern Indian borderlands. This was the same area that Colonel Robertson – one of the founding fathers of military intelligence in the last third of the nineteenth century – had seen active service. The two officers did indeed find out that the Russians were on the move. So nervous were the Russians that they had suspected the Indian traders in Tashkent of being British spies ('news writers') and had ordered them to leave.

We also learn something about the network and recruitment of spies and informants in the last years of the Great Game from Sykes's life. When he was in Meshed – a town close to the Russian and Afghan borders – Sykes was in the heart of a recruitment territory; Ney Elias had been there for some time, and the place was a centre for arms smuggling as well. But according to Anthony Wynn, the place became Britain's 'most important and sensitive consulate in Persia' and that life there was 'a heady cocktail of power politics mixed with religion, espionage and arms smuggling'.[11]

All these British officers – from Conolly to Sykes – were individual adventurers from the officer class. But there was also another major intelligence arm – the 'pundits' recruited by Captain Thomas Montgomerie. A pundit, in Hindi, refers to a learned or a scholarly person. But in the context of military intelligence in the British Raj, the explanation given by the reference work on the – *Hobson-Jobson* – helps to direct attention to another element in the business of information-gathering at the height of the Empire: '...the term has acquired in India a peculiar application to the natives trained in the use of instruments... surveying regions inaccessible to Europeans'.[12]

In a more direct field operations sense, there were spies in the ranks of the Indian Army, controlled by the Quartermaster General. In William Howard Russell's account of his travels in India just after the Mutiny, *My Diary in India* (1860) he gives out the details of these activities; the people concerned were not involved in the geographical work of Montgomerie's men, but they were the same breed with similar training, and they had to travel very long distances and report back to the base at regular intervals. Russell notes the following in his account:

> Long practice has made the natives very expert in concealing despatches, and we have unfortunately been reduced to many makeshifts to carry our meaning from one part of the country to another without any chance of detection, or, if detected, without exposing ourselves to the risk of information being given to the enemy. Our officers brushed up their recollection of the Greek characters and of French, which is not so much known in India as in Europe... I have a suspicion that our spies are impartial in their services to both sides.[13]

But, not so with Montgomerie's men. He recruited men with the primary motive of sending them to explore the territories of China and Tibet which remained still unknown at that time. For that kind of intelligence work he needed a special kind of man. The land they were to go into was 1.4 million square miles in the Himalayas and Karakoram. First, the men had to be Bhotias: these were people with Tibetan blood who had lived on the border regions with India. Then, he had to have men who could handle his own tough training course – one that lasted for almost two years. The focus of this was the craft of surveying, but along with that came all kinds of related skills which were necessary in order to carry on with the explorative work in areas where there would be suspicion and indeed great danger. Essentially, Tibet was closed to foreigners. The entry into the land would be possible using certain designated trade routes, but only for a particular set of people. Montgomerie had to devise methods of storing materials for transport, such as carrying the quicksilver for thermometers. However, the more difficult task was to determine the appropriate disguise since his spies had to convincingly be acceptable as men of specific groups or areas. On top of that he had to have a way of measuring the distances they had covered. Montgomerie devised a stride of 33 inches, and he used Tibetan prayer beads that could be slipped, one for each 100 paces. In that way proper measurement of the distance covered was possible. But sometimes his men were discovered and identified and had to return home. They had to be fearless, intrepid and had to have immense stamina. He found his ideal spies in Nain Singh, his cousin Mani and his brother Kalian. They each took a name for military use in which the initials were merely reversed. Therefore, Mani Singh assumed the name GM – that referred to the reversal of the first two letters in his name when uttered.

The Singhs' first journey represents the template of the typical journey for information-gathering in the far north. Nain Singh travelled for 1, 500 miles, and in terms of his prayer bead countings that was 2.5 million slips of the bead. They had to carry heavy equipment as well, such as sextants and compasses. They had to return at times and restart their journeys. Subsequently, Nain had to adapt to survive in unfamiliar places, such as the time he had to teach in a school at Shigatse because he had run out of money. However, it must be taken into account that these expeditions involved physical dangers also: their were always bandits around and the spies had to attach themselves to other caravans on the move, and use guides (*vakeels*) wherever possible. At one point, Kalian and his men had been attacked by a gang of armed robbers.

The achievement was remarkable: their survey had covered 1, 200 miles and they had ascertained exactly what the route from Kathmandu to Lhasa was like. The Singhs' had also determined the river course of the Brahmaputra from its source. The star figure was Nain Singh – who was recalled in 1873 almost at the age of 50 – to help with a mission to Yarkand. It was his last mission and it was a considerable achievement, involving entry into Tibet in the darkness of the night; he had carried a pack of £25 on the journey and covered a 1, 000 miles across the gold fields plateau, where he could monitor and describe the string of lakes and rivers as he surveyed the route from Tawang to India. Singh was given a substantial pension and even won the Royal Geographical Society's Patron's medal, along with the award of Companion of the Indian Empire.

All these exploits and adventures are stories of individuals, either in terms of the organizers or the explorers and even the travellers themselves. But this makes the history of espionage in the main phase of the Great Game seem to be little more than a chronicle of gentleman-officers and local men undergoing great hardships to locate places, log information and extend military knowledge for the supposed future confrontations with the Russian Empire. None of these tales relate to any central political energizing principle generating tactics, policies or aims in the territories of the Raj and beyond. But in the years immediately following the establishment of the Intelligence Branch at the War Office in 1873, with Major General John Ardagh in command, there were considerably ambitious and important initiatives being taken, generated by the dynamic and intellectual Lord Salisbury, with his Russian policies and moves towards achieving more by means of secret intelligence. A look at these policies gives an insight into the broader picture, the world in London and beyond at the time of some of these espionage adventures on the far fringes of the Empire.

Here we have a world of intrigue and complex strategy which impinges on the world of diplomacy as well as on the actions and attitudes of the military high command. The clearest way to see this is to keep the attention on Disraeli's government at this time: the mid to late 1870s. A basis of the thinking in this context was the issue around the Middle Eastern Islamic nations. The old problem of deciding exactly which borderlands were potentially the seat of the main Russian threat was at the centre of the diplomacy. The issue was whether or not the then Russian regime was prepared to do more than simply infiltrate Persia and leave Afghanistan to a future time – this was at the heart of the two schools of thought in Britain. While the 'Forward School' supported the idea of creating a defensive area beyond the North West Frontier, which in turn meant that Afghanistan had to be retained in some way, beginning with diplomacy, the 'Closed Frontier School' on the other hand, favoured maintaining alliances with the states located at the borders of India, stretching from the north all the way down to the west and Persia.

Salisbury – Disraeli's Foreign Secretary – managed to discuss what eventually became the 'eastern question' at length with the premier and they began to agree on some key issues. Salisbury was of the opinion that the way to control the border states and in particular the Islamic fringe was by the 'moral authority' of the British officer or delegate. In 1878, he wrote: 'An intermediate course between military occupation and simple laissez faire... The principle is that when you bring the English into contact with inferior races they will rule, whatever the ostensible ground of their presence'.[14]

He observed that there was a certain degree of power in the mere presence of British personnel in these bordering states, irrespective of whether they belonged to the military background or other categories such as engineers or businessmen. All this implies that Salisbury was counting on non-military means of implementing intelligence measures in places from Tashkent to Odessa. But there was much more than that; in fact there was a well-established network of spies in all the major cities and there was considerable funding for the enterprise. Salisbury was sure that secret intelligence activity was the answer to the challenge of this eastern question; during that time there was a Secret Service Fund (SSF) with a total amount of £25, 000. Naturally, a large part of this would have to be used for bribery – simply distributed to the locals in a whole range of regions in these eastern states who kept a network of informants going. The way this worked had to be ad hoc most of the time: if there was a certain category or source of information needed at a certain time, then spies were contacted who in turn were asked to supply the relevant information. There was no permanent arrangement in this context. When intelligence did arrive, it was assessed by a group of professionals, ranging from military personnel to diplomats of various capacities. There was always something 'dirty' and unacceptable in the Victorian period about the nature of a 'spy'– as Lord Cranbrook – the India Secretary wrote: 'I am rather suspicious of the nation who offer their service as spies upon Russia and masters of espionage... These dirty weapons must be carefully handled'.[15]

As the decade progressed, Salisbury and his contacts in India and in the Middle East discussed the varying arguments about Russian intentions: was there agreement in Russia that Afghanistan was a target in imperial expansion, or did some Russians believe that greater presence in the Middle East was the priority? A crucially important phase in this was the period in which the military attaché in Russia – Sir Frederick Wellesley – became an active spy. From

1872 he had been stealing official papers in Russia. He became spymaster with the Russian War Office as his terrain. He was instrumental in raising other agents to do similar work in divergent areas, such as in naval intelligence. Salisbury, therefore, in the years between 1872 and 1877, knew a great deal about the Russian troop movements, the correspondence of diplomats and was even aware of some of the letters that were exchanged between General Milutin and the Tsar.

Disraeli had famously announced that 'Our duty is to maintain the Empire of England' and he was always in favour of supporting Turkey and of settling the issue of the North West Frontier. Espionage was looking increasingly like the best way to do the latter, rather than any ambitious notions about controlling Kabul, although it annoyed Salisbury to think that no 'white man' could negotiate the Khyber Pass with impunity. Ideas about the Russian Empire in this decade were apparent largely through the work of Wellesley, a man who had led a chequered career, finding his foothold in St Petersburg because he married the daughter of the British Ambassador there. Earlier he had run off with an actress and blotted his prospects in diplomacy, or so it seemed at the time. Nevertheless, he discovered his real talents when it came to photographing the Russian documents or when he found enough time to sit and transcribe them.

He also became involved in the risky business of code-breaking; naturally both Britain and Russia knew that code-breaking was going on, so often the use of misleading and fabricated documents would be encouraged. In 1876, the Russians were becoming more aware of what he might or might not be doing and did produce unreliable communications. But Wellesley progressed; in 1876 he became Military Secretary to the Viceroy. Disraeli himself used Wellesley's materials and information to develop his military attitudes and statements with regard to Russia's imperial intentions.

What the British government really wanted to know was whether or not Russia had any intention of taking Khiva and holding on to it. If they did, then any large force from them in Afghanistan would have a supply base closer than any point within the Russian lands. Hence the journeys to Khiva earlier by the individual officers have their place in the story. But in this period, years after that first phase of the Great Game, a general thought began to concur that Russia was more interested in consolidating what she had, notably in Asia Minor – until, of course, Wellesley told Salisbury something different. This happened in 1878, when Wellesley communicated notes on a Russian plan to mobilize and move towards Bokhara.

The problem in London was about how much of Wellesley's reports should be believed and acted upon? Specialist historians on his work and achievement tend to agree that what Wellesley did was to enlighten people in power as to the nature of the Russian mindset when it came to deciding on strategy. What his reports did certainly do was convince the two powerful viceroys – Derby and Lytton – that their attitudes towards Russia were right. One of the most influential governors in India at the time of the Mutiny, Lord Lawrence, had represented the older approach towards Russia that they would not and could not venture beyond the North West Frontier. But, by the 1870s many were imagining a world in which Cossacks would fight alongside Afghanistanis against the British Army of India.

Espionage undoubtedly played a major part in that extended diplomacy during the reign of Alexander II when Russian intentions in the Islamic states were unknown. But Salisbury was always convinced that Russia simply did not have the right level of resources to trouble Britain. Arguably, when Britain is compared with other European nations in terms of espionage in this period, no other country there could be said to have a better system. The real achievement of Wellesley is that his lines of thought and his commentary on the sources he used dieted attitudes to Russia for the remaining years of the century.

Notes and References:

[1]   John Hughes Wilson, *The Puppet Masters*, Cassell, London, 2005, pp. 246–247.

[2]   See Charles Allen, (note 7, Introduction), pp. 47–88.

[3]   Ibid., pp. 47–88.

[4]   Frederick Burnaby, *A Ride to Khiva*, OUP, Oxford, 2005, p. 97.

[5]   Ibid., see chapter 3.

[6]   Ibid., p. 238.

[7]   Ibid., pp. 238–240.

[8]   Ibid., p. 98.

[9]   Ibid., For more on the foregoing notes, see the final chapter.

[10]   See Michael Alexander, *The True Blue*, Hart Davis, London, 1957, pp. 209–212.

[11]   Antony Wynn, *Persia in the Great Game – Percy Skyes: Explorer, Consul, Soldier, Spy,* John Murray, London, 2003, p. 129.

[12]   Jules Stewart, *Spying for the Raj: The Pundits and the Mapping of the Himalaya,* Sutton, Stroud, 2006, p. 50.

[13]   W H Russell, *My Diary in India*, Warne, London, 1860, p. 331.

[14]   See John Robert Ferris, 'Lord Salisbury, Secret Intelligence and British Policy Towards Russia and Central Asia 1874–1878' in Ferris, *Intelligence and Strategy,* Routledge, London, 2005, p. 13.

[15]   Ibid., p. 17.

4

The Crimea and the Mutiny

When the writer and traveller, A W Kingslake, visited the holy places of Palestine in 1844, he wrote the following about his time in Nazareth:

> I had fasted perhaps too long, for I was fevered with the zeal of insane devotion to the Heavenly Queen of Christendom. But I knew the feebleness of this gentle malady... let there but come one chilling breath of the outer world and all this loving piety would cower and fly before the sound of my own bitter laugh.[1]

This is from his book, *Eothen*, and this reflection evokes a strong irony when we recall that later, in the battle of Alma in the Crimean War, Kinglake would be caught up in a madness largely stemming from the access and status of that Holy Ground with regard to Europe and Russia.

The Crimean War (1853-6) was known at the time as 'The Russian War', and much of the political substance beneath the conflict relates to the discussions about Russia in the previous chapter. However, the history of military intelligence in the nineteenth century contains some of the classic exemplars of what went wrong in terms of field knowledge in the attitudes and conduct of war during that period.

It is useful here to recall that military intelligence has three areas of field, diplomacy and context. That is, the knowledge required to be successful in a war in the Victorian period can be easily applied to the theatre of war itself; to the diplomacy in the high society and to the areas of knowledge in geography, surveying and cartography so essential to military information. The Crimean War provides a melancholy template of the nature of all three domains. It started with a great deal of diplomacy and espionage long before a war became inevitable. The war has become attached to the notions of military incompetence and intelligence (or lack of it) has, in some ways, dominated the later interpretation of the conflict.

The focus of attention was Palestine – part of the declining Ottoman Empire; Napoleon III – who had then recently come to power – made it clear that France would have the right to guard the Christian holy places. Tsar Nicholas I too thought in much the same way. Therefore, the foundation for the conflict was laid as matters started escalating. Nicholas clearly mentioned that he held Russia responsible for the protection of the Christians within the Ottoman Empire, and naturally, Turkey was suspicious of such a Russian move. When Sir Hamilton Seymour – the Foreign Secretary – reported these words spoken by the Tsar, other reasons for Russia's pressure on Turkey came to light: 'Now Turkey has by degrees fallen into such a state of decrepitude that, eager as we are for the continued existence of the Man [Turkey, 'the sick man' of Europe] he may suddenly die upon our hands... if the Turkish empire falls, it falls to rise no more. It could happen that circumstances put me in apposition of occupying Constantinople'.[2]

Gradually, the diplomats of the four nations directly involved negotiated and searched for an agreement over Russian aspirations and Turkish independence. The various visits made by Russian envoys to the Turkish court led to complex and sometimes farcical intrigue, particularly when Menshikov tried to exclude Turkey from playing any part in appointing the Greek Patriarch, there was a spy hidden in a wardrobe in the Russian Embassy.

Before the outbreak of the war, Colonel Hugh Rose assumed the centre stage in terms of his principal role of supplying information about Russia to those who were embroiled in the diplomacy. Rose was sure that there was a need for a British squadron in the Dardanelles; he had one eye on the commercial interest in the area and another on the military possibilities. What was to be done about Turkey became the media issue of the day and when a partition of that land was suggested, Rose began to see how quickly and effectively European media were absorbed in St Petersburg – something that would later become an important intelligence issue when Russell of *The Times* began his reports from the front. But, as the talks about the holy places and the position of Turkey went on, everyone knew that really, under the talk, the fear of Russian expansion and her presence in the Middle East was the problem. The British fleet – under Dundas – was ready for entry into the Black Sea any time, and preparations for war were going on as the verbal wrangling became more heated.

On the surface, Britain and her ally France seemed to have had plenty of intelligence information regarding Russian power and positions. Seymour sent reports on this, particularly on the size and capabilities of the Russian Baltic fleet. These influenced Admiral James Graham in his future planning regarding the Baltic. But Seymour noted something else of more threatening import – something that would be crucially significant if war broke out. This was that there were Russian forces in the borderland principalities such as Wallachia. Although Nicholas had problems with a few rebel leaders in some of these states, generally, Nicholas wielded enough control in these states in order to easily preserve the lines of communication to the Black Sea. In the lines with what the Tsar had been planning, he sent a note to Britain informing the latter about his ambitious design of maintaining those forces.

A large part of Nicholas's policies was, arguably, due to the influence of the pan-Slavists at the time. The French Ambassador in 1853 thought so, and he was aware of these forces in Russia. Basically, the influence here was that both the Ottoman Empire and the Austro-Hungarian Empire were ruling over Slavic peoples; pan-Slavists argued that the foreign states were oppressing the Slavs within their borders. Prominent pan-Slavists thought that the opportune time had arrived to liberate the Slavs who were residing in the neighbouring states. Ivan Aksakov wrote: 'God has assigned a lofty task to the Russians; to serve the liberation and rebirth of their enslaved and oppressed brethren. There is in Russia no desire for usurpation, no thought of political domination... It desires but freedom of life and spirit for those Slav peoples which have remained faithful to the Slav confraternity'.[3]

There was a certain degree of counterbalancing influence with Nicholas though, and that was in the person of Nesselrode – his negotiator in Turkey – a man who understood the European position. The British diplomats thought that there the best hope of avoiding a war came with Nesselrode's influence, but it was not to be. Nonetheless, war came, and in February 1854, the advance contingents sailed for Gallipoli. Britain and France declared war on Russia on 28 March the same year and after a bright start by the allies the British forces were encamped at Balaclava by late September. The ensuing confrontations, principally involving the cavalry, were to steal the limelight in terms of the part played by intelligence in the war.

The British leader – Lord Raglan – had been Military Secretary to Wellington in the Peninsular War and he was highly rated as a tactician, though his experience had been largely in administration. Part of his attraction with regard to leading men was the amazing tale of his having lost an arm in a battle and then asking for it to be returned as the hand had on it a ring given to him by his wife. There were other virtues: he spoke French well, and though he was 65, he was a man who would command respect. One fundamental aspect of the war, however, was the point that the French were then allies, not enemies. Raglan and other senior officers were going to have to work with Leroy de Saint-Arnaud - the French commander - and his officers. The French had recent experience of war; they had been on campaign in Algeria. They had organized their quartermastering systems much better than the British.

But only two of Raglan's six divisional generals had commanded brigades; all his senior men were over 60, except for the Queen's cousin - the Duke of Cambridge. Whatever was going to happen in that war, Raglan was going to stand where responsibility lay, and he had a great deal of worry there, with so many men under his command and so many allies to work with. Initially, in the broader operations of intelligence, Raglan had plenty of information; some of this came from the embassies in the Balkans and some from the agents. These reports were proved correct in the first phase of the war, as Russian troops moved towards Silistria, where a Turkish force with British officers in charge, had been positioned.

With complete knowledge of Russia and Russian militarism in mind, one of the other mythic names from the war - Lord Lucan - was appointed in charge of the cavalry division. Lord Lucan who had been a Staff Officer in 1828, was familiar with the land of Turkey at a time when she had been the enemy of Britain. Since the influence of Best Jervis and cartography had not yet arrived and no accurate maps of the Turkish theatre of war were available to the British forces, Lucan's knowledge, therefore, seemed to be of vital importance at that moment. But as Lord Cardigan - an enemy of Lucan - whose younger sister Cardigan had married, was to be in charge of the Light Brigade, this relationship was not a good basis for the conduct of a war.

History has made Raglan, Cardigan and the Charge of the Light Brigade at Balaclava the centrepiece of the Crimean War, and the interest in that is partly one of military intelligence. Even the earliest writing about Raglan's behaviour notes his responses to reports by spies. Balaclava – a small port close to Sevastopol – had been picked as a suitable base for communications to the front. Raglan had placed a cavalry division to the north of the place and also defended the Causeway Heights with redoubts and infantry. His intelligence was good; a Tartar spy brought news that 28, 000 Russians were heading for Balaclava. But it appears that Raglan had no confidence in the reports of spies. It is not certain why he did not act on that occasion; certainly there had been some misleading reports from spies not long before this. Possibly he did not wish to withdraw any men from Sevastopol just ten miles away. However, as a result much reliance was placed on the Ninety-third Highlanders – the infantry force holding the heights – and on the cavalry in the valley.

Of course, in keeping with their reputation, the Highlanders shocked the Russians into retreat and then the Heavy Cavalry charged the Russian cavalry and dispersed the ranks. So, at that point all seemed well with regard to defending the port of Balaclava. But the famous blunder was about to occur, which was to become the most powerful lesson regarding the neglect of intelligence in the nineteenth century imperial wars. The basic error – the Light Brigade command was sure that they had been told to advance on the main Russian artillery position rather than wheeling round to go towards the redoubts – ended in glorious courage and of course though this is often forgotten, a sort of pyrrhic victory.

On a wider scale, it has to be said that no real thinking had been applied to most of the military actions of the war, from the action at Sevastopol to the supply of provisions and tents for the men. As the war gathered momentum and William Howard Russell of *The Times* began his despatches, the topic of intelligence received great attention as Sevastopol was about to be attacked. This was because it took only a week for copies of the newspapers to reach St

Petersburg. Nicholas's famous remark that he could read about the next strategy in *The Times* appears, with hindsight, to be an ironic extension of the established nature of intelligence work in wars at the time – merely extensions of diplomacy or amateurism. But to the British troops in the thick of the action, it seemed no joke when told that their enemies had come to know of the British plans through the newspapers. The men's attitude to Russell changed markedly after that.

Though all this is a part of the story of intelligence on a general level in the Crimean War, there was also another aspect of the work done, and this was something far more relevant to what was actually learned about information-gathering at that juncture. This hinges on operations undertaken by Charles Cattley. Before he arrived, Raglan had not really had access to any reliable topographical information, and nor did he know anything about the manpower of the enemy. Estimates differed markedly, giving figures up to 100, 000 men.

Until recent research, there has always been some confusion about Cattley, who had been British Vice Consul at Kertch. This confusion arose because a family of diplomats called Calvert were also working as consuls in the Dardanelles, and Cattley used the name 'Calvert' in his undercover work. One of the culverts – Frederick – began to take control of supplies and provisions for the army in the area, notably at Abydos. Frederick set-up a network of transport provision and made sure that supplies arrived at the front.

Cattley began his activities after being commissioned in August to ascertain details of the topography of the area. He started the process of questioning Russian prisoners and this became one of his primary information sources. In addition, Raglan had the local spies of course and he was never really convinced of their usefulness. The leading diplomat – the Earl of Clarendon – expressed his concerns abut the lack of intelligence in a report: '... it is deplorable that we should be so totally uninformed about the numbers of Russian troops there or indeed anything about the country...'[4]

It soon became apparent that the workings of the intelligence would have to be bolder and also involve the soldiers themselves as a sideline. As a result, small detachments of Light Brigade men began to be deployed with the purpose of observing and monitoring the enemy. But Cattley, on the surface a man described as a civilian interpreter who was working with Raglan's staff, had a profound knowledge of all Russian activities and naturally, he began to leave a deep impression. However, the achievements of Cattley were not restricted to this alone.

Raglan had learned many things from Wellington, and one of these was the necessity of a Secret Intelligence Department. Initially, a man who died of cholera – Colonel Lloyd – had been in charge, but after his untimely death Cattley took over. After years of diplomatic work in St Petersburg and subsequently in the Crimea, Cattley gained considerable experience with regard to the working technique of Russia in a war situation. Therefore, his reports, always as far as we know sent directly to Raglan, indicate what methods he saw to be the easiest to attain given that there was no platform on which previous information could be fabricated. However, it was essential that the information always came directly from the Russian ranks. Consequently, Cattley set the cavalry to work on observations and note-taking. Prince Menshikov, who was leading the Russian Army in the Crimea, was a prime target for observation; Cattley realized that local spies would need to be used in that locale, and he began a network, much as Napoleon had always done, relying on good pay and rewards for fidelity and courage.

It was an infiltration task for the local spies and a reconnaissance command for the patrols of cavalry. The latter would need to penetrate the Chernaya, which was a pass on the course of the River Traktir, some six miles south of Sevastopol. On one occasion, a patrol of ten men were frighteningly close to a formidably large group of Russians and retreated sharply. Some of the patrol were cornered and killed. Clearly, these risky forays were being noticed by the Russians, and the area involved was not vast, so every brief Cattley gave was a dangerous one.

Where Cattley shone was in the interrogation of prisoners. During the siege of Sevastopol, he reported to Raglan that after questioning two deserters he had gathered very valuable information. That was an understatement. Regarding the long siege, what the two seamen told Cattley was that massive numbers of Russian reinforcements were on their way, and that Menshikov's intention was to send another force to the rear of the British. Again, Raglan decided to forget Cattley's information. Raglan's stupidity was astounding. There had been an earlier report - from a naval source - saying similar things about the Russian movements. On top of that, his reasons for mistrusting the sources of Cattley's report were nonsensical. Since Cattley's information was gathered from two Polish sailors who were simple townsmen and were not taken from the ranks of Menshikov's force, Raglan concluded that such a report cannot be relied upon and therefore, decided not to take any action. But, as Terry Brighton has pointed out, even Russell of *The Times*, knew that this information was sound. He wrote: 'I was told that the Russkies are very strong all over the place, that reports had been sent to headquarters that an attack was imminent'.[5]

Everyone but the commander it seemed, expected the huge Russian attack. He must have been shocked when it came, early in the morning. The Russians had gathered for an attack just beyond the Chernaya Pass, so no doubt Cattley's outriders would also have confirmed the sailors' reports.

The Crimean War constitutes a fascinating part in the history of Queen Victoria's spies for several reasons. First, it was a chaotic campaign from the very beginning, so the shortcomings of supplies and provisions were sure to have spin-offs in other areas of ineptitude. Second, it was conducted with very little advance knowledge of the terrain. Finally, it was a war on a massive scale involving high-level sharing of command and decision-making; since that command was mostly in the hands of the foreigners who practically had no local knowledge, in such situations trusting their Turkish allies seemed to be of foremost importance. Yet, Raglan did not do so. The natural conclusion to this thinking is that as a check on Russian imperialism the war had obvious reasons and aims, yet the rationale of how it was to be conducted was done weakly, with too much reliance on men with long-standing reputations from another age. The army that fought the Crimean War had not materially changed from the army of Wellington. It still operated on the buying of commissions and flogging. The reliance on *esprit de corps* and personal courage was still at the ideological centre of the army's sense of identity. Nowhere was this more apparent than in the Highlanders and Sir Colin Campbell. One of the collections of war stories – written around 1900 – emphasizes the drama of that achievement:

> Whatever resistance was to be made depended on the 'thin, red line'. Sir Colin, as was usual with him, spoke a few words of warning and encouragement. 'Remember men,' he cried as he rode along the line, 'remember there is no retreat from here. You must die where you stand'.[6]

It is difficult to avoid the conclusion that intelligence work, in the eyes of the commander and his staff, was something best left out of the balance of thought until there was an extreme demand or a crisis. But paradoxically, when one thinks of Raglan's methods, Wellington's quartermaster generals had used light cavalry for short-range reconnaissance, cultivated deserters for intelligence information as well as had acted on captured despatches. It has to be said, however, that maps were still low on the list of priorities even with Wellington. But Wellington's intelligence systems worked very well on the whole. One soldier wrote that 'If the French army had been in the bowels of the earth Lord Wellington would have found them out'.[7]

The significant fact about Cattley's contribution to the work of the spy is that he taught the staff officers lessons that would improve their performance in the remaining years of the war in the Crimea. His activities meant more sense of security and preparation when men were on the move or preparing for action.

Naturally, Russell's reports on the privations suffered by the men in the Crimea had an effect on future-thinking, and there was a logical link between the causes of the problems he witnessed and the presence (or lack of it) of a coherent intelligence structure. Raglan had made sure he had a Special Intelligence Branch, but then restricted its use and applications. In some ways, Russell was one of the best witnesses of the state of affairs with regard to Raglan's shortcomings. As Nicolas Bentley observed:

> In his reports from Gallipoli and Varna, the Bulgarian Black Sea port used by the allies as a springboard for the Crimea, he began to give his readers some idea of the inadequacies and unnecessary hardships from which the army was already suffering. At the headquarters these reports created furious resentment. The reaction was understandable, but it was unjust. Russell saw clearly and made it apparent that the conditions of which he complained were... the faults of... the departmental chiefs at home...[8]

What Russell's presence at the Crimean War affirms is that from that point on, intelligence in its widest military sense and applications would in the future have another dimension, and that would relate in part to propaganda as well as to mediation of facts. In addition to Russell's criticisms was the inescapable fact that the war had cost England 25, 000 men and £76, 000, 000. Related to Russell's achievement in showing some of the incompetence behind those losses was the element of documentary evidence in relation to warfare and its intelligence systems. In other words, the jokes about the Tsar knowing what the British high command were thinking by reading the papers was in truth a part of something much wider and entrenched in everyday European culture and communication. While at one level it expressed in the open the free attitudes of Russian officers about troops and ships when talking to the British officers; at another level, it exposed the confidences exchanged in diplomatic circles when 'off the record' subjects were broached. This laxity in the ranks of the diplomats had always had its dangers as well as its eccentricities. In the memories of naval administration produced by Sir John Henry Briggs in 1897 – covering the years 1827-92 – there are some insightful remarks in this context, and these were by a man who retired in 1870, after joining the Admiralty in 1825. For instance, during the administration of the Earl of Haddington in the years 1841-5, he writes:

> I was consequently placed in personal communications with the French officials, and was not a little surprised to find that a complete register was kept of every ship in our navy. Her tonnage, armament and complement, when she was launched, upon what station she had served, what repairs she had undergone, and whether she was fit for further service or not.[9]

Briggs goes on to say that the French were so interested in our navy that every scrap of information printed in the *Hampshire Telegraph* was cut out and placed 'under various headings of intelligence'. We can only be glad that ten years later in the Crimea, the French became the allies of Britain. But this highlights something very important in the area of exchange of information. In the case of Anglo-French naval rivalry at this time – the middle years of the nineteenth century – it was a feature that there was indeed an exchange of information between rivals, and that was the case in all military spheres.

This tendency may be seen more clearly in a maritime context, as scholars have studied the exchange of information in visits to ports. Some dockyard visitors were spies, and that was apparent. At the time of the Crimean War, for instance – a man called Eugene Sweny who worked as a spy for England – was sent to French dockyards on information trips. In 1859, he actually supplied plans of a ship – La Gloire. More significant was the case of Lord Clarence Paget, who was a Secretary to the Admiralty in 1859. In plain clothes he walked freely into the dockyards at Toulon and went on board a battleship that was being built. He 'began measuring the height of her battery with his umbrella'.

Related to this, and in part very much linked to what Russell was doing, is the fact that the middle years of the nineteenth century were the years of print revolution; states would learn of scientific advances that would have a bearing on military affairs by means of the printed word in all kinds of forms and places, often in scientific or technical language. As one historian puts it:

> Here lay one of the reasons for the efforts made in both navies [French and English] to teach the officer to read and speak the rival's tongue. Many officers were thus able to keep up with new publications in both the important naval languages of the time.[10]

The same historian points out that an English translation of *Tactique Maritime* appeared in 1857 and conversely, *Naval Gunnery* by Sir Howard Douglas was printed in French in 1853.

The same kind of interchange of information was bound to go on in military matters also. One only has to look at the publications of the Royal Geographical Society, for instance. In the year 1837, not long before the Crimean War, there were such travel features as 'Memoir on the Northern Frontier of Greece' by Lieutenant Colonel Baker 'with a folding map' together with 'Notes on a Journey to the Sources of the River Orontes in Syria' by W Burchardt-Barker. The sheer pressure of dealing with huge amounts of information in various places turned out to be quite problematic for the Intelligence Branch in 1873 – but in many ways this was a welcome problem.

In future the news reporter would have a part to play in the nature and functioning of intelligence in war.

In some ways, Russell is a useful link to the events in the Indian Mutiny just a year after the end of the Crimean War. He travelled to India just a year after the Mutiny and his book, *My Diary in India* (1860), is crammed with insights into the workings of the spies at work, both pundits and lesser figures who merely reported on everyday facts about whoever was in opposition to the army in the uneasy months after the Mutiny. In this work, Russell tells us a great deal about the military actions and initiatives taken in the years immediately after the Mutiny. However, Russell in his book did not provide any explanation with regard to the causes of the Mutiny.

What interests the historians of military intelligence is why it happened. The causes are manifold but the rebellion is easy to summarize: mutinous native soldiers (sepoys) staged an uprising in northern and central India and the aftermath of the harsh reprisals and ensuing repression meant that the long-standing power and status of the East India Company in the Indian subcontinent was transferred to the army of India and the British Crown. But with the common practices of the interchange of intelligence being established, why did the revolt take place and consequently escalate into a major problem for the Empire? One of the principal historians of this vent is Saul David, and he points out that certain parties were well aware of the coming Mutiny:

> According to the King's secretary, however, the Red Fort received intelligence that the troops would mutiny at Meerut, a full twenty days before they did. Three days before the outbreak, he added, the King's personal attendants were predicting that the army would soon revolt...[11]

An active and important spy called Jat Mall and another spy, Ahsanullah Khan, reported on conversations with the sepoys about the certain revolt that would come if the contentious greased cartridges were forced on them. Ahsanullah even went to the extent of noting that the sepoys he had interacted with had divulged to him that there had been a long-standing correspondence with the other indigenous troops across the subcontinent, and accordingly, a convergence of rebels was planned – with Delhi as the focal point. Therefore, the most baffling question that loomed at large was the lack of any response to this.

Naturally, as with all the major events in history, there were several contributory causes to the Mutiny. Fundamentally, there had been a steady process of annexation directed by Lord Dalhousie and particular local or regional power bases had been threatened and indeed erased, such as the sons of the King of Oudh, the Rani of Jhansi and Nana Sahib. There were also tax collectors in Oudh, the *talukdars*, and they had lost income and status as land ownership and settlement had been transformed. In a military context, the Bengal Army, with a strong presence of Brahmins in its ranks, was disaffected for various reasons, including undoubted inequalities in the treatment of the natives as opposed to the British troops. In the course of military duty, the Brahmin soldiers had to often mix with men of lower castes. Besides, the enrolment of Sikhs in the ranks also caused much resentment within the different native troops.

In the larger picture, there was also considerable decline of British prestige and self-confidence after the Crimea and also following the Afghan War of 1841-2. Fundamental to the way the army operated was the essential moral strength and power of command in the ranks of the British officers, but not all of them knew the Indian languages nor very much about the cultures, beliefs and traditions of the people they lived amongst.

The issue of the greased cartridges became the light for the powder keg in effect, with all these factors underlying that final outrage. The word was spread across the military establishment that the new Enfield rifles being issued were greased with a mix of cow-fat and pig-fat. The former animal was of course sacred to the Hindu and the latter repulsive to the Muslim. As mistrust grew and statements denying the grease were made by the officials, the thought began to persist that British ideology was being percolated into the ranks, quashing the native faiths within the army. As with all such panics and rumours, the suspicions grew and soon afterward it came to be rumoured that human bones had been ground in the flour that the sepoys consumed.

With these various factors in mind, it is not difficult to see why the Mutiny occurred, but in order to understand the basis for the events we need to summarize what the East India Company had been doing, along with the support from an army comprising Indian manpower, to acculturate native communities and to influence the power base in certain key areas. The Company had taken all kinds of measures to tighten control over the vast subcontinent, mostly by non-military means. They had applied a British administration which was concerned with private property in land, and they linked this to military security. The first wave of control was either military or economic; revenues could be withdrawn and any resistance from small-scale rural chiefs was dealt with by the sword and the cannon.

In addition, the wastelands and forests had been attended to with the intention of fragmenting any centres of power on the margins of the vast areas of arable land. At the heart of the economic changes brought about by the British rule was the increase in security on the major roads and lines of communication; house prices increased notably in Delhi in the decades before the Mutiny and other smaller but valued work was done on making travel and movement of goods easier, such as the efforts made by the Britain to repair the ruined rest-houses used in the Mughal days, along the main routes. In all regions in which their control was strong the Company administrators worked hard to stabilize the running of the rural communities.

Knowledge increased with all this administration. As C A Bayly noted:

A vast array of statistical information poured into Calcutta Secretariat as the Company's charter came up for revision in 1813 and as new revenue assessments were introduced throughout much of the North Western provinces and Madras. By the mid-1820s almost all districts had revenue survey maps going far beyond the earlier Mughal route maps...[12]

In the decades before the Mutiny, the British rule in India had been basically stable because there had been efforts to use diplomacy, mainly in the second-level bases of power in the states where the stirrings of rebellion would often start. The administrative focus was always on a flexible method of liaison and control. A case in point that supports the viability of the system in place before 1857 is the 'White Mutiny' in Mysore in 1809. This conspiracy, however, could be prevented because one of the major players in this Mutiny – Purniya – ultimately turned out to be faithful to the Crown. This in turn became possible as the British through means of diplomacy and efforts to understand the native ideology were able to successfully stall the White Mutiny. The fundamental aim was to neutralize the Indian states which might be potentially oppositional to the British rule.

Yet, at times there was confrontation, and from these much should have been learned that would have helped the Company authorities who ruled over in India in 1857 to perceive the forthcoming upheaval. An instance of this was in Gwalior in 1843. A constitutional right of interference in writing allowed the British to intercede in the internal affairs in a particular state as and when a call for British assistance arose from the native rulers there. When an intriguer Dada Walla succeeded in attaining power in Gwalior, with the expulsion of Mama Sahib, a delicate diplomatic and military situation was created. In bordering Scind the Maharajah was under British protection. When there was a development involving the succession in Scind, the cooperation of the Gwalior regime was needed along the borders. Since Britain increasingly felt the need for their intervention in the kingdom of Scind, they decided to introduce a document under the Treaty of Burampur of 1804 which would support the call for British interference.

From this a diplomatic situation emerged in which Britan was defined as a 'guardian' in Scind and from that situation came an impasse: the Governor General wanted to meet with the Maharajah, but the intelligence made it clear to the army command that a British Army must not enter Scind until that meeting with the Maharajah had taken place. Advice dictated that the advance of the army across the River Chumbul should be delayed, for the same reason. The Company resident – Colonel Sleeman – made the matter of protocol very clear:

> When I mentioned his Lordship's intention to cross the Chumbul on the 22nd, Suchurun Rao, the brother of Ram Rao Phallthea and Bulwunt Rao, who had come to meet me, expressed a very earnest desire that this might not take place, as it was unusual for his highness to pay the first visit to the governor-general on the other side of the river...[13]

Eventually, the river was crossed; the British Army entered Scind and the result was disastrous. Some men who had been previously friendly to the British crossed the line into the rebellion. The treaty that was supposed to take place never did, and a battle was on the cards. Communication had not been successful, and as a chronicler writing just a decade after the battle wrote to explain the nature of a despatch into the military command: 'Despatches like that of the commander-in-chief in this instance, are not written for the information merely of the individual to whom they are addressed; they are framed for the public eye...' In other words, he was questioning the use of the intelligence information, gleaned by diplomats and Company administrators, in the field.

There was a confrontation and it was a bloody one. Of special interest was that of all the various regiments involved in the battle in Scind following this blunder, the Indian centre was to be attacked by the native troops: Brigadier Stacy's contingent of infantry primarily consisted of native infantry and was led by Lieutenant Colonel Gairdener.

This case study explains how the always delicate balance of administrative logistics and military presence in the native states could lead to major problems if information was not absorbed and used in the right way.

In the build-up to the Mutiny one of the most prominent spies in the story is Jat Mall again. He figures in the escalation of the *chapatti* communications as the mutinous ideas were spread. The *chapattis*, with their symbolic significance, are still an enigma to the historians. One early reaction to their appearance typifies the mystery and unease at their significance. This was a magistrate – Mark Thornhill – based in Mathura, who found some *chapattis* lying on a table and described them as 'dirty little cakes of the coarsest flour'. Although numerous people responded lucidly to such remarks, major newspapers considered the cakes to be indicative of something very serious yet to come – a foreboding of a large-scale disaster.

There were several good reasons for spies like Jat Mall to live in Delhi as spies like him gathered information successfully from street gossips and from conversations in the eating-houses/restaurants. He claimed that 'some people regarded the *chapattis* as a warning of an impending calamity, others that their purpose was to warn against the government's plot to force Christianity upon the people...'[14] Officers from various parts of the land had also had encounters and conversations which, with hindsight, were far more important than they realized at the time. Colonel George Carmichael-Smyth, for instance, commanded the Third Light Cavalry at Meerut. In March, he had been in the Himalayas and there he had conversed with an old Indian soldier who had told him: 'I have been 36 years in the service and am a *havildar* [a sergeant] ... but I still would join in a mutiny and what is more I can tell you the whole army will mutiny'.[15]

In the course of the rebellion, the only kind of intelligence of any import was information about how, when and where troops could be moved to the front lines where sepoys and other disaffected men were active, together with despatches concerning small triumphs and disasters. A central concern was the transport of European troops, often being done in small detachments by *dak* carriages. But in the aftermath, when forces were on the move against remnants of dissent, the intelligence was once more of the kind reliant on well-guarded despatches with information on the size, composition and strength of the enemy. Russell witnessed one such event in this process, when the despatches arrived, reporting on a scrap with Bainie Madho's sepoys:

> This man made his appearance almost about the same time that an Emissary arrived from Evelegh, carrying a despatch in a quill Concealed about his person, in which the Brigadier gave an Account of an action he had just been fighting with this very Bainie Madho's sepoys. Long practice has made the natives Very expert in concealing despatches, and we have unfortunately Been reduced to many makeshifts to carry our meaning from one Part of the country to another without any chance of detection...'[16]

Clearly, the subtle devices of Nain Singh and Montgomerie had some parallels in the more directly military arm of the intelligence as practised at various stages in the history of the Raj.

The rebellion began in the Bengal regiments of the East India Company, where only 18 out of 74 regiments remained loyal. Fortunately, the Mutiny did not move into the Company areas of Bombay and Madras, but it took two years to combat and suppress. In 1860, the Company's regime in India ended.

It is typical, and also ironical that the years following the suppression of the Mutiny and the re-establishment of British control in India should reflect the massive transformation in the nature of military intelligence begun by Russell of *The Times*. This indicated that all non-military personnel surely had a say in matters relating to espionage, information-gathering and basic diplomacy. Examples of this are legion, but one man in particular represents this trend towards wider commentary on military matters by journalists, writers, travellers and artists. This was G W Steevens – the man best-known for his book – *With Kitchener to Khartoum* (1898).

Steevens wrote a short book on India in 1905, published simply as *In India*. In principal, this is an assessment of India written 20 years before, in the 1880s. The Mutiny in the 1880s was not so distant and therefore, the memories of the rebellion remained deeply entrenched in the minds and hearts of the then Indians. Steevens in his book assesses the military situation keeping in mind that repetitions of such large-scale rebellions do not occur in the future. He saw the problem as one connected to the logistics of troop movements, and this was true to a large extent, but mutinies had happened before, and sometimes over other more easily definable things, such as the one at Vellore in 1806. The cause of this trouble was an attempt to try and compel the sepoys to wear round hats and leather stocks. This meant that the sepoys had to do away with their distinctive facial markings, earrings and necklaces, which were worn by them as a mark of religious significance.

But Steevens is eager to put forward a rationale of what is needed so that things do not go wrong in these affairs. He says: 'How can even a proper regimental feeling be maintained when officers and men are forced to grow strangers?... What is to become of the senior officers, deprived of their chances of learning to handle a regiment'? He was anxious after reading that the Royal Warwickshire regiment had arrived in India after service in Khartoum, only to find that 'it had been sent there by mistake or prematurely'. Steevens also found out (we don't know how or where) that half of the regiment was 'dumped down in Fort George, with no ground for manoeuvring or shooting within miles, and the other half at an obscure place called Bellary'.[17]

What had been happening in the 40 years since the Mutiny and the Crimea was that amateurs of all kinds and backgrounds were becoming 'informed commentators' and the comments from the Tsar about learning the allies' tactics from reading *The Times* was becoming a prophecy on the shape of things to come in terms of intelligence and war.

What Steevens did understand, however, was that the largest military problems in the past had been the ones exacerbated by profound divisions and oppositions in the mindsets of soldiers. He writes: 'It may be true that a Mussulman may never quite surmount a feeling of antipathy – at any rate strangeness – to a Christian... But it is also true that if the breach between races forbids intimacy, it leaves room in the army for comradeship, and even nurtures the personal devotion of men to officers'.[18]

But 'John Company' had gone by 1860 and Queen Victoria had been proclaimed the sovereign of India in 1858 and then, the Empress of India in 1877. This was all about trying to restore some self-belief and prestige after such shameful loss of face in the Empire. From 1860 onwards, things were to be very different in the advance of the pink on the world map, and the focus, in many ways, was to shift to Africa.

Notes and References:

1   A W Kingslake, *Eothen*, Nelson, London, 1910, pp. 120–121.
2   Trevor Royle, *Crimea*, Abacus, London, 1999, p. 99.
3   See Waldron (note 7, chapter 2), p. 123.
4   See Royle (note 2 above), p. 56.
5   Terry Brighton, *Hell Riders*, Penguin, London, 2005, pp. 197–199.
6   Archibald Forbes *et alia*, *Battles of the Nineteenth Century*, Cassell, London, 1902, p. 528.
7   Philip J Haythornthwaite, *The Armies of Wellington*, Brockhampton, London, 1994, p. 158.
8   Nicolas Bentley (ed.), *Russell's Despatches from the Crimea*, Panther, London, 1966, p. 13.

9   C I Hamilton, *Anglo-French Naval Rivalry 1840–1870*, OUP, Oxford,
        1993, pp. 281–282.
10   Ibid., pp. 275–276.
11   Saul David, *The Indian Mutiny*, Penguin, London, 2002, p. 99.
12   C A Bayly, *Indian Society and the Making of the Empire*, CUP, Cambridge,
        1988, p. 68.
13   A Thornbury, *History of the British Empire in India*, Cassell, London,
        1880, p. 509.
14   Saul David, (note 11 above), p. 65.
15   Ibid., p. 79.
16   See Russell (note 13, chapter 3), p. 331.
17   G W Steevens, *With Kitchener to Khartoum*, Blackwood, London, 1903,
        pp. 64–65.
18   G W Steevens, *In India*, Nelson, London, 1901, p. 357.

5

The Intelligence Branch and Professionalism

In 1903, a special publication, *The Report of His Majesty's Commissioners on the War in South Africa*, criticized the organization and management of the Anglo-Boer War. Every contributing department of the military machine of the Empire was called to question, with the exception of the Intelligence Branch and its leader. As historian Correlli Barnett has noted, as early as 1896 the Department of Military Intelligence had informed the General Staff that it would take two months for reinforcements to reach troops in South Africa, and that at that time there should have been an increase in manpower in that region. That detail might not sound like such a momentous fact, but it was, and the reason for that was even after 23 years, the Intelligence brains were not necessarily awarded any status or seen as particularly noteworthy by many in positions of power.

Yet, over that 23 years there had been a quiet revolution. Before the founding of the Intelligence Branch in 1873, the so-called 'Long

Peace' between 1815 and the Crimean War had been largely a matter of complacency and neglect in terms of the growth of intelligence as a respected department of a war ministry and military structure. The Great Game – in one sense – was peripheral, rather amateur and always somehow overshadowed by the machinations of diplomacy. It is not difficult to see the activities of the spies and surveyors out in the Raj and the Levant as secondary to the larger questions of maintaining the power base nearer home.

Of course, the Crimea and the Mutiny changed all that. Despite the poor reputation that posterity has given to Lord Raglan, at least he saw the importance of military intelligence. As John Hughes-Wilson wrote: 'The fact was, in the long peace, the British Army had forgotten how to collect intelligence. The Great Duke's legacy has much to answer for. Lord Raglan... railed at his lack of intelligence. The truth is that Raglan was a calculating and sophisticated commander'.[1]

By 1870 that type of commander was exactly what was needed. The Franco-Prussian War had taught the rest of Europe a lesson about how to conduct warfare: the Prussians had beaten France because of their short-term service system and their reservist corps. They had seen the value of streamlining provisions, from uniform victualling to transport, and they had highlighted the value of having truly professional soldiers. In Britain, in 1870, the army still worked by the system of purchase of commissions. The Empire was ticking over with surprising ease when one considers that most British officers bought their commissions, as they had been doing for as long as there was an Empire. But at the time when the Intelligence Branch was set-up, the new theorists and army professionals were beginning to be a presence, and much of this change was down to the Gladstone ministry and in particular, Edward Cardwell who became Secretary for War in 1868. In addition, to eradicate the flogging that became a common practice in the army, Edward took Gladstone's help in abolishing the purchase system. When the Lords blocked his Army Regulation Bill in 1874, Gladstone went to the

Queen and used her power to see the legislation through. Victoria agreed to Gladstone's suggestion as she could not bear the terrible row this subject had caused in her government factions.

Cardwell has been called the armourer of Britain; in his Army Enlistment Act of 1870 he introduced short-service and in many ways, this was to open up possibilities of radical change in the perception of the place and importance of military intelligence. Prussia had benefited from a large reserve of experienced men who had done a limited term service and yet were standing by for action when required. Cardwell brought in a six-year term and opened up a more rigid selection procedure. The army had long been defined as the depository of criminals and renegades, the tough types who had won the field at Waterloo, perhaps, but in late Victorian years it was perceived that there was more to being an officer than dash and horsemanship, and there was more to being a squaddy than drill and hard-drinking.

It was in these momentous years, c. 1870-4 that the Intelligence Branch arrived, and following Sir Richard Brackenbury in 1887 - a man named Sir Garnet Wolseley - whose attitudes towards the army matched the new thinking soon came to the forefront. One man who was to become a principal figure in many of the departments of army functions was future Brigadier William Robertson - a person who hailed from a modest background in Lincolnshire. In his memoirs he writes of the birth of this Branch:

When first formed in 1873 it was a branch of the Quartermaster-General's Department; later it was placed under the Adjutant-General; and was, when I joined it, more or less under the commander-in-chief, Lord Wolseley. It Had a staff of about sixteen officers and, with the 'Mobilisation Section' Of three or four officers, was the only semblance of a General Staff then in existence. The Mobilisation Section had originally been under the Director of Military Intelligence, was afterwards absorbed by the Adjutant- General's department and then, like the Intelligence Branch, came under the commander-in-chief. [1]

Robertson added that the two branches had been 'constantly tossed over from one high official to another'. He noted that intelligence organization was therefore always going to be influenced by whoever was in charge at one particular time. Clearly, there was a problem in how the department and its work were seen by the top brass. What Stieber had achieved in Prussia was certainly interesting in its outcomes, but the thinking was that there was no way that Britain was going to ape the Prussians in Stieber's own brand of espionage. The bottom line was that the most useful intelligence work since the war with Napoleon had been achieved by individuals – like Cattley or Abbot – and so, it took some time for the new department to have a clear identity. Robertson explains the early work done there – in the office at 29, Queen Anne's Gate – as primarily the collection and collation of information on foreign countries. He also notes that such knowledge was somehow to be processed, taken into the catalogue of current information on every state that might play a part in conflict, and kept for reference.

Before this new departure, according to Sir George Aston, the prevailing attitudes had been more domestic:

> The military authorities were still under the influence of the Palmerston Royal Commission of the early sixties, which was responsible for the idea that fortifications could do the work of warships, the theory being that the introduction of steam propulsion had rendered obsolete Raleigh's old principle that it was better to deal with foreign invading armies at sea... intelligence in those early years, was mainly devoted to studying how to deal with a foreign invading army...[3]

In the 'long peace' the army had been more interested in tactics than in strategy, but that was going to change. The initiative began with a memo from Stanhope (who later became Chairman of the Central Committee) in June 1888. This defined the aims of the new Branch in three main functions: (i) the support of the civil power, (ii) the provision of staff for the India garrison and, (iii) the capability of mobilizing corps of regular and auxiliary troops. What was happening behind all this was the emergence of forward-planning with regard to geopolitics: the event of a war with a European power or in the Raj. The subtext, we might guess, was again something gleaned from Prussian professionalism: to have an intelligence arm of the forces that would have an important status and that would be part of an organic function in time of war.

In 1875, came the Hartington Commission which recommended a War Office department with a Chief of Staff whose business would be largely that of collecting information. In fact, in the person of Wolseley this kind of function had begun, as he set about creating a fresh breed of officers and placed intelligence within a generally more forward-looking and educated elite of senior staff. However, the new Branch was initially under Sir John Ardagh's command since at the time of the Branch's formation Wolseley was in West Africa leading the expeditionary force against the Ashanti. This provided an enlightening case study in which one could observe the new attitudes at work, particularly as Wolseley was destined to take over the Branch later. Wolseley, in the words of one of his biographers, saw that 'War was a serious business and soldiering a profession, not a pastime for dilettantes. The days of playing at soldiers were over. Education in the army, still at a dangerously low ebb, should permeate through all ranks'.[4]

Cardwell and Wolseley were an alliance, and they were not alone. Other officers had been nurtured into supporting roles. Cardwell, when the Ashanti problem became a most urgent one, made sure that Wolseley would lead the force out there and we have to reflect that both were out to prove something about the new methods and attitudes. The Ashanti king – Kofi – and other warlords were conducting a brutal and inhuman regime of terror along the coast and into the territory of Fanti. Their militaristic structures combined with bloodthirsty acts of murder and repression led to a state of emergency in which the various British administrators of smaller protectorates feared that a very large-scale emergency might arise if some immediate action was not taken.

Wolseley emphasized gathering the right team of officers around him and then planned to use native fighters, with a request to the high command that regular troops would be ready to arrive, if needed. He even gave his superiors a quote for the job of £150, 000. Wolseley also involved the navy, for diplomatic reasons and therefore, the force that eventually arrived and set about marching on Kumasi – the Ashanti main settlement – was a mixed one in which some of the fiercest African warriors were travelling along with a naval detachment and Fanti people. But, Wolseley realized at a later stage of planning that he would need some professionals from Britain and he had no less a force than the Black Watch with him.

Wolseley had officers whose task was to survey the local conditions and also to collect a viable force of indigenous fighters. Indicative of the new thinking was the nature of the key men in the Wolseley team. There was Lieutenant Maurice who was an instructor from Sandhurst; Captain Buller, Major Colley and the future principal of the Intelligence Branch, the vibrant Captain Brackenbury. Perhaps, the most significant feature of the early phase of the Ashanti campaign was Garnet Wolseley's own habits; he studied blue books and reports assiduously and he worked his way through all the information about the place and people that he could find. As Joseph Lehmann noted: 'For the first time in the history of the British Empire, a general appointed to command an expedition sat down to a table at the War Office with the Secretary for War, the Secretary for the Colonies, the First Lord of the Admiralty and the various heads of military departments to discuss the necessary arrangements'.[5]

There was a library of books on topography and history available for the staff to peruse. Not to put too fine a point on it, this was *intelligent* intelligence in war.

One of the heroes of the Ashanti campaign – Sir Henry Brackenbury – took over the Army Intelligence command in the 1880s and according to Sir George Aston, a significant change occurred:

> ... it began to be realised that gathering information about foreign armies was only a means to an end. The next step must be to make the best possible use of whatever army Parliament consented to provide, and at last the question of speedy 'mobilisation', which Prussia had taught to the world in 1870, was grasped...[6]

This implies that Robertson's narrative does not make it clear that it took a good ten years for the lessons from Prussia to be learned. In fact, when Robertson talks about his training course at the Staff College, the importance of the Franco-Prussian War for the changes in British intelligence becomes clearer. Robertson was taught at the College by Colonel George Henderson, whom he refers to warmly as 'Hender' – the man who was to be Director of Intelligence with Lord Roberts in the Boer War.

Robertson and his fellow students were taken to see the battlefields of the Franco-Prussian War, notably to Woerth and Spicheren where the French had been defeated and the action was followed by very demanding armistice terms by Bismarck. Robertson's account of the Staff College education provides a clear example of the new attitudes in practice. He spends a lot of time in his autobiography recalling his efforts to learn foreign languages and to master administration, yet intellectual discourse on tactics and on the application and use of intelligence is always balanced with this theory. He gives a clear impression of the kind of mindset expected of the young officers attached to intelligence work, based on a conversation he had with Henderson:

> Having passed into the college without the help of a crammer I was anxious as to how my work there would compare with that of the other officers, and so I told the commandant at the first interview...

His encouraging reply was that the lack of this form of education need not necessarily be a handicap. 'We do not want crammers here – we want officers to absorb, not to cram'.[7]

But the new department still needed to be placed somewhere in the structure of the army. By the time of the office of Sir Henry Campbell-Bannerman in 1892, the Intelligence Department was put as so often in the past, under the Adjutant-General. Since the 1880s, the department had been streamlined in many ways, and there is ample evidence to show that its briefs, assignments and staff were busy doing what intelligence outfits have always done when there is too much to cope with: prepare voluminous reports. For instance, in 1882 John Frederick Maurice, Secretary to Wolseley with the Ashanti, wrote a *History of the Campaigns of 1882 in Egypt*. This was prepared specifically for the Branch. Best Jervis's lessons on cartography had been absorbed by this time, as the volume has 11 maps on no fewer than 16 folding sheets. Maurice even appends a map illustrating the attack on Tel-El-Kebir.

We have to ask, though, about the other side of intelligence, the one involving people rather than paper. What was happening out in the field of operations at the same time? A rare insight is provided by Wolseley himself, writing in his campaign journal while in the relief expedition to Khartoum in 1884. Just before Christmas, when he perhaps had a little more leisure to fill a few pages, he wrote:

It is always difficult to get information in a country where money is no temptation to its people to betray it, and the cruelties of barbarous people not only to the spy but to all his family make men hesitate before they undertake to give the invader information. In Europe or America of course money will provide the energetic man with any amount of information...[8]

He and his fellow officers were learning in these years that understanding the cultural and ethnic lifestyles and relationships in the localities of warfare was more complex than previously thought. In fact, the Raj in India had become a touchstone, a model of how to do things in this respect. But as with all templates of the kind, the situation prevailing in the British Raj did not necessarily influence other contexts. There was no 'John Company' in Africa and comparisons with European races and traditions, as Wolseley was realizing, had no value in places such as the Sudan. In that same journal he assesses the place of Mahdi - the leader of the Sudanese rebellion - in this respect:

> Of course native rumours are important and generally contain some grains of truth in them but they are apt to frighten those whose nerves are not the strongest. One day I hear the Mahdi is surrounded by thousands of warriors longing to die for him... the rumours and stories I hear seriously repeated by fairly sensible men very often here are to me simply ludicrous...[9]

Under two men, Major General Sir Patrick MacDougall (who had been in charge of the Camberley Staff College) and Captain Wilson, the new Branch really went into full throttle by the time of Wolseley's relief assignment in Egypt. That expeditionary army took with it several copies of a massive 400-page volume called the *Handbook on Egypt* which had in its covers almost everything a traveller might need to know about that country, from food to protocol and camels to dervishes. One of the highlights of the Branch's early history has to be the part it played in the diplomatic success in the Congress of Berlin in which Disraeli had faced a potential war with Russia, but he came home and made his famous statement that the nation had 'Peace with honour'. Following this, the Secretary for India - Salisbury - wrote that the Intelligence Department of the War Office had played a major part in the success of the 'preceding diplomatic negotiations'.

However, William Robertson did point out one shortcoming in this period. He wrote that a properly equipped department, led by the Adjutant-General, 'could collect all information and place it at the disposal, not of one officer or department alone, but of all the military heads...' But he notes that even by 1895 nothing had been done in that respect: '... although there was a change of government in 1895, nothing was done to introduce the system recommended until the necessity for it was forced upon us by the costly experience of the South African War'.[10]

It is arguably Wolseley's modus operandi regarding his staff that formed the most important influence on what eventually turned out to be the efficient central 'engine room' of the new Branch. After all, in the 1870s Wolseley had complete support of both Brackenbury as well as Maurice. Brackenbury typified this approach, in which the commander took time to select the right man for each particular role in his team. As Wolseley's biographer has written: 'Henry Brackenbury would never have gained appointment on either his looks or social gifts. In uniform he appeared to be a businessman in disguise'. What Wolseley rightly observed was Brackenbury's special talent for articulating the bearing of theory on practice warfare.

The man – the team called *him* 'Brack' – developed into a hard worker and a superbly gifted organizer, very much what we now think of as a 'personal assistant'. But he was not always sitting at a desk or taking notes: he was one of the first men to walk into Esaman in the Ashanti campaign.

The Raj was very much in step with these advances in intelligence as well. In 1878, an Intelligence Branch was developed in Simla under the initiative of Brackenbury. This was one of the points of real crisis on the North West Frontier. In Robertson's memoirs, he makes a point of noting that it was the quality of the staff running intelligence that needed most attention, exactly as Wolseley had done:

Apart from the faulty organisation of headquarters as a whole, the Intelligence Branch had suffered because of the inadequacy – and of the inferior quality – of its personnel. Although much had been done by the commander-in-chief, Lord Roberts, to ensure that priority for staff employment should be governed by professional capacity, favouritism and social influence were not yet deemed by the outsider to be extinct.[11]

Robertson is keen to inform the reader that in Simla, up in the hills where life was rather more leisurely. But there was more to the northern Indian town than amateur theatricals and dinners. In 1864, the Viceroy – Sir John Lawrence – had made Simla the summer residence for the government of India. Northern India at that particular time was of great strategic importance, and in a more practical sense, the climate was better for getting down to administrative work. This would have been a shock to many residents there, as it had attained the nickname 'Olympus' because of the self-indulgent and languorous Greek gods who ruled man from their heights. But Robertson's criticisms were based on his fundamentally serious and ambitious nature. He personally welcomed the fact that the town had a new status and importance.

From that base, Robertson's mission into Pamir territory is very informative about the way that the sheer vastness of India impacted on the work of an intelligence officer. From his reflections on this situation around 1880 it is probably the case that he knew little of the work of men like Younghusband and all the other loners, though he was aware that 'travellers' had been to some of the uncharted lands towards the Himalayas:

When I went to Simla there was no good information available as regards much of the vast area for which the Frontier Section was responsible. We had to rely largely upon the reports of travellers, and these seldom gave the kind of intelligence that was needed, much of it was many years old, while some of the travellers were themselves renowned for their powers of graphic description than for the accuracy of their statements.[12]

What this meant for the Simla Frontier Branch was that apart from conducting topographical surveys the Branch had to perform additional duties. Robertson was bewailing the lack of directly gathering strategic information such as assessments of manpower strength, weaponry and so on. The work usually performed by the pundits and by individual officers was, by this time, viewed as too marginal in terms of the feared confrontation with Russia on the North West Frontier.

Robertson travelled up the Kashmir Valley, after going first by rail and then by *tonga* – a covered two-wheeled vehicle. He eventually learned as much about brigands operating within the Hunza and Nagar areas as he did about anything directly military. In fact, Robertson's criticisms of the existing information chain in northern India is interesting when we compare what tended to happen when the East India Company had to cope with the thuggee murders back in the first four decades of the nineteenth century. Counteracting these murderous gangs meant police informers in a network, with rewards. Finally that had worked, but unfortunately the same methods did not carry over into major international conflicts. Robertson had a subtext and this had been made simple to him on his arrival in Simla: there had always been ad hoc decisions and a mindset of mere pragmatism when dealing with intelligence across the vast areas of the northern borders. In the past, various commanders had relied on Abbot, Conolly and Burnes and their ilk; clearly by 1880 that mode of action was being retained, but only marginally. The Great Game, in short, was becoming too leisurely in a military world that had been transformed by the mobilization and reservist practices of Prussia, combined with Russia's new imperialism that had led them to extend their lands to Vladivostok – located close to the fringes of Manchuria.

The converse was also true: British travellers were writing about those far Russian provinces, the lands which were across the mountains from where the Frontier Section of the Intelligence Branch found itself. But these were foolhardy and headstrong individuals such as Harry de Windt, who travelled from New York to Paris by land, travelling by sledge across Siberia. Gentlemen such as Harry played a minor part in matters of intelligence like coping with Yakuts and Inuits, collecting all kinds of obscure anthropological data, recounting their experiences to the police and other officials. However, the real work was done (by the last two decades of the century) by men like Robertson and Younghusband.

The nature of the various armies involved in these power struggles was changing also, along with the political climate in the capitals of the empires involved. Mechanization and more sophisticated weaponry was having an influence, as was the more advanced technology in communications that would have had an impact on the way a war was being conducted. As Trevor Fishlock has explained:

> One effect of the Mutiny was to spur the British to forge ahead with building railways over which they could send troops quickly in case of trouble, and stations which could double as fortresses. Lahore railway station was built in 1864 in the form of a medieval castle, with musket loopholes and iron gates.[13]

On paper at least, the new intelligence work may have appeared to be a structure very much dictated by the attitudes and ambitions of a new breed of officers, and to some extent that was true. Young officers such as Robertson were certainly impressed by the likes of the studious Brackenbury and the meticulous Wolseley. They were receptive to the idea of learning several languages at least to an everyday functional level and they were mostly open to the efforts of understanding foreign cultures. But, when it came to actual warfare in particular terrain and conditions, the intelligence personnel still had to be present and had to move along with the regiment.

Certainly the new technology applied to transport and communications was beginning to have an influence on the work of men like Robertson, but we still have to consider that the different varieties of intelligence are always there, even up to today as I write this book, and Britain is still fighting in Afghanistan. A useful distinction is to separate two basic areas of intelligence work in the nature of a military expedition against an enemy. There is what might be called 'paper and science' work done with maps and field reports, and there is the observation and support for the 'knowledge of the enemy' aspect of a fight.

Again, in Robertson's memoirs we have a case study of this, because he was part of the Chitral expedition in 1895 which was organized after a political assassination in Chitral that led to a situation of emergency proportions.

The area around Chitral had been the focus for a series of coups attempting to wrest power from the inheritors of the throne of the Chief (known as a *mehtar*) who had died in 1892. The *mehtar's* brothers and an uncle who had been based across the border in Afghanistan were all involved in the former's murder therefore, an alliance between the uncle – Sher Afzul – and an ally became extremely necessary. Francis Younghusband was the political officer at the time in Chitral and there was a brief respite before Afzul took over, by murder. When two chiefs combined forces, they had enough manpower to overthrow the British garrison and a British force was besieged in the fort. Following that, another British detachment was under siege at Reshun, so things were hotting up when action was decided; there would be a punitive expedition. It was at this point that Robertson became involved and we are able to gather much information about the role of intelligence from his actions in that confrontation.

The plan was put together: three separate groups to converge on Chitral. The main fight was going to involve the First Indian Division and the Thirty-Second Pioneers. The management was in the hands of the Quartermaster General's department, and specifically by the Intelligence and Mobilization Branch. Robertson's part in all this, as appointed by Sir George White, was to collate – with some haste – the various sources of intelligence required. First there was the topography; there was very little available except for those from native sources, so the old problem was there again: how much of that was to be trusted? What he did know was that there were four mountain ranges in the route and that there would be tribal opposition during the march.

The spies' job was therefore, to obtain knowledge of the three passes which would be encountered. The charismatic Chief of Staff – Sir Bindon Blood – made sure that there was an application of false intelligence, as it was absolutely essential that the enemy remained unaware of which pass the British Army was to take. Everything in these situations depended on surprise and misinformation, even to the extent of officers such as Robertson being misinformed. But he was beginning to learn the essence of doublethink and when instructed to prepare for a march to Shakot, Robertson surmised that the real target was Malakand. He writes: 'I laid my plans accordingly, and next morning when the brigade was about to move off, and I was ordered to conduct it to the Malakand and not to the Shakot, I greatly enjoyed seeing the look of surprise on the Brigadier's face at the readiness with which his order was carried out'.[14]

What Robertson was engaged in, in terms of the greater scheme of things, was the 'forward policy' – that of making punitive expeditions across the border, making Afghanistan (and Russia) aware that Britain was active, not merely complacently sitting pretty in Simla and similar places, waiting for others to take the initiative. Winston Churchill, then a cavalry subaltern and a reporter, and his conception of the part played by intelligence in imperial conflict was largely formed in the Malakand campaign. Churchill, learned a great deal from Captain Henry Stanton, who was one of the intelligence officers alongside Robertson in Blood's force. The situation in which Churchill,

Robertson and the others learned so much about the nature of spy networks is well described by David Stafford:

> Everything about the Malakand Field Force engaged his [Churchill's] romantic spirit... Here for a brief moment he was to play the Great Game, a world of intrigue where every man was a warrior, every house a fortress, every family waged its vendetta... Agents and informers for the Indian Army, like Kipling's *Kim*, provided eyes and ears throughout the land, and political officers exploited enmities between rival factions to maintain an uneasy imperial peace.[15]

It was Captain Stanton who wrote the official report on the Malakand campaign and the functions of the Intelligence Department in that enterprise. From here, we can learn a lot about the kind of men who were in those ranks of native 'agents and informers'. One such was Abdul Hamid Khan – a man from an Afghan refugee family – a family that had for three generations supplied reliable advice for Britain, and the man's skills were very impressive. Abdul Hamid Khan could speak English, Hindi, Persian and Pushtu. He knew all the frontier tribes and had also learned what kind of information was wanted by the British commanders over the years.

Churchill, in his account of the Malakand campaign, was aware of the achievements of such men and of the ways in which they worked with the Intelligence Branch. He learned that, as Stafford puts it: '...intelligence and operations were intimately linked, and that the former should be firmly controlled by those who had to act on it'.[16]

Reading between the lines with regard to the view of these border events as recalled by Churchill, Robertson and Stanton, there is a valuable insight to be gained from a consideration of the bigger picture, and that means the 'Forward School' – in particular a cabal of three powerful men in the context of the Great Game and Russian threats on the North West Frontier: these were the foremost British authority on the Indian subcontinent, Sir Henry Rawlinson, Henry Bartle Frere (who is prominent again in the next chapter) and Sir Robert Montgomery. In Gladstone's first ministry a Council of India (1858) was created as one of the political repercussions of the Mutiny. The Council was a consultative body comprising ranks of retired administrators from India, whose primary function involved studying, evaluating and formulating important despatches in the interchange of information between Britain and India. The cabal of three had their main attention on Afghanistan. The head of the Political and Secret Department at the India Office was Sir John Kaye, and he clearly had a good working relationship with the cabal of three elder statesmen. It was Kaye's job to handle state drafts replies to secret and political letters from India.

What becomes apparent is that this group of men knew all about the content of secret material that other members of the council could never see. Their exercise of powerful information in the context of the border expeditions in the decades preceding Malakand set a precedent for such involvement in the encroachments into Afghanistan that many aspired for. Frere, for instance, had pushed hard for the establishment of a British settlement at Quetta, which is in fact, 200 miles over the frontier into tribal lands.

This group first worked together in 1869 and at that time it was a unity founded on the Persian policy. As Britain at the time was reliant for information on a scattered band of agents and spies in a vast area (the one travelled later by Percy Sykes) there was a perception that something more solid and permanent should be put in what was, to all effects, a buffer state which Russia was keen to control. The 'forward policy' regarding India by c. 1890 was a natural result of this thinking.

It is stunning to contemplate the machinations of the London-based Political and Secret Department alongside the daily work of intelligence officers and regional political officers, not to mention the work of Montgomerie and the pundits: such a multiplicity of intelligence elements had to work across the vast area of India and her bordering states and had to do so in such a way that when something like the Malakand emergency arose there would be a degree of unity of action and swift communication. As more historians search for meaningful answers to questions about how these elements worked together, the more confusing it becomes. This all helps to explain why the new Intelligence Branch was an expression of the new faith in professionalism in Whitehall.

Sir George Aston sums up this new feeling that there might be something worthwhile in listening to men like Wolseley or Brackenbury; he writes about his work at the new headquarters in Queen Anne's Gate, set up in 1884:

> There, in 1886, I began to spend many profitable hours learning from the Army Intelligence officers, with the gathering force of experience behind them, how to get great government departments to do things, instead of perpetually discussing them without doing anything... the late Sir Henry Brackenbury, an artillery man equipped with good brains and great administrative capacity, became the head of the department in Queen Anne's Gate... [17]

Aston locates the central reason for success: a combination of new organization with man-management from officers of both field experience and theoretical ability in terms of warfare and strategy. Yet, the new cast of thought about intelligence was to have several shock in the years between 1870 and the end of the century, making it clear that there was still a long way to go in mastering the effectiveness of field-intelligence and local networks of informants.

Notes and References:

[1]   John Hughes Wilson, *The Puppet Masters*, Cassell, London, 2004, p. 212.

[2]   William Robertson, *From Private to Field-Marshall*, Constable, London, 1921, p. 91.

3   Sir George Aston, *Secret Service*, Faber, London, 1930, p. 20.
4   Joseph H Lehmann, *All Sir Garnet*, Cape, London, 1964, p. 307.
5   Ibid., p. 301.
6   Sir George Aston (see note 3 above), pp. 21–22.
7   Robertson, (see note 2 above), pp. 83–84.
8   Lehmann (see note 4 above), p. 233.
9   Ibid., p. 244.
10 Robertson (see note 7 above), p. 94.
11 Ibid., p. 83.
12 Ibid., pp. 55–56.
13 Trevor Fishlock, *Conquerors of Time*, John Murray, London, 2004, p. 367.
14 Robertson (see note 10 above), p. 61.
15 David Stafford, *Churchill and Secret Service*, John Murray, London, 1997, p. 15.
16 Ibid., p. 16.
17 Aston (see note 6 above), p. 20.

6

The Zulu Wars and Egypt

In 1879, two of the most memorable imperial military battles took place in Zululand: one has gone down in history as one of the most embarrassing defeats of a British Army at the hands of native warriors and the other, as arguably the one siege in imperial history that exemplifies the spirit that created the Empire in the first place. While Isandlwana was the defeat, Rorke's Drift was the victory. The year proved to be the decisive turning point in the long period of confrontations with the martial Zulu nation – the inheritors of Shaka's Spartan-like war-centred state. Following the British response in which the Zulus were crushed, at Ulundi, in only another five years there would be another tough campaign with an equally high-profile setback in the death of Gordon at Khartoum in 1885.

Gordon had been a map-maker as well as a leader of men, and his achievement in mapping the upper reaches of the Nile while he was the Governor General of the Sudan gives him a part in the chronicle of military intelligence. That work also reminds us that in the war against the Zulu and the struggle with the Mahdi in the Sudan, Britain learned a great deal about the value of having an established database of information. In fact, as the British Empire with its pink hues on the maps was so huge, we have to ask why no one considered the value of such knowledge long before these campaigns.

In the context of Africa, one of the answers was that no one really considered that any native tribe there could take on the might of Britain. Wolseley's defeat of the Ashanti proved this. But the historian Ian Hernon has graphically reminded military historians that there were several small wars in the Empire against native forces in the Victorian period, and some of these were in progress close to the time when King Cetshwayo of the Zulu too on the redcoats and the Natal forces in 1879. There was a war in Belize in 1872; a Modoc Indian War in 1873 and the Fenian invasion of Canada in 1866. The elder statesmen running foreign policy in the middle years of Victoria's reign assumed that, broadly, field operations would be enough to contain dissent; only the large empires such as Russia merited the organization of any intelligence work mustered against them. After all, it was often asked that strong individuals, usually British officers, had managed well enough the leading local detachments in combat against insurrection in many areas. Gordon himself had led such a force in China at the time of the Taiping Rebellion in the 1860s.

The Zulu War of 1879 illustrates the disastrous consequences of this kind of arrogance and nonchalance. There was at the time a certain overconfidence about the situation in the mind of Bartle Frere – the man who was the Governor of the Cape and High Commissioner for South Africa. Britain annexed the Transvaal and the Boer settlers were seen as only minor irritants in the general picture of the time: the geopolitical problem was understood as being difficult mainly because of the Zulu kingdom to the north. The Boers had encroached inland along the Tugela River and there had been a string of small incidents and skirmishes between the

Boers and the Zulus. But with an annexation taking place thereafter, Frere could not risk having such a strong nation in close proximity.

The interest in this situation for the history of Victoria's spies is that Frere's commander, Lord Chelmsford, became the quintessential representative of that mindset of easy supremacy that left intelligence matters low down the list. The notorious defeat at Isandlwana not only revealed his weakness as an overall commander with an eye on the work of the Quartermaster and the auxiliary command, but as someone whose intelligence functions were surpassed by the Zulus. Chelmsford did apply himself to understanding the geography and the overall nature of the land he found himself in. But in terms of field-intelligence and of direct knowledge of the kind of army he was against, he fell short. The Zulus were unlike any other African nation in respect of warfare.

The latter had always put significant thought into that element of war. On the surface, it appears incredible that the battle at Isandlwana should have been such a massive defeat. There were border agents whose knowledge was available to the military commanders. One of them was F B Fynney in Natal, who had produced a report for Chelmsford on the Zulus and their structures of warfare and tactics. He understood the depth of the military ideology in the Zulu nation and therefore, explained this very well, noting that the Zulu Army had virtues and strengths that would not normally be met with in colonial conflict:

> ...the Zulu army has gradually increased, until at present it consists of twelve corps, and two regiments, each possessing its own military kraal. The corps necessarily contain men of all ages, some being married and wearing the headring... each of these fourteen corps or regiments have the same internal formation. They are in the first place divided into two wings – the right and the left – and in the second are sub-divided into companies from ten to two hundred in number...[1]

Fynney even gave Chelmsford the important figures of the Zulu manpower: 33 regiments, but 'in practical purposes not more than twenty-six Zulu regiments were able to take to the field'. He noted that the total number of fighting men was 40, 400.

The central Zulu tactic in the field was *izimpondo zankomo*, 'the beast's horns'. The principle seems simple, but what was not fully realized was that it was adaptable to almost any situation. The main body (composed of the die-hard experienced men) would confront the enemy while the horns, the quicker, younger men, would run around and create flank attacks. Then the 'loins' of the beast would be available for solidifying the main body as they closed ranks and inevitably lost some men. Even before the attack at Isandlwana, a Lieutenant Hamilton, in his notes, summed up the situation with regard to intelligence: 'They know a great deal more about our movements than we know about theirs; they could not well know less, and will probably attack the convoy...'[2] What was destined to happen, then, at Isandlwana, was that Chelmsford did not fully understand the implications of splitting his large army into smaller units, and he did not comprehend the swiftness and efficiency of the Zulu spy arrangements across the mountain terrain in which the armies were to clash.

Fynney's information during the whole period of the movements prior to the battle was accurate. A massive Zulu Army of 28, 000 men was preparing for war when it was clear that Chelmsford's army was invading their land. The British force consisted of two battalions of infantry (regulars); a Royal Artillery battery; two battalions of the Natal Native Contingent (NNC) and a mixture of various volunteers. The total was 4, 700 men. The force had to carry their guns and equipment across the Tugela River and into the mountains. The fundamental problem was in Chelmsford's attitude to the movements at each stage of the advance towards the enemy. Not only had he found it hard to absorb and act on the border agents' information; he loaded his men with unnecessary orders at the level of basic movements and protocol, such as the fact that at each halt there had to be entrenchment or laager. On the surface, the tactics in terms of pushing into the Zululands for reconnaissance seemed practical and sensible; this involved pickets going well in advance of the main force. The key figure in this initiative was Colonel William Durnford of the Royal Engineers.

Durnford was to lead the detachments of the Natal Native Horse and a rocket battery (something that had been used marginally since the Napoleonic War). There was also Major Dartnell with his cavalry unit. Along with Lonsdale and the NNC, these two were given the brief of exploring the hills and ascertaining where the main Zulu Army was located. By the time any of the scouting detachments found a large enemy force, it was too late to act. Chelmsford had somehow come up with the idea that if he scattered his army in small units about the valleys leading towards the Zulu centre, he would be able to act quickly when there was a confrontation. However, his analysis turned out to be totally incorrect.

When Dartnell did find a large Zulu Army, his messenger could not reach Chelmsford's camp until midnight. What then happened – and it was the primary reason why Isandlwana turned out to be a terrible defeat – was a matter of poor communications. He divided his main column in order to send one force to meet the Zulus that Dartnell had found. Using pickets and vedettes along the route to where the enemy were, Chelmsford relied on reinforcing Pulleine, who was going to meet the enemy head-on. Subsequently, when Durnford took some of Pulleine's men to meet a force of Zulus he thought would be moving elsewhere, this drained Pulleine's force further.

The Zulu regiments came in vast numbers towards Pulleine's position. Various smaller British forces had to shift as quickly as possible across the area to find the most productive places from which to fire. The story of Isandlwana was one of disjointed forces and desperate ad hoc measures against a well-organized enemy. One of the most desperate of all was Pulleine's gallant attempt to take some artillery to a plateau from where he could have some effective fire on the Zulus as they moved.

But then the infantry companies began to need more ammunition. When the covering fire of Durnford's men, who were in advance of the infantry, ceased as they pulled out, the infantry were to be surrounded. The defeat was certain from that point.

There was then a systematic massacre of the British and the native support forces as the Zulus ran riot. From a force of 17, 000 men who had been with Chelmsford, only 55 whites survived. The Twenty-Fourth Foot were all slain. On the Zulu side (a fact not often absorbed) there were around 1, 500 men killed.

One notable reason why Chelmsford's thinking was wrong is that he acted on the intelligence from border agents as if the Zulu positions would remain unaltered. So, he then developed strategies on that information when he wrote to his officers. For example, he wrote to Durnford on 19 January:

> No 3 column moves tomorrow to Isandlwana hill and from there, as soon as possible to a spot about ten miles nearer to the Indeni forest. From that point I intend to operate against the two Matyanas if they refuse to surrender. One is in the stronghold on or near the Mhlazakazi mountains, the other is in the Indeni forest...[3]

This is reminiscent of a games room in toy-soldiering. The Zulu positions, as implied by the note, are taken as static, as if they have no detachments watching the British movements and acting accordingly.

In fact, the Zulu spies were very active. Lieutenant Hamilton's journal has an entry that shows how active they were; he recounts a time when two messengers from Cetshwayo arrived at his camp and asked them to leave. He notes: 'Colonel Pearson did not believe they were from the king at all, but made prisoners of them for being spies. They tell us we are surrounded by three armies, numbering in all 35, 000 men...'[4] This seems fairly near the truth.

Chelmsford, well behind the battle positions, of course survived. In the phase of the war after Isandlwana, when the tide turned, it was in part due to the activities of the most notable spy of the campaign: John Dunn. Dunn had actually been made an ally of Cetshwayo some time earlier, being given the task of liaising with and supervising the various white settlers and visitors to the area of Zululand along the coast. Dunn's family were in Port Natal but he went closer to being a hybrid, absorbing the native culture to a large extent. He had swayed back and forth across the two cultures and in a civil war between Zulu leaders he chose the wrong one and was almost killed. But to all intents and purposes, he was appointed a General with Cetshwayo. It was he who had obtained weapons for Cetshwayo and thereby, became the chief intelligence source regarding the British when trouble was brewing.

But when it came to reprisals after Isandlwana, and Chelmsford needed information, Dunn had re-crossed the line. It was due to Chelmsford that Dunn became an ally. His involvement was highly significant, as he had a corps of spies who could venture into the interiors easily and with a sense of normality. Donald Morris has written an account of when and where Dunn sided with Chelmsford:

> On the twenty-first of February the General was riding back to Durban from a visit to Fort Pearson, when he encountered a smart gig driving north. John Dunn, the unhappy occupant, had been dreading this meeting... Dunn was well aware that the war could only have one outcome, and he naturally hoped to return to Zululand once the war was over... Chelmsford now forced him off the fence. Chelmsford was sufficiently sympathetic to his problem not to force him to accept an official post... and when the troops entered Zululand John Dunn marched at the head of 244 armed retainers, officially listed as the Head of Intelligence.[5]

In the build-up to the fight at Eshowe, Dunn formed units of supporting fighters and when the time was right, he supplied a detailed report on the situation in Zululand for Chelmsford, from material originally gathered by a spy – Magumbi. The report gave very specific information about where the enemy was placed and in what numbers. Magumbi estimated that in the area in which Chelmsford was to move, there were some definite indications that some of the army which had been around at Isandlwana had moved north. It became a matter of some urgency to move onto the offensive.

Chelmsford knew from the reports that his best route was close to the coast; he then could predict more or less where he would be most likely to be attacked. This time he knew what the problems linked to moving supplies and arms would be and he put special attention on that issue. It was also not absolutely certain that the report from Magumbi could be trusted, so there was caution in every small move from then on. But as he advanced, aware of Zulu scouts, he was attentive to the messages from border agents. The column stayed together; at the Nyezane a force of about 11, 000 Zulus had gathered to meet the column. The odds were now two to one and there was no dispersal of British forces. Chelmsford knew that he had a relief column behind him and he laagered the column to meet the Zulu attack. It was a case of traditional defence and rifle-fire. This time, the Zulus retreated and threw away the weapons in panic.

How much of the success at Eshowe was down to John Dunn and his agents? Arguably, a great deal is the answer. Dunn, who rode beside the staff some of the time, actually fired at Dabulamanzi – his former ally – as the fight receded. He had become a turncoat, of course, but he was a pragmatist who wanted his lifestyle to continue in the place he loved, and he sided with the winners. His network of spies had played a major part in the turning of the tide against the Zulus. Credit must be given to Chelmsford as well, in having to cope with a plethora of information. In one report he notes: 'The report of Mr Fynney is diametrically opposed to that which I have received from the border commanders during my numerous visits to that part of the country...'[6]

It was down to John Dunn also that the pockets of Zulu power in the coastal strip were suppressed. In all the work of the Eshowe relief column Dunn rode with them, along with his scouts. He had been in Zululand since 1853 and knew it very well, as no British officer could have done. The official Army Records Society volume on the war notes that Dunn was accused of treachery by Cetshwayo's advisers, and that it was in late 1878 that he 'threw in his lot with the British'. If so, we can only regret that he was not active in the party that left Rorke's Drift on that fateful day when the column moved towards Isandlwana. He had a good life, and lived until 1895, leaving behind 49 wives and 117 children. It might well be asked whether any of his sons continued his work and made a living spying for the government; in fact, none did. Many of his daughters married Europeans, and they settled down in Dunn's land, but the family scattered far and wide.

The other main player in the intelligence network in the war was Frederick Fynney. He was an interpreter for the Natal government who became a border agent in the lower Tugela Division; he was the main source of military intelligence in Zululand in the period, compiling a list of headmen in the Zulu Army. As he also commanded the border police, he would have had ample opportunity of questioning captives and Zulu criminals on the run who would have had information about important developments in the interiors. Chelmsford, predictably, preferred and trusted his reports above many of those from native sources. It was at the meeting that Fynney interpreted Frere's ultimatum directing Cetshwayo to 'alter his military system' and therefore, initiate the war.

The spies, agents, scouts and surveyors in the Zulu War were particularly valuable in such terrain; the British were fighting a campaign in land totally unlike the previous sites many of the combatants knew, and even more important was the fact that the extent of Zululand was covered by a military network of both active fighters and reservists. In their own way and with the methods of

King Shaka of the previous generation, the Zulus had established a very powerful army machine, with all departments catered for. When they stepped up their intensity of operations to cope with a British Army rather than a native one, their tactics worked extremely well. One has to reflect that a Wolseley would almost certainly have not made basic mistakes in terms of communication and troop deployments, but on the other hand, in spite of his disgrace, Chelmsford redeemed himself to some extent in his work with Dunn later, showing that he had learned some lessons. By the time Wolseley had assumed command, when all was settled really, it was a landmark in the military administration of the place, but it was only after a prolonged hunt for Cetshwayo and a desperate series of small fights that a political settlement was reached under Wolseley. He divided the Zulu kingdom into 13 tribal units and gave control to people who had run areas in pre-military ways. He also gave Dunn another special role – policing some of the regions.

Frere wanted direct control, with a Resident similar to the system used by the East India Company in its successful period. What was destined to happen was, naturally, a complete dismantling of the old warrior caste and the military ideology. Wolseley wanted 'Zululand for the Zulus' but there was always going to be tight control and military presence of some kind.

In the Zulu War there had been a meeting of almost medieval attitudes to war embodied in personal heroism and a special kind of brotherhood present in the Zulus, as opposed to bullets and steel in the British. It had been a war of courage and subtle strategy on both sides, and the intelligence men had hastened the end of it all. In the figure of the enigmatic duel-identity – John Dunn – we have that rare variety of agent, the 'Gone native' European who made friends and enemies on both sides.

It is difficult to bring to mind any figure comparable to Dunn in the annals of Victorian intelligence; what he does represent is the tendency for the use and amalgamation of any local sources by the imperial armies in a campaign. He is closer to the American frontiersmen who worked as scouts for the US cavalry than to any European character who might come to mind. The new Intelligence Branch, just four years old when the slaughter was taking place in Zululand, would have found it hard to categorize the man; yet, of course, he had much more to offer than even the border agents. In all respects, the Zulu War came at a very inappropriate and difficult time for army command. It was really Frere who desperately wanted it to happen and he had the stature and influence to do so.

Just three years after Wolseley was in Zululand, he was called on again to sort out another crisis, this time in Egypt. The Suez Canal, which was completed in 1869, was built by Ferdinand de Lesseps. In 1875, Benjamin Disraeli bought 40 per cent of the shares from Khedive Ismail and suddenly Britain found that it had a genuine interest in the Canal, though earlier it had been unconcerned. Since the Canal was a short-cut to British India, its control became of utmost importance to the British. The Khedive Ismail after having squandered money in vast amounts also fought a very costly war with Abyssinia. As a result his financial situation deteriorated to such an extent that Britain and France stepped in to take hold of the Canal.

At the time, Egypt was technically a part of the Ottoman Empire. Both the economists as well as the diplomats saw brilliant opportunities coming their way when Ismail made a mess of his government and failed to control his State. Egypt became subject to a Commission for Debt and that meant that creditors had first claims on income from Egypt and the Sudan. When the humiliation of this European control became too much to bear, the Khedive Tewfik, who had taken power after Ismail, was ousted by a military nationalist party led by Arabi Pasha, also known as Ahmed Arabi. What he fronted was no less than a rampant rebellion with the aim of killing or terrifying all foreigners. He was one of the *fellahin* – a manual worker – and eventually, had made his name and gained high status in the army from his lower class origins. There had to be British military involvement; apart from the Canal and the passage to India, there were almost 100, 000 foreigners in the country and they would all be in danger from Arabi.

Wolseley was to lead the expedition and it was another instance of his mastery of intelligence that led to success, particularly his use of misinformation. He gathered around men who came to be known as the 'Ashanti Club' as he knew extremely well as to who could be relied on to perform specific tasks that featured in his plans. Vast numbers of military men of all backgrounds wanted to join the expedition as the campaign attracted all kinds of adventurers and reputation-seekers. The first phase of the war and then, the escalation of events up to the battle of Tel-El-Kebir, are of special interest to the theme of this history. The reason for this lies, surprisingly, in a book written by Major Alexander Bruce Tulloch, and with his papers now lying in the archives of Gwent in Cwmbran. Tulloch wrote his *Recollections of Forty Years Service*, published in 1903 and it is clear from that and other sources that the new commander at the Intelligence Branch, Major General Sir Patrick MacDougall, travelled to Egypt with two other officers (one of whom was Tulloch) ostensibly 'for his health' nevertheless, his travel attracted enough attention as well as suspicion.

MacDougall wrote a report of this fact-finding trip and Tulloch clearly found the experience to be a very useful basis for his spying and reconnaissance in the Tel-El-Kebir battle. Tulloch was to play a significant part in the Egyptian war with Arabi; he approached Wolseley and offered to run his intelligence arm. His improbable disguise was to be as a hunter – a man going snipe-shooting in the area. Major Tulloch who was 44 in the year 1882 was often confused with the famous Sir Alexander Murray Tulloch – a prominent army thinker and adviser in and after the Crimean War. As James Exelby has said, it is in the affairs Tulloch involved himself with that we learn how intelligence officers worked in the field at this period; from the Tulloch papers, Exelby writes:

> ...we learn how Tulloch investigates the coastal defences at Alexandria and Damietta, gathers information on the Suez Canal, Egyptian army and its supply base, and reconnoitres the ground at Tel El Kebir in the desert east of Cairo where the decisive battle of the Egyptian Campaign was fought.[7]

In fact, Tulloch had an encounter with none other than Herbert Kitchener in the early stages of the campaign. Kitchener had been involved in surveying work at nearby Cyprus and wanted to be where the action was. Obtaining a leave of absence for a week, he crossed over to Alexandria and there he met Tulloch. As his first biographer wrote of Kitchener at the time: 'On board a steamer in the harbour the eager young officer seriously meditated disobedience by breaking his leave'.

Leaving the flagship *Invincible*, Kitchener looked for Tulloch, who was described as the Military Liaison Officer. Kitchener told the intelligence man that he spoke Arabic and Turkish and asked if he could be engaged in some way in intelligence work. It is quite stunning to learn that in fact, even during a leave of absence for a supposed rest, Kitchener accompanied Tulloch by train well into the area controlled by Arabi's army. Tulloch was disguised as a Turkish minor pen-pusher and Kitchener as a man on holiday of course. Undoubtedly, Tulloch and Kitchener had risked their lives by entering the enemy's territory. The risk involved in their expedition was validated by an account of a Syrian who had been kidnapped from a carriage and ruthlessly killed by slashing his throat. Tulloch himself had recorded the above incident in his memoirs as that of a mistaken identity, in other words, the Egyptians had killed an innocent Syrian traveller as they were under the impression that the man was Tulloch – the British spy.

While Wolseley was executing a daring and efficient ruse, informing (even to the newspapers) that a fleet was about to attack Aboukir Bay, Tulloch played his part by telegraphing *The Standard*, pretending to be a journalist of the same paper, telling them that all rumours about the British taking over the Suez Canal were untrue. Of course, in a swift and stealthy action, Wolseley had the Canal under gunboat control, with deployments of men and guns at every defensible spot on that stretch of water. It also seems to be the case that Tulloch devoted abundant time and energy in order to explain plans for major undercover espionage and bomb attacks, such as noting that it would not be difficult (by use of bribery) to blow up the Arabi forces' magazine at Tourra. Tulloch had obviously done a close study of all sites of enemy strength or interest, even down to the minutiae of which places would be most vulnerable to attack and by what means.

When Alexandria was later annexed in the campaign, Tulloch had led the advance and because of his action, he was rewarded with a promotion. He was even in the thick of it at Tel-El-Kebir: he brought up an escort of marines at a point at which Wolseley himself was in a dangerously vulnerable situation. He had seen the imminent danger and shouted to his comrade, Butler, 'Good God... Wolseley will be cut off!'[8]

Sir Garnet himself has to be credited with one of the most efficient and successful ruses in the Victorian wars; he wanted the enemy to think that his main sea-based attack would happen at Aboukir so he even had ships appear as a distraction, strike their top-masts as if they were about to do something, and then disappear. He had even had a Staff Officer make an announcement of the attack, and naturally, because Aboukir Bay was a famous scene of a battle in Nelson's day, it was easy to believe the announcement. Sir Garnet realized on his arrival, and after taking advice, that his most promising plan was to grab Ismailia as a base rather than travelling down to the south or moving upwards towards the Nile delta. That position would also bring him close to Arabi's main base at Tel-El-Kebir. The enemy had already moved into a camp close to Ismailia at Nefiche.

The Wolseley phoney war had a terrific impact. In the moonlight the main strength of the British fleet, as the ruse at Aboukir was taking place, moved off to Suez. At the break of the day, there was no fleet for the Egyptian troops to see; the ships and troops took Port Said without a shot, as sentries were disarmed and captured. It was destined to be one of Wolseley's most effective military actions in terms of the kudos it won him back home. The press had a fascinating tale to tell and the Queen was most pleased, though there was a report about her not approving of the lies told to the newspapers.

Therefore, with the first steps taken, Ismailia was occupied. Ferdinand de Lesseps was living there and did not approve of what was happening regarding the Canal, but he could do nothing; Wolseley eventually paid him a visit. The advance was now to begin; hundreds of citizens had left the country and even Kitchener's leave was over and he had to return to Cyprus.

There was a deep irony in the reports published in *The Times* that year. First, it was revealed that Cetshwayo had been to London and John Dunn went with him as an interpreter. They travelled down Kensington Gardens and visited the bears, lions and monkeys; 'Cetewayo [sic] and the chiefs appeared highly amused with all they saw', *The Times* noted. Then, just a month later, on 14 September, the headline was 'Rout of Arabi's forces' and Wolseley received his praise:

Cheer after cheer was raised for Sir Garnet Wolseley and the British soldiers, and General Ponsonby, who was present on behalf of Her Majesty, expressed the Queen's gratitude for the strong display of loyalty. Bonfires were lit, and the dark hills round Lochnagar and Balmoral presented a weird appearance.[9]

As the Highlanders had been in the vanguard in the dawn attack on Tel-El-Kebir, the setting was perfect also. As James Cromb wrote in 1902, the Gordon and Cameron Highlanders had been a force to be reckoned with in the battle. The author was a witness to the battle and he wrote:

> I never saw men fight so steadily. Retiring up a line of works which we had taken in flank, they rallied at every re-entering angle at every battery, at every redoubt, and renewed the fight... The victory at Tel-El-Kebir was gained in a short half hour. The battle was fought and won ere yet the dawning morning had broken into daylight.[10]

The total number of British victims – both dead and wounded – in the Highland Brigade was 258, including 23 officers. In the night-time walk to the Egyptian positions, they had faced 30, 000 men in the enemy ranks.

Behind all this – in the shadows where special agents belong – was Tulloch. But all did not go smoothly with him. Although he had been recommended for a Victoria Cross, and although his memoirs were backed by colleagues, the book caused a stir. After all, there was in the Intelligence Branch a 'Code of Silence'. When the Branch was introduced in 1873, as Robertson has written, there was a sense of anew beginning and a chance to be truly organized and professional in intelligence work rather than operating in every crisis with sheer pragmatism. One of the key rules was broken by Tulloch: he had printed his memoirs, revealing some of the ways he had participated in the Egyptian campaign. As James Exelby wrote: 'He gleefully tells the reader how over lunch he personally hoodwinked de Lesseps himself as to the British intentions regarding the Canal's neutrality'.[11]

Whatever the moral and political topics around this point the fact remains that Tulloch was a remarkable soldier and a first-class spy. He had risked his life in venturing into the interiors of Egypt and had arguably only come through that ordeal because there were large number of foreigners moving around the country at the time – men with fair skins and light hair – and so to a certain extent he could fade into the shadows and do his work. The fact that, in his memoirs, he can place a picture of himself in uniform, medals lined across his chest, is the paradox. It would have been very unlikely for such a publication to appear under a Stieber regime or in the Russian Cheka.

However, by 1882 the Intelligence Branch had emerged as a recognizable presence and men like Tulloch and Robertson played an instrumental role in showing that the intelligence staff could do much more than mere Arabic translation and map-making. MacDougall – the Chief – had summed up what could be achieved when he wrote, after he and Tulloch had entered Egypt in their 'civvies':

> ... arriving in Cairo as I did shortly after the purchase of the Suez Canal shares, I was led to conclude from the remarkably polite but at the same time reserved manner of the Egyptian militaryauthorities that the presence in Egypt of one of the principal officers of the English Head Quarters Staff was regarded with suspicion.[12]

The bottom line then was that Britain occupied Egypt and came to control the Cape and Cairo – the two crucially important strategic places – at that point. What has become known as the 'scramble for Africa' arguably began at that point in 1882. The repercussions of the battle won by Wolseley were that Arabi was sent to Ceylon, well out of the way, and of course the official status of Egypt was then a protectorate. Diplomats – as Niall Ferguson noted – were eager to point out to the neighbours that the Cairo occupancy was merely a temporary measure. Ferguson comments that this was 'a reassurance repeated no fewer than sixty-six times between 1882 and 1922'.

The French – who had also been a presence in Egypt – had some of their fleet moored off Alexandria, but when the war was imminent, their fleet left. At first it had been assumed, when the Khedive was first assailed with the Europeans to exploit his debts, that the diplomacy would be both British and French.

What had seemed to Gladstone in 1881 as a minor coup on the part of Arabi as an event quite understandable and fine – in terms of 'Egypt for the Egyptians'– was a viewpoint he had gleaned from the Arab scholar Wilfred Blunt. But that was before the coup had led to vicious anti-foreigner riots in Cairo in which 50 people had died and the British Consul had been severely injured.

These political factors had meant that, as with the Crimea, a long diplomatic wrangling could well have taken place, but the aggressive acts of Arabi meant that Wolseley had to be brought in. We have to reflect on the difference between Wolseley and Raglan at this point, and to note that although Raglan considered intelligence work to be an integral part of a campaign, yet, unlike Wolseley, he failed to amalgamate the two. After the triumphs with the Ashanti and then in Egypt, Sir Garnet had shown that all the elements of a military command had to work together organically and that these functions depended on key men in charge of each aspect of the work in hand.

Apart from this, Wolseley also made his presence felt on the battlefield. Despite criticism easily levelled against him in terms of old-fashioned strategy, here was a man who had initiated some really vital work for the new Intelligence Branch to carry on with. Thomas Best Jervis and his cartography would have been green with envy. Wolseley's belief in the right men for the job began in the Red River in his North American days, and the 'Wolseley Ring' of men became – in the words of Jan Morris – 'the most influential cabal in the Victorian army'.[13]

Notes and References:

1   *Lord Chelmsford's Zululand Campaign*, Army Records Society, Sutton, Stroud, 1994, p. 129.
2   Donald R Morris, *The Washing of the Spears*, Cape, London, 1965, p. 339.
3   *Lord Chelmsford's Zululand Campaign*, (see note 1 above), p. 73.
4   Morris (see note 2 above), pp. 451–452.
5   *Lord Chelmsford's Zululand Campaign* (see note 1 above), p. 177.
6   Ibid.

7   James Exelby, 'The Secret Service Major and the Invasion of Egypt' in
     History Today, November 2006, pp. 40–41.
8   See Lehmann (see note 4, chapter 5), p. 327.
9   Ibid., p. 407.
10   James Cromb, *The Highland Brigade: Its Battles and Heroes*, Mackay,
     Stirling, 1902, p. 303.
11   Exelby (see note 7 above), p. 41.
12   Ibid., p. 40.
13   Jan Morris, *Heaven's Command*, Faber, London, 1988, pp. 510–513.

7

Spies, Informers and the Fenians

The 1860s, in England, restored the kind of intelligence work that had not only been the order of the day during the French Revolution but also existed when England's domestic front witnessed massive political dissent. In the period of Peterloo (1819) when a crowd at a peaceful political meeting in Manchester had been attacked by hussars, sedition was a common offence and small presses and republican clubs were the subject of double agents and *agents provocateurs*. Throughout the years c. 1790-1820 there prevailed a general fear of revolution in the streets of England. As time passed by and the Great Reform Act of 1832 failed to empower the common people – i.e., leaving out the bulk of the middle classes, and permitting the rich alone – with voting rights, the Chartist Movement for suffrage reform became the next threat to public order.

All these aspects of life in the years of the Regency and into Victoria's first years of reign meant that security and the prevention of crime became the order of the day. But, these matters also involved military issues. Until Sir Robert Peel's Police Act of 1829 meant that Britain was to have a professional police force for the first time, in the years during the revolutionary ferment the army had been the main force of repression. Militia forces had been active in most areas, but particularly in the north where the new concentration of industry and cheap labour led to the militancy of mass groups of the proletariats.

All this was reflected in Ireland too since the year 1798 was regarded by the Irish people as the year of rebellion. For instance, in the Wolfe Tone Revolt or the Irish Rebellion of 1798, the French troops were also involved. Then, in 1848 the members of the Young Ireland Movement had reminded the authorities that there was a groundswell of nationalistic fervour, at least among particular social classes or minority intellectual factions, although its influence had never really spread far beyond Dublin. Although much of this popular feeling was little more than talk or myth-making the attention of the army and the British government had been constant and usually efficient. The unrest was partly concerned with the land system, with the 'absentee landlord' tendency and the nature of English landowners who had no real knowledge or awareness of the nature of farm labour in the Irish context. Of course, there was a great deal of ignorance about the real condition of Ireland across the Irish Sea and representations of the Irish people were generally distorted and negative.

In addition, the 1840s witnessed the Great Famine, which was followed by a mass migration to America. In 1858, when the forerunners of the Fenian Movement emerged, attempts were made to form associations with the Fenians based in America. This, in turn, resulted in the increased talks of armed insurrections. The Fenians – a name derived from the Irish warriors the Fianna, who were ardent followers of the hero Fiona MacCumhail – demanded an independent republic of Ireland free from the English dominance. The first leaders – James Stephens, John O'Mahony and O'Donovan Rossa – had mixed backgrounds but their combined talents led to the formation of a paper – the *Irish People* – and also a determined appeal to the labouring class across the country, with Stephens, a man with experience of French politics, walking thousands of miles in order to talk, convert and speechify.

It took years of false starts, inaction and theorizing, with constant promises of arms and men from across the Atlantic, before anything serious began to happen, and that came with the replacement of Stephens with Colonel Kelly. By February 1866, the government suspended habeas corpus and gave the administrators in Dublin Castle the extraordinary powers of arresting suspects. A debate arose on this very extreme reaction to talk of open rebellion. John Bright attacked the bill and soon after the bill was passed a large number of American Fenians felt that the time had arrived to leave Ireland. The plan was to stage an invasion of Canada. Nevertheless, the Fenian rising failed to occur on a large-scale, as planned, since the English spies and informers performed their duties with sincerity in lines with the continuing *agent provocateur* tradition.

Stephen's men and Rossa's – the Phoenix Society from Skibbereen – merged in 1856 to give birth to the Irish Revolutionary Brotherhood, which was later christened the Irish Republican Brotherhood. We need to understand how this developed with a spy network functioning in its ranks, in order to see how the Fenian events influenced military intelligence in general. It was a slow progress for the republicans; between 1858 and 1864 only £1, 500 came to them from their colleagues in America. Stephens had felt sure that 1865 would be the year of insurrection; one reason for this was the American Civil War ended in that year and many soldiers who had fought in that conflict would be looking to Ireland to continue their careers, and of course many were Irishmen who had learned to be soldiers in that war.

Another reason why Stephens was quite confident about gaining success was due to the crusade – whose mission was to convert numerous Irishmen belonging to the different ranks in the British Army into Fenians. At various points during the build-up to the 1865 rising, it was claimed that as many as 20 per cent of the Dublin garrison were Fenian sympathizers. Indeed, when Stephens was arrested, due to the work of an informer, it was clear that two prison warders who helped him escape were Fenian men. Lord Wodehouse, who was running things at the Castle, assured Whitehall that he had 18, 000 men ready to suppress any nationalists who might take to the streets. Yet, there was still a feeling of a general threat. In September 1865, Ireland was in a tense, expectant state. In August, \$30, 000 had been raised in America and the Fenians had new, more militaristic leaders. One was John Devoy, who had served a year in the Foreign Legion and had brought a gang of deserters from the British Army with him to Dublin. These were intended to drill the amateur soldiers of the new republican army.

Captain T J Kelly had fought in the Tenth Ohio Regiment of the Union Army in the Civil War; he came to participate in March 1865. But there were also other adventurers: a Frenchman – Cluseret – joined in. In 1848, he had been a member of the *Garde Mobile* in the Second Republic and had in fact, earned the medal of *Legion'D'Honneur* in a storming of a principal barricade. He had also actively served in the Crimea and in the colonial wars in Algeria even earlier. After that he struggled against Garibaldi for Italian Unification and still restless for another clash he crossed the ocean and subsequently came to support the Union. He actually did become a real General, whereas, as might be guessed, the formation of the new Irish Republican Army (IRA) – destined to fight its first action in Canada – was largely a fantasy at first, opening up playful adventure to dreamers as well as genuine military men. Cluseret, as the proven military commander, agreed only to lead a force in open attack if he had 10, 000 men.

But from the outset, the activities of spies and informers beset the whole Fenian Movement, and it is precisely in this context that the history of military intelligence is principally observed. Britain was not, clearly, opposed to a genuine army, so it was able to maximize its use – and payment of – a team of spies. The years of the development of both Stephens' and subsequently, the more militarily experienced leaders' activities provides a very informative case study of how the English establishment, in the shape of the War Office and the new Scotland Yard Intelligence Branch, learned and adapted to the new context of intelligence: the domestic front and the more European 'insider' work. In short, the work of the double agent had arrived.

There was a long tradition of informers in Ireland, back to decades before the 1798 rebellion; often this was ad hoc, with payments made to anyone who came along with a convincing status, identity or track record. In Dublin Castle in the late eighteenth century there was a department of the Whitehall secret service. A succession of spies was busy for the Castle as paid informers like Samuel Turner who was eventually given a pension of £300 a year – as much as Dr Johnson received for his work on the *English Dictionary*. William Pitt who was the organizer must have observed with some concern the transitory phase his agents faced – when they reached the end of their career as a spy and thereafter had to find an alternative means for survival. Many fled into distant anonymity but some adopted a disguise and started a new life under an assumed identity within the Irish borders. Arguably, the most reviled (and successful) spies in this earlier period was the man who double-crossed Robert Emmett – the Irishman who became a folk hero and martyr. This was Leonard Macnally, who operated as 'Robert Jones' and was paid £1, 000 to turn in Emmett. Not only did he do that: he even defended his victim in the court and Emmett remained unaware of the fact that his lawyer had betrayed him.

During the years leading up to the 1867 rising though, various spies worked among the Fenians in Ireland. They are mostly shadowy figures (for obvious reasons), but the manner in which they gained information played an imperative role in the formation of the liaison between the detectives and the intelligence officers in the near future. For instance, it was two spies called Pierce Nagle and Head Constable Talbot who put paid to the intended rising of 1865. Talbot reported that there were no less than 120, 000 Fenians being drilled for insurrection in 1865; he found out where arms were stored in Dublin and a rising in Cork in which 200 men were involved was disclosed to the Castle. Lord Wodehouse swung his police into action and premises were raided; then it emerged as the trials of the prisoners drew near that there had been a long observation of the principles, largely due to the work of Nagle, who was paid off in July but wrote a begging letter, stayed under police protection and managed to move to London, existing with periodic payments until the government finally gave him a final *ex gratia* sum of £250 in 1866 and he disappeared into obscurity. In his letter to the Castle, which he signed, 'Pierce Nagle, English and Mathematical Instructor, Dublin Mechanics Institute' he wrote:

> The labour of fidelity to the state and throne exhausted my private means so that I had to be supplied with funds by the Government to continue the good work. My entire ambition is to be a useful public servant in the employment of her Majesty's government... In the next place I have to inform your Excellency of the fact that those revolutionists in conjunction with their Fenian brothers in America contemplate an uprising this year.[1]

Nagle had indeed been running some risks in his undercover work. In September 1865, Stephens wrote a letter to his peers in Clonmel in which he wrote that 'There is no time to be lost... this year must be the year of action... the flag of Ireland – of the Irish Republic – must this year be raised...'[2] The plan was for this letter to be delivered by a member of the group, but the man drank too much, and as he passed water in a drunken state, Nagle took the letter. This was easy because Nagle was actually a trusted clerical worker for the *Irish*

NARRATIVE OF A JOURNEY

FROM

HERAUT TO KHIVA, MOSCOW,

AND

ST. PETERSBURGH,

DURING THE

LATE RUSSIAN INVASION OF KHIVA;

WITH

SOME ACCOUNT OF THE COURT OF KHIVA AND THE
KINGDOM OF KHAURISM.

By CAPT. JAMES ABBOTT,

BENGAL ARTILLERY,

Author of the " T'hakoorine," and lately on a political Mission.

IN TWO VOLUMES.

VOL. I.

LONDON:
Wm. H. ALLEN AND CO.,
7, LEADENHALL STREET.

1843.

1. Frontpiece of *Narrative of a Journey to Khiva, Moscow* and
St. Petersburg by Captain James Abott. One of the very first narrative
texts of the Great Game.

2. Summud Khan — Abott's Steward.
He was valuable as a linguist and guide on the Khiva expedition.

3. Captain Thomas Montgomerie, who raised the pundit corps.

4. Nain Singh — a principal pundit who worked with Montgomerie.

5. General James Walker, Surveyor-General of India.

6. William Howard Russell of *The Times*.
His despatches from the Crimea are classics of war reportage.

7. Lord Raglan. Criticised for orders leading to the
'Charge of the Light Brigade'.

8. The Sobraon Barracks, Lincoln: a survival to remind England of one of the most significant battles of the First Sikh War of 1845–6.

9. The return of the spies. In Russell's diary of his Indian journey, this picture shows the military native spies back at camp, working with the Quartermaster General.

10. From the same memoirs, 'Good news in dispatches' shows General Mansfield and Lord Clyde studying intelligence notes.

11. Dalhousie Barracks, Fort William, Calcutta.

12. Sir Garnet Wolseley. Won fame in the Ashanti War of 1873–4.

13. Lord Chelmsford from *The Illustrated London News* 1879. At the time, news of the disaster of Isandlhwana had not reached the press.

14. Gonville Bromhead, one of the heroes of Rorke's Drift.

15. Wolseley in *Punch* just before Tel-El-Kebir. Here he is 'The Modern Caesar'.

16. Gordon as sketched in his journals in the first edition.

17. Gordon in his robes when he acquired the name 'Chiness Gordon'.

18. Rex Wingate – Kitchener's Chief of Intelligence.

19. Rudolf Slatin – Intelligence second-in-command in Egypt – in chains being shown Gordon's head.

20. Kitchener on 'Democrat' in *Vanity Fair* magazine, 1910.

21. Kitchener saves Conder's life in Palestine, from the first biography of the master tactician.

22. The Khoord Khyber, Afghanistan, from *The Illustrated London News* 1879.

23. G W Steevens, spy, military theorist and journalist.

24. Sir William Robertson at the time of the Great War.

25. Robertson at the Army Manoeuvres, 1913.

26. Robertson at the time he worked in the new Intelligence Branch in 1902.

27. 'The death of two Japanese spies', a sensational story from *The British Workman* magazine 1907.

28. Rufus Isaacs, later Lord Chief Justice, involved in spy trials.

29. Mata Hari, spy destined to be shot.

30. Gustav Steinhauer, the Kaiser's Master Spy, from his memoirs.

31. Dublin Castle – British stronghold and Jenkinson's
base against the Fenians.

People. Newspaper and he would, naturally, have been a familiar sight in and around the offices.

Another informer – a man named James MacDermot – also known as 'Red Jim' who worked for the British secret service and was responsible for passing on all valuable information to the British Consul in New York was to play a vital part in a fiasco at Liverpool during the Fenian bombing period in Britain.

But as the news filtered through to Whitehall that the Fenians were to start bombing in England in 1867, a secret service operation was initiated under the command of Lt Col. W A Fielding, who was directly accountable to the Home Secretary. His counterpart in New York was Edward Archibald – Consul and Intelligence Chief. It appears that he was seen as a useful source of income for all kinds of men who realized they could earn a few dollars for information on any actions or meetings involving Irish republicans in the city. But just before the campaign in England, the Irish Army had their first encounter in an invasion of Canada. Intelligence in that phase of Fenian events was no problem. The President – Andrew Johnson – knew all about it, thanks to Archibald and others.

At that juncture, the most significant figure in military intelligence with regard to the Fenians – Thomas Beach – also known as Major Henri le Caron, appeared on the scene. Beach who had started out his military career as a Private was gradually promoted to the rank of Major at the time when he was serving in the American Civil War. Even after the Civil War, Beach who was still living in America wrote to his father in Colchester informing him that dollar bonds were in circulation there and was often exchanged for cash from the newly settled Irish immigrants. From this, Beach concluded that a network of republicans were at work in America. Beach not only disclosed his observation to his father but also duly passed on the information to the Home Secretary. Subsequently, Major Beach came to be known as Major le Caron and henceforth, was entrusted with the responsibility of supplying vital information to the British government.

It was at this point that the invasion of Canada was planned and Beach gave out the details. Nevertheless, the whole enterprise was a fiasco. Colonel John Roberts was O'Mahony's rival for the overall military leadership, and Roberts thought that a move across the border to Canada would be far more worthwhile than a massive and risky investment of a fleet of privateers and thousands of armed men setting sail for Ireland. His thinking was that even the smallest foothold on American soil in which an Irish flag could be raised would be a huge achievement, an encouragement after so many frustrating years of planning and talking that had come to nothing. The so-called 'Right Wing of the Army of Ireland' gathered at Buffalo – a city in Western New York state – and prepared to cross the border. O'Mahony had just failed in a seaborne attempt to take the island of Porto Bello off New Brunswick, so Roberts had the incentive of one-upmanship. Colonel O'Neill, leading 800 men, crossed the Niagara River and took possession of Fort Erie.

At a place called Lime Ridge, or Ridgeway, the Irish force met a Canadian volunteer force. At Ridgeway there was a confrontation, or better still a skirmish that concluded with the death of eight men on the Fenian side and 12 on the Canadian, and 60 Irish were taken into captivity while many retreated. The Ridgeway farce was, paradoxically, still some kind of a significant gesture that could be used as propaganda, and the spin given on the defeat was one of claiming that the Fenian flag had been raised, albeit as a mere gesture. It was, in its reverberations across the Atlantic, at least a spur to some kind of response. Colonel Kelly was leading matters in Ireland, and after the Canadian adventure, the appropriate time had arrived in England itself to launch a campaign.

There had been a detective branch in the new Metropolitan Police since 1842 and they had coped well with daily crime, including some good work on prominent murder cases, but how, with a terrorist threat, there was a new threat for them and they were not ready for it. The Earl of Derby, campaigning for the Commissioner of Police - Mayne - to resign, wrote:

> It is really lamentable that the peace of the metropolis, and its immunity from wilful destruction, should depend on a body of police who, as detectives, are manifestly incompetent; and under a chief who, whatever may be his other merits, has not the energy nor apparently the skill to find out and employ men fit for peculiar duties.[3]

What had happened was that there had been a failed attempt to attack Chester Castle, which was in fact, a barracks and a prison. But the authorities knew about it, as the Irish spy network had done its work well. Subsequently, this had been followed by one of the most significant events in Irish republican history: in September 1867, a Police Sergeant, Brett, had been shot dead in a prison wagon while taking three Fenian hostages to the prison. The armed attempt to free the men failed and the prisoners were hanged: Allen, Larkin and O'Brien were executed and the martyrdom was encapsulated in the media accounts in Ireland and elsewhere - they were the 'Manchester Martyrs' for evermore.

After that in December 1867, an attempt was made to blow up the Clerkenwell House of Correction. It was a sensational and terrifying failure: terrorism had come to the streets of London. Two Fenians, Burke and Casey, were held in the prison, and Dublin Castle warned the London police that an escape attempt was to be made. At the second attempt, the bombers managed to destroy 60 yards of the wall; six people were killed and over a hundred others injured. The detectives stated that they had not been vigilant in that instance because they expected an underground dig and an attempted breakout from that.

Le Caron/Beach infiltrated the IRA in America and even established a headquarters in Lockport, Illinois. He was a remarkable individual with a genuine flair for espionage; he even managed to meet the President to discuss the Canadian invasion. It was down to le Caron that, just three years after the London bombings, Fenian activities in Canada were phased out. A communication network with Ottawa and the Chief Commissioner of Police was effected, and this was very much needed because the Fenians still had designs on entering Canada, this time to use it as a focus for all moves against Britain by sea. O'Neill was to lead this coup attempt, and le Caron's information led to his arrest by General Foster.

One might expect a beam of suspicion to be directed at the spy by that time, but in fact le Caron's infiltration was intensified, and to such an extent that he even became a member of a secret group within the Fenian Movement called the 'Knights of the Inner Circle'. This was Masonic in format, as the spy recalled:

> I have often laughed to myself at the surprise shown by some Masons on the occasion of their initiation to Clan-na-Gael clubs - for there are Masons in the Clan – at being brought once more into contact with the familiar procedure. One great feature of similarity exists between the two ceremonies. In both the candidate is impressed with a deep sense of awe and respect, to learn subsequently that nothing very mysterious or wonderful is to come within his knowledge.[4]

Beach was well aware that there was a resurgence of Irish Fenianism ten years after the failures of the 1867 events. In 1876, there were 11,000 revolutionaries who were busy as usual with correspondence, theorizing and planning subversion. The primary obstacle that the revolutionaries faced was Beach who observed all the communications minutely and made sure that Sir Robert Anderson came to know about their activities. Anderson who was initially based in Dublin was transferred to London in 1876 and henceforth he operated from within the Home Office team as a specialist on the Fenian Movement. He was the spymaster working with Beach and others for ten years up to 1876. He later became the Assistant Commissioner.

Developments in London were to be decisive when the next and most widespread Fenian campaign began in the early 1880s. Just before the Irish Branch of Scotland Yard was formed, there was a notable murder in Phoenix Park, Dublin. Lord Frederick Cavendish and Thomas Burke were killed there and it was this event that triggered the formation of the Irish Branch. The Branch emerged on 17 March 1883 as a special section of the Criminal Investigation Department (CID). The future Special Branch came from this first outfit, led by Adolphus Williamson (known as 'Dolly'). Williamson along with Anderson and Vincent of the CID were responsible for the management of the team. Nevertheless, there was a remarkable man in Dublin – Edward Jenkinson – who became one of the real players in the espionage game in the Fenian years.

Jenkinson apparently questioned Anderson's skill in this Irish context; but then Jenkinson was critical of many others. By 1884, the British government employed Jenkinson in London, working with Major Nicholas Gosselin, who had been a magistrate in Ireland. From 1884, Jenkinson was running the whole counter-intelligence network against the Fenians. He had been educated at Harrow and was given the post of Assistant Undersecretary for Police at Dublin Castle after the Phoenix Park killings. His attitude towards the organization of his agents was antithetical to the Scotland Yard view of things. Jenkinson wanted his spies to report to him personally rather than for them to be checked, known and directed by any superior at the Yard. His work was certainly eccentric and often flamboyant. Jenkinson has been seen as the forerunner of a future breed of spymasters, at once devious and charming, with a knack for cultivating 'sleepers' as they are now named.

One of the most remarkable episodes in his work at the Home Office occurred in July 1884 when one of his agents – a woman named Tyler – during her stay at the Gresham Hotel in Dublin enquired about bombings and spoke of revolutions. After she had checked out of the hotel, detectives found letters/telegrams from the Home Office in her room. Such a discovery made it quite evident that she was a 'spook' in Jenkinson's network. However, her true identity could not be discovered. What she clearly appeared to be was some kind of *agent provocateur* – something always frowned upon in open debate despite the fact that such a practice had been followed since Elizabethan times.

Another crisis in Jenkinson's regime was in January 1883 when we have a detail that reminds us that this spying and double identity work was no playground. An agent – Joseph Phelan – was stabbed to death in the office of *The United Irishman* newspaper in New York. Jenkinson was genuinely disturbed; he said that he felt he could go on with 'this horrible work'. Jenkinson always mentioned that his man – Phelan – was a quiet family man who had been employed because of his strong views about the dynamite campaign.

These London bombings in the 1880s, organized by the Clan-na-Gael, the Irish–American republicans, were more successful than the Clerkenwell bombing of 1867, though the latter had had some impact. At the time of the first campaign, Karl Marx had seen the results of a bomb in London streets: 'This latest Fenian exploit in Clerkenwell is a great folly. The London masses, who have shown much sympathy for Ireland, will be enraged by it and driven into the arms of the government party'. He was right, and more so when we look at the 1880s events. The first bombs were left at the offices of *The Times* newspaper in March 1883, but they virtually failed. This first failure must have brought about a tremendous disappointment to the chief dynamiters, however, with the passage of time they did continue to inflict terror campaigns.

A bomb exploded in Whitehall, and others followed at railway stations and 60 casualties resulted from a single attack on Praed Street station. In 1884, there was a definite result for the bombers; after failing to blow up Nelson's Column, they did succeed in placing some dynamite in a toilet at Scotland Yard and a fairly large part of that building was destroyed. On that occasion, a man working late at the Yard was John Sweeney, who later wrote his memoirs as a detective. He had just left to go home when the bomb exploded. The office he had been sitting in was totally destroyed and the public house next door – the Rising Sun – was severely damaged. Extreme attacks meant extreme responses; an act was passed, the Explosive Substances Act, Royal Irish Constabulary men were drafted in for duty in London and counter-subversion became a major part of intelligence operations. The various forces lined up against the bombers were, as Clive Bloom has written:

> ... a civilian spy network in the professional police cadre... uniformed police on guard duty at public buildings; port of entry officers including plain clothes detectives; special duty Irish Branch men stationed at Central Office; two intelligence sections and the RIC.[5]

It is worth recalling at this juncture that a war with Russia seemed to be imminent at the time. This was one of the factors that encouraged the Irish bombers as they thought that 'the Russian Bear' would distract military attention in London. The Fenians even made an effort to start talks with the Russians, and Beach was thoroughly convinced that such matters had sufficiently progressed in Europe. One of the Irish leaders, a Dr Carroll, communicated with the Russian minister based in Washington. As research by Christy Campbell had shown that there were several ambitious plots to assassinate Queen Victoria. Michael Davitt, who had been active in the work of gun-running around Chester, was imprisoned at Portland and he also was a target – a plan to free him was set to happen but he was released.

The sure sign that extraordinary measures were needed to challenge the extraordinary attacks at the very heart of the country and the Empire was that, in addition to Jenkinson's team, a 'secret intelligence' network was established under James Monro. He was appointed Head of the 'Secret Department' in 1887. From that year he had sources that enabled him to work with (and often in opposition to) Jenkinson. He was particularly efficient at receiving intelligence from America. The Clan-na-Gael Congress of 1886 in Chicago was clearly of profound interest to the British agents, and Monro in May, reported to the Foreign Office on what the repercussions of a Fenian appeal for help and funds to that Convention were. For instance, he knew that the ships were to arrive at Le Havre that would have explosives loaded on them. Once again, it was surely Beach who had supplied the information.

Monro and Jenkinson were destined to express deep animosity to each other. When Monro learned that Jenkinson had put together a cadre of London-based detectives who were easily seen as being independent of the Yard, it was then that real trouble started brewing. Someone had reported to Monro that, after answering an advert for a porter's job (aimed at Irishmen in London) he had been recruited to a net of agents working against the bombers. The fact that this had been done without the knowledge of the Yard was alarming to Monro. Some of the agent's men had even been instructed/briefed to observe the Yard detectives. Basically, Jenkinson had become convinced that the detectives in the CID were mostly corrupt. The basis of the conflict was that Jenkinson had a European attitude to espionage; he saw that working with *agents' provocateurs* and double agents was a customary practice, as it had been under men like Stieber in Prussia and Fouche in France.

Jenkinson was dismissed. But the fact is that Jenkinson was legally compelled to give all information he gathered to Scotland Yard. Jenkinson had no other alternative but to follow the instructions. Monro had removed his chief irritation in his work at what was now known as Section D – the 'confidential branch' in other words. This latter force was directly answerable to the Home Secretary, and was separate from the Irish Branch led by Williamson.

Monro placed William Melville in France as his main agent and he met with Millen, the soldier adventurer who had taken the role of a double agent. The spine of the American intelligence process was Beach and Millen, moving separately and with distinct roles. But Monro had chosen his men well; Melville, as the European contact, was a very talented and able detective. He later became head of the Special Branch and the War Office Intelligence Department after the turn of the century. But Beach/le Caron was at the centre of almost everything at the time. Not only was he inside the American Fenian ring; he was active in a wider arena, even finding out about a plan to build a torpedo boat in Jersey that would smash the Royal Navy. The most staggering aspect of Beach's work here is that his report about the ship, passed to the Royal Navy, eventually became the source of the blueprint for the first British submarine in 1901.

The five years of the 'dynamiters' in Britain had included the development of a bomb factory in Birmingham, but Beach and the others in Monro's network gathered the required information and hence action could be taken quite promptly that ultimately resulted in the arrest of the plotters. Beach writes about the trial and about the probable designs of the Birmingham factory terrorist group:

> Quite sufficient for the public must be the fact that so enormous was the quantity of nitro-glycerine discovered that, according to experts, it was quite equal to the blowing up of every house and street in London, from one end to the other. Pleasant discovery this for the ordinary British citizen who laughs at dynamite and poohs-poohs the the existence of any condition of things calling for a more elaborate Secret Service.[6]

Beach was active in the secret service for many years, his final involvement being one that necessitated his retirement. He left America in 1888 and at that point some evidence was needed that Parnell had been implicated in terrorist plots because Irish Home Rule was looking very likely. The Times produced a series of pieces on Parnell and crime, and a letter was discussed which was allegedly written by Parnell linking him to the assassination plot against the Queen. A journalist called Richard Pigott based in Dublin, had been paid to produce any documentation that would substantiate these allegations. At the centre of these machinations was Thomas Beach of course. The outcome was that Beach would have to appear in the trial as a witness. Then, when Pigott was in the witness box, he was tested on his orthography, so that his link with the supposed Parnell letter could be established. He misspelled some key words and a forgery was revealed. This blunder led to a dramatic end to Beach/le Caron's career.

At the close of Beach's memoirs, *Twenty-Five Years in the Secret Service* (1893), he writes:

> I have no stronger, no sincerer wish than to see an end put once for all to the delusion which is practised upon thousands of poor Irishmen throughout the States by the men of whom I have written. With the Rank and file it has assuredly been a case of 'theirs not to reason why, theirs but to do and die'. I hope it may not be so in the future.[7]

What Beach had done was to take on what some have called the 'neo-Fenian elite' who came into prominence after the failures of 1867. This came about after the release of some of the Brotherhood men in 1869. As Major Henri le Caron, his amazing adventures make dramatic reading today, portraying him almost as a Victorian counterpart of the 'Reilly Ace of Spies' myth similar to the ones we find in popular narratives.

In the first years of the decade, after the battle of Tel-El-Kebir, the press had been brimming with the optimism of Wolseley's victory. Papers such as *The Graphic* enjoyed depicting the General with his administrators around him, pouring over despatches and reading reports. The mainstream arena of military intelligence – the kind operating in the vanguard of the imperial structures – was the familiar one. But now, in the middle years of the decade, an enemy had struck at the heart of Victoria's domains. A bomb had destroyed much of Scotland Yard. The general public had no idea that this new world - one in which the military and the police detectives were beginning to amalgamate - had arrived. 50 years earlier it had been a matter of suppressing such entities as corresponding societies and Chartist meetings. Now it had become a case of locating an enemy within who was apt to create an army in the midst of the civilized world. Fighting what Wolseley called 'the barbaric foe' was one thing, but having to understand and react to enemies of the throne and government on home ground was inconceivable. Yet, it had happened. Military intelligence was marked as an activity which would need more men like Thomas Beach - men who would have to be transmuted into officers in distant armies or who would have to learn skills of infiltration and subterfuge in new, subtle ways and for quite different ends.

Perhaps, the most formative event of the whole 1880s Fenian dynamiting episode was the attempted 'Jubilee Plot' in which the plan was to plant bombs in Westminster Abbey during the Golden Jubilee thanksgiving service on 21 June 1887. Monro had details about Millen (and no knowledge that Millen was not what he seemed) and enquiries traced two men who were implicated in the plan. One, known as Melville, was actually John Morony, a Clan-na-Gael man; the other principal activists were Thomas Callan and Michael Harkins. Monro always insisted that he foiled the plot, but most writers on the subject agree that there is no certainty about the real intentions and whether or not it was really going to happen. Monro in his autobiography does reveal something that points to a more dark and sinister set of intentions from America; he explained that the Fenians wanted to establish a system of assassinations of famous people and that the killers would be Irish, not American-Irish. He wrote: 'The agent chosen for this rascality was J S Walsh, resident of Brooklyn, and a well-known ruffian who had been concerned in the Phoenix Park murder'.[8]

It is not beyond logic that the scheme to be formed around Walsh was something peculiarly modern in the amoral world of espionage

141

as used in revolution: a network of double agents, trusted men in familiar roles who would have access to places such as Westminster Abbey, and even to the Houses of Parliament. That is the way the fabric of threat and disturbance was going at the time of the second wave of bombings by the Irish republicans.

The learning curve for British intelligence was only just beginning, both in the theatre of war and in the combat zones on the home front. In terms of the Fenian story, it had started with certain features of black comedy and ended with undoubted terror. Lord Frederic Hamilton in his memoirs published in 1920, reflected on the skirmish at Tallagh in the 1867 rising:

> The authorities had heard that part of the Fenian plan was to capture the Viceregal Lodge, and to hold the Lord Lieutenant's children as hostages.. That night an engagement... did take place between the Fenians and the troops at Tallagh, some twenty miles from Dublin... as a result of this fight, some three hundred prisoners were taken and Lord Strathnairn, Commander-in-Chief in Ireland, was hard put to find sufficient men to escort the prisoners to Dublin. He had every single button, brace buttons and all, cut off the Prisnoers' trousers. Then the men had to hold their trousers Together, with their hands, and I defy anyone similarly situated to run more than a yard or two...[9]

There we have the farce: but 20 years later that threat was as real as it could get and it was functioning in such a way that the defence was one of undercover work, something familiar but never perhaps so urgent.

Notes and References:

[1]   Christy Campbell, *Fenian Fire*, Harper Collins, London, 2003, pp. 58-59.
[2]   Leon O'Brien, *Fenian Fever*, Chatto and Windus, London, 1971, pp. 46-51.

3   Douglas G Browne, *The Rise of Scotland Yard*, Harrap, London, 1956,
     pp. 144–151.
4   Major Henri le Caron, *Twenty-Five Years in the Secret Service*,
     Heinemann, London, 1893, pp. 194–196.
5   Clive Bloom, *Violent London*, Pan, London, 2004, pp. 247–248.
6   Le Caron (see note 4 above), p. 241.
7   Ibid., pp. 279–280.
8   Campbell, (see note 1 above), p. 207.
9   See O'Brien (see note 2 above), pp. 112–113.

8

Adventurers and Advances

Anyone reading a chronicle of the men involved in the branches of espionage and military intelligence at this point in the story could be forgiven for thinking that the century in which the British Empire reached its zenith was chaotic in that respect. Indeed it was, up to and including the Boer War. But that chaos is a word only to be applied in terms of any expectation of a workable, uniform system. How could such a concept be transformed into practical realities with such a massive stretch of land and peoples to be comprehended in those pink areas on the world map? It is unthinkable that such huge continents could be handled smoothly by agents, officers and individual spies. The reality was more a series of pragmatic decisions as each new crisis came along.

By c. 1880, however, Britain had – as we have seen – proved that its resources in respect of intelligence in both domestic and foreign areas could be handled well. As the new Special Irish Branch was coping with the Fenian outrages in London and elsewhere, Major le Caron was in Canada, infiltrating the American Fenians; Wolseley was defeating Arabi; the talk of war with Russia and Afghanistan once again became a hotspot, with the pundits and the bold explorers such as Sykes and Younghusband heading northwards. It seemed at the time, to some observers, that the loose fraternity of officers and administrators were managing well, but in their own ways, and these methods sometimes defied analysis. At the very core of this operation was a brotherhood – a sense of enterprise that meant an officer or indeed a regiment, could be transferred from India to Africa at a fairly short notice. Rudyard Kipling, in his short story – *The Mark of the Beast* – explains this well:

> It was a very wet night, and I remember that some of us sang 'Auld Lang Syne' with our feet in the Polo Championship Cup, and our Heads among the stars, and swore that we were all dear friends. Then Some of us went away and annexed Burma, and some tried to open up The Sudan and were opened up by fuzzies in that cruel scrub outside Suakim and some found stars and medals and some were married, Which was bad, and some did other things which were worse and the Others of us stayed in our chains and strove to make money on Insufficient experiences...[1]

For the officers it was that kind of brotherhood, and the imprint of empire-building was deep in their character. But not all the men active in spying and intelligence work were regular officers. The wars of the period, together with the European diplomacy, meant that other personalities would be enmeshed in espionage. The wars in Egypt and indeed in Europe itself gave such men a part to play.

The larger picture in the 1870s, as the new Intelligence Branch was put into operation, was one of an expectancy of war. Otto von Bismarck had brought about the unification of Germany and that would later have an impact on British colonial aspirations. His foreign policy was partly a strenuous effort to ensure that France, defeated in the Franco-Prussian War of 1870, could not find a new ally; Russia was a threat on the other side, and they were likely to be antagonistic towards the weakening Austro-Hungarian Empire centred in Vienna. It was even mooted that there might be a Franco-German alliance or even an Anglo-German alliance. But more pertinently, Germany had designs on Africa, though somewhat limited at that time. But colonial enthusiasts often thought differently from Bismarck, as his often-quoted remark suggests: when asked about his map of Africa he said: 'Your map of Africa is all very fine but my map of Africa lies in Europe. Here lies Russia... and here lies France, and we are in the middle that is my map of Africa'. He worked hard to cause certain colonial confrontations between Britain and France, as distractions from any talk of open rivalry in Africa.

The Berlin Conference of 1884-5 led to The General Act of 26 February 1885, which stated that there would be 'spheres of influence' for each of the European powers involved, and that the Belgian-owned Congo Free State would be created. The provisions relating to African possessions were phrased in such a way that future aggressive acts were defined: 'Any power which henceforth takes possession of a tract of land on the coasts of the African continent outside of its present possessions... shall accompany either act with a notification thereof, addressed to other signatory powers, to enable them to protest against the same if there exists grounds for them doing so...'[2] In effect, just three years before this, Britain had occupied Egypt when the benefits of the Suez Canal were fully realized, and had insisted that the control of affairs was temporary. It was a precedent. But it was also an impasse, so attention on Africa was not a pressing concern at that time. The attention was directed elsewhere.

For these reasons, the focus of attention for much of Europe was the Balkans and the repercussions of the weakness of Austria in the face of the Russian pan-Slavic threat on her border. In that context, we have the first of a fascinating collection of men involved in an assorted range of espionage in the second half of the nineteenth century. This was the military historian and academic – H Spenser Wilkinson. A number of military men who were involved in intelligence work took to writing military history and tactical analysis; some of Wolseley's team did so, of course, notably Brackenbury and Maurice. Later, after having drawn considerable experiences from the Boer War, G F R Henderson became a notable leader in these ranks. Nevertheless, Wilkinson (1853-1937) who later became a Professor of Military History at Oxford was an exceptional case. He was a military reformer who knew many influential people on the scene in the last decades of the Victorian period, including Alfred Milner.

Wilkinson was trained as a lawyer but began a journalistic career in 1882. He was also the brother-in-law to the Secretary at the Foreign Office, Sir Eyre Crowe and he also became a friend of Sir Ian Hamilton and of Lord Roberts. But in his younger days, Wilkinson strayed into espionage. In his memoirs – *Thirty-Five Years 1874-1909* – he writes about a world in which a man of respectable and gentlemanly appearance could attempt to walk into a city preparing for war and travel to gather military information. He very nearly lost his life in that endeavour. This was in 1887 when Germany might well have been involved in a war with Austria–Hungary, or even a war between the latter and Russia was possible. Wilkinson initially planned to go as a war correspondent with the German Army, but instead found himself in Cracow en route to Vienna. Even with letters of recommendation, he suffered from overconfidence. He thought it would be useful to visit a frontier fortress and learn details of strength, deployment and the general resources of the forces potentially involved.

Wilkinson wrote that he had no intention of getting into trouble, yet his preparations were not convincing; he adopted a schoolroom attitude to the dangerous trade of spy, reading the code books of civil and military regulations in order to find out the definition of a spy. His only conclusion was that a spy was someone with a 'characteristic mark of... the secrecy of his acts and movements'. He checked into a hotel and he noticed that earthworks were being constructed at a point beyond which visitors were allowed to go.

He noted: 'On the great north road a large new fort was being constructed... Everything pointed to a great effort to have the place ready to meet an attack within as short a time as possible'.[3]

He was surprised when, as he sat in a refreshment room, two men approached him. He had been warned by a Frenchman that the police were looking for him, thinking him to be a Prussian spy. But the police arrived before he could do anything:

> When I had been sitting about five minutes, two young men of a better type than most in the room, dressed in fur coats, came up to me... one of them, lifting his cap, said in polite German, 'The Commissary of Police would like to speak to you.' Then.... 'Will you be good enough to come with us? [4]

Wilkinson's account of how he coped with the dangerous situation is a paradigm of the mental combat required in such diplomatically tough situations. He played every card he could think of, including the 'fellow officers and gentlemen' one; he also spoke coolly about his role as a war correspondent and then about his deep sympathies with Austria. None of this had much effect and he was asked to produce his papers. But the Commissary was a tough man to deal with. It was when his property was searched that Wilkinson must have feared the worst: 'Now began an examination of papers from my bag; and to tell the truth my heart sank within me as the Commissary took up a handful of greetings cards'. There were two cards from Prussian high-ranking officers. He had even bought some maps of Cracow. Even the most youthful tyro in the ranks of the police would have failed to see Wilkinson as a guilty man. When Wilkinson was taken to a citadel to make written depositions, he must have felt the shadow of a firing squad over his destiny at that moment.

The situation grew more ominous when a clerk changed his statement to make the words read as assertions that here was a spy.

Luckily, Wilkinson who was fluent in German must have worked quite hard to put that right. His original words were written down in the nick of time. The occasion became one of a battle of wills and intellects between the prisoner and the Commissary. After a night in a cell, Wilkinson was told he could walk free for some hours if he swore to return to the office that afternoon. This was the turning point of the spying adventure and it was sheer brainwork to extricate the man from his captivity:

> I replied, I think not. You publicly arrested me last night as a spy. All the Cracow papers this morning will announce that you have caught a spy. Now you want to turn me out on the mob. That does not suit me. You will have to take care of me 'yourselves' until you have quite done with me...[5]

The conclusion of the tense arrest and inquisition was that his cultural acquisitions and fluency with both language and thought extricated Wilkinson. His account of dining with the Governor and Commissary reads like an episode from a James Bond film. He had stayed calm, and as the Governor admitted, the general perception was that Wilkinson must have been a Russian spy since the Cracow authorities had captured several such Russian secret agents. However, Wilkinson was followed and observed all day by the authorities who expected him to fight his way out since his captors realized he was British. His calmness and frankness had won the day. Not only did he go free and continue his journey to Vienna, but he also asked his captors if there was anything about their preparations for war in Cracow that they did not wish to be printed.

The Wilkinson adventure illustrates that element in espionage at the time that might be called the 'dockyard visit' experience. Notable people, from the royalty down to the top industrialists and financiers, could make official visits to dockyards, take notes, ask questions and return home with details of ships, guns, tonnage and so on. This was the same strange kind of candidness that Younghusband came across when some Russian officers in Manchuria invited him to tea and furnished him with some military statistics.

But there were also men who, as soldier–adventurers, played major roles in the British military occupation and government of the Empire. Such a man was Rudolf Slatin, Reginald Wingate's deputy in military intelligence in the Kitchener reprisal expedition after the murder of Gordon. Slatin was the chief person in charge of information-gathering initially for Gordon when the latter tried to govern the Sudan, and subsequently for Kitchener in the events leading to the battle of Omdurman.

Slatin was born in Vienna in 1857 and his first education was commercial. This led to the first link with Africa in his life, as he acquired a post as an assistant to a bookseller in Cairo who needed a clerk and a tutor. He worked with an explorer for a while and then worked in Khartoum and in the Nuba mountains. He was gaining a great deal of local knowledge when General Gordon arrived on the scene. Gordon gave Slatin a government responsibility: first the work was in financial administration and later it involved inspections of the outlying areas. This led to his most powerful position under the Khedive (the ultimate ruler of the Sudan): Governor of Dara in Dar Fur. Gordon, operating under Khedive Ismail, needed Europeans in his management team and so, Slatin was a valuable acquisition in that respect. But it was tough for Slatin who soon found himself acting in a military capacity. He had experience in Austria, as he had served as a Sub Lieutenant in the forces of Archduke Rudolf (the Nineteenth Hungarian Infantry). But his troops in Dara were unreliable; though he had fought several battles, eventually his men left and he had to surrender to the Mahdi. The Mahdi was Muhammad Ahmad - a man who had won power and influence leading a jihad against the 'infidels'. The word 'Mahdi' means 'guided by God' and Ahmad convinced his followers that he was that man. What could Slatin do to survive and still play a part in the war against this charismatic figure? He converted to Islam.

In a letter to Gordon on this he wrote:

> After several battles, all more or less unsuccessful, the Arabian officers who bore me a grudge and who firmly believed in the victory of Achmet el Arabi over the Europeans, gave out among the soldiers that the cause of my defeat lay in being a Christian. In order to stifle these injurious opinions, I gave out that for some years I had already practised the Mahomedan religion...[6]

Slatin had a very hard time trying to make Gordon see that he had been more sinned against than sinning. His letters – some in French or German as an attempt to reduce the chances of being read by undesirables – are usually in a begging tone, pleading for a proper understanding of his position. He says desperately: 'Should you accept my services, I beg your Excellency to write me an answer in French...'[7]

But Slatin began to show his real worth when it came to knowledge of the enemy. In another letter he did have something very important to convey: 'Your scribe has written a dispatch in cipher, half Arabic and half cipher, so badly, that they have been able to decipher it, and so they have found a key to your despatches... and have deciphered your Excellency's despatches to Towfik Pasha'. Throughout Gordon's correspondence and in his journal, Slatin – through Gordon's eyes – comes across either as an extremely useful intelligence agent or as a rather eccentric and amusing figure. The great man appears to have been very hard on the Austrians at that time. In one journal entry he writes that Slatin had written a letter to the Austrian Consul saying that if Slatin went over to join Gordon there must be no surrender because he (Slatin) would suffer terrible tortures and death. Gordon comments: 'He evidently is not a Spartan'. Gordon would not consider Slatin coming across to Khartoum; his reason was he would be breaking a parole, something 'sacred when given to the Mahdi'.

Slatin who lived in captivity in a mud dwelling remained in chains until the death of the Mahdi. A painting has been found in which 'Slatin Pasha' is staring at the displayed head of Gordon that is being carried by two Mahdists. But this amazing character began a new role when Khalifa Abdullahi succeeded the Mahdi in 1885. Slatin who was impoverished by then, however, managed to realize a role at the court despite many believing him to be a British spy. He did actually send a number of reports to Cairo over that long period in subjugation.[8]

Between 1884 and 1895 Slatin was a prisoner of the Mahdi, but when the army under Kitchener came to the Sudan to retake Khartoum and crush the Mahdist forces, Rudolf Slatin was, in a sense, reborn. Subsequently, he became the intelligence officer he was always meant to be: he had incredible local knowledge. As one early writer on the events wrote: 'He knew the workings of the native mind, and he suggested that the best way to prevent the Dervishes from launching a night attack was to give them the impression that their stronghold would itself be attacked that night'. Kitchener had learned well from Wolseley the value of a ruse and Slatin was as wily as the enemy themselves. In fact, it was the brilliant combination of Slatin and Major Reginald Wingate that came to play a significant role in the success of Omdurman, as will be seen in the following chapter.

William Sleeman is arguably more famous for police work than for military exploits, nevertheless he demonstrated some working methods that would influence all kinds of practitioners in information-gathering and field-intelligence. Sleeman was born in Stratton, Cornwall, in 1788. In 1809, he joined the Bengal Army and became a Lieutenant in 1814. In 1854, he was promoted to the rank of Major General. His talent was first displayed in 1835 as a political officer in the Central Provinces where he had to work against the formidable army of murderers known as 'thuggee'. These troubles were usually caused by organized bands of killers who would select their victims from amongst travellers, rob them and brutally take their lives. The thuggee moved in large numbers and were difficult to track down. Sleeman managed to find and hang or transport for life over a thousand of these killers, and the reason for his success was the use of 'approvers' – informers. In 1830, for instance, in Jubbulpore there were reports of a band of thuggee who were active on the roads. Four approvers in the gang were, however, arrested and the case taken to court.

One of Sleeman's most remarkable talents was his skill as a linguist. All political officers had to learn the usual Hindi and sometimes some Arabic, but Sleeman had become fluent in Hindi even before he arrived and even before he turned 30 he was, according to one report, 'Probably the only British official ever to have addressed the King of Oudh in correct Urdu and Persian'. He could also get by in Nepali and Gurkhali. So enthusiastic was he for gaining and understanding of India that he even wrote a voluminous journal on his time in Oudh and developed a deep interest in the poor land-workers of the country. In this way he could become the eyes and ears of the foreigners, in a military capacity when needed, in a wide range of contexts, in the field with the poor or in the salons and messes of his peers and compatriots.

Sleeman represents the typical political officer of the time: someone profoundly located in the civic and economic life of the local community, paternalistic and knowledgeable. He would have had to travel around a massive area that was his responsibility and also act as a magistrate. It was quite evident that when wars came along, a man like Sleeman would indeed become indispensable to the army in the battlefields. He became the Political Resident in Gwalior between 1843 and 1849. He was a notable success, but incident and danger were never far away from him. In 1851, an attempt was made on his life. Nonetheless, before the crisis arrived, Sleeman had performed a vital task of report-writing for Lord Dalhousie and it was that kind of labour that made Dalhousie offer Sleeman the

Residency of Lucknow. Thereafter, in 1854, he had to retire north to the hills as he was an ailing man by then. A couple of years later, in 1856, he died on board ship on his way back home.

Basically, his success against the thuggee was based on his questioning of captured men who would turn approvers. However, he was up against far more than a system like the British one. Sleeman had to understand and exploit the Islamic courts. His approach was to communicate with men captured who would subvert the enemy if handled properly, with discretion and patience. The Islamic law did not emphasize witness testimony, so Sleeman, on signing up his agents, made sure that they knew what was needed to overcome the testimony problem. There were conditional pardons for approvers who did the witness statements given in the 'contract' with Sleeman. There was also a small amount of money given to the approvers' dependents. The approvers were questioned in Hindi first and only then the testimony was written down in Persian.

Sleeman's achievement highlights the nature of the place of political officers in the functioning of the Raj administration, yet, it also points to the crossover of police work and military intelligence that increasingly occurred over time. Besides, certain methods were sought that helped to streamline the workings of the officers of the new intelligence departments, like in the case of William Robertson.

But the role of secret agent as opposed to military intelligence officer was something entirely different in conception, and the concept was widely seen to be unacceptable, ungentlemanly. Diplomats such as military attachés and envoys had a problem with the very idea, as one said: 'I would never do any secret service work. My view is that the military attaché is the guest of the country... Certainly he must keep his ears and eyes open and miss nothing, but secret service is not his business'.[9]

In addition to the adventurers who pushed forward the boundaries of espionage in the context of double-agent activity and the manipulation of spy networks and informers, there was the important matter of technology being applied to military intelligence and espionage. Undoubtedly, the innovations achieved by individuals in the American Civil War, notably with signalling and cryptography, had an impact generally in military affairs. Major Albert Myer (1829-80) introduced a hand-held signalling system into the American forces in 1856, and within the next four years there was a regular and mainstream signalling corps. In the 1861-5, conflict between North and South, Myer and the Secretary for War – Thomas Scott – put a telegraph signal attachment to every army.

The origins of the telegraph are with the Chappe brothers in France; Claude Chappe, in 1793, showed how a system of mechanical signalling could be used, sending a message over a distance of 20 miles, with a telescope being used to read the message. In 1794, the British forces captured a prisoner who had details of the Chappe methods on his person, and a clergyman – John Gamble – produced his own version, applying it first in 1795. By the next year there was a relay of signals extending from London to Deal, in Kent. But after military uses, there was the commercial application, and in 1827 a string of signalling stations were placed along the Welsh coast, from Holyhead north to Liverpool.

Nevertheless, the telegraph had been used in the Indian Mutiny before that; there was a telegraph placed between Agra and Calcutta in 1854 and Sir William O'Shaughnessy had started the whole technical improvement of this facility in the 1830s. When the sepoys revolted in 1857, it was quite evident that the sepoys had realized the importance of the telegraph by then; the sepoys, therefore, made the telegraph offices the primary target of their attacks at the start of the rebellion.

Alexander Graham Bell invented the telephone in 1876; steam-powered ships and locomotives appeared in the 1860s. Technology came with the large-scale escalation of population in the great cities. In 1900, London had a population of 4.7 million. Wireless telegraphy came in 1896 with Marconi; in this setting it has to be noted that in this new world, military intelligence embraced not only knowledge of the enemy but also tactics, manpower, weaponry and technology. By 1882 the Admiralty had made sure it was in step with these developments: the Naval Intelligence Department was created in 1887, growing out of the former Foreign Intelligence Committee.

There was also a profound influence on the business of military intelligence with the advent of the railways throughout the Empire. When Kitchener came to the Sudan with the objective of reclaiming Khartoum, the railways had already come into existence – something that Wolseley was not privileged with 14 years earlier. In 1882 when Britain had moved into Egypt after the war with Arabi, Uganda and Kenya – situated in the south – were converted into protectorates; it was imperative to keep the Nile as a British preserve and line of supply. Consequently, a railway was built extending from the north of Egypt to Mombasa, 600 miles south. The line ran through wild, uncharted terrain. When intelligence units or agents needed to move into such areas (as Slatin had to do at times when governing Darfur) the railway revolutionized movements, and Kitchener was to find that, along with gunboats nearby, that transport technology was to play a major role in the reconquest of the Sudan.

Finally, in the setting of the new arena for espionage work across the Empire and Europe, there was the issue of competition, and what Britain was learning from her rivals. Foremost in this respect was Prussia. In 1866, when Prussia was tempted to expand, looking keenly at Silesia (which was part of the Habsburg Empire) it created a counter-intelligence organization called the *Abwehr*. Stieber, discussed in Chapter 2, made sure that his agents were placed in all the European cities that might have had important bearings on potential national aggressive movements. The new initiative certainly played a large part in the speedy defeat of the Habsburg forces at the battle of Koniggratz in 1866 – a battle involving half a million men. In the 1870 Franco-Prussian War, the infamous spy August Schluga (known as 'Agent 17') was active in France gathering information, and did so until 1917. Schluga was also very much present in the scene when the famous 'Dreyfus affair' came to be published in all the newspapers in 1894. Schluga was very impressive in his use of cipher-texts, and that was certainly indicative of how professional and successful the Prussians were in contrast to France.

Stieber had explained the need for a network of agents by explaining that reliance on a limited number of spies was not feasible; he insisted on the need for a 'multiplicity of spies' that would enable his state to 'penetrate the best-protected secrets'. He also noted that, 'The importance and accuracy of each piece of information collected by an army of agents can be more carefully analyzed in terms of the other pieces of information which verify or contradict it'.[10]

The Dreyfus case pinpointed the dangers of counter-intelligence within a national intelligence system if not properly patrolled and organized. Here was an instance in which a spy scanning waste-paper basket in the offices of the army found screwed-up notes about France's military secrets. The work of the intelligence staff had been so haphazard that the resulting sensation and the use of Dreyfus as a scapegoat highlighted these fundamental failures. Europe would learn professionalism from the Prussians and bungling slackness from the French, at least in their public images. But in fact, the *Service de Renseignement* or SR was most effective, with representatives in Berlin and Vienna. They actually acquired details of the German mobilization plans. Yet, paradoxically, Dreyfus – the stooge was qualified to be a first-class officer in this line of work; one of his accusers wrote of him: 'We would add that Captain Dreyfus, whose field of knowledge is very wide, possesses a remarkable memory; that he speaks several languages... Moreover that he is by nature very pliant, even obsequious, a quality which would be much appreciated by foreign agents...'[11] In other words, here was a definition of the kind of man they should have been nurturing.

The persistence of the individual adventurer in the ranks of military intelligence, together with technological advances and foreign influences, all happened with a backdrop of economic stress and strain. After all, Britain had to continue to find the resources and financial support to maintain an ever-increasing Empire. Naturally, the policy of creating satellite states and protectorates makes sense in that framework. Gordon in Khartoum typifies this; men like Lord Salisbury had always put forward the view that colonies entrenched in British ideology would survive and even prosper with a nucleus of British officers and administrators at the helm. But the fact remains, as historian E J Hobsbawm has pointed out, there was a 'flight into dependencies on the part of the economy at the centre of Empire':

> From the 1880s 'imperialism' – the division of the world into formal colonies and 'spheres of influence' of the great powers, combined with the attempt to establish deliberately the sort of economic satellite system which Britain had evolved spontaneously – became universally popular among the large powers.[12]

In the increasingly complex world of espionage, the repercussions of this policy led to a reliance of individual men of genius, enterprise and resourcefulness. Naturally, there had always been a plentiful supply of such men, but from the turning point of the early 1880s, arguably, the combined effects of technology, Realpolitik and more sophisticated diplomacy meant that agents working both at home against the anarchists and overseas against such enemies as the Mahdi would find themselves being asked to exist and operate in a bewildering microcosm of doubletalk, subtle communication and multiple managers and administrators. The old view of secret service work being somehow unethical was destined to be untenable at the *fin de siecle*. Quite simple everyday factors were impacting on the work of the spy: such aspects of modernity as faster transport, rapid communication and a large-scale increase in the sheer volume of information being exchanged. These developments explain why the earlier attitudes of openness and the ideology of the fraternity of the officer class across national divides was becoming a thing of the past.

An overview of the last quarter of the nineteenth century, with an understanding of military intelligence and secret service work in mind, would have to account for both professional and most successful undercover work of Thomas Beach, the explorations of Francis Younghusband and the new sense of purpose and identity in the Intelligence section of the War Office.

However, first the conclusion of the Egyptian campaign along with the truly innovative achievements of Baden-Powell need to be considered.

Notes and References:

[1]   Rudyard Kipling, 'The Mark of the Beast' in J J Strating (ed.), *Oriental Tales of Terror*, Collins, 1971, pp. 20–31.

[2]   See The Berlin Conference: General Act of Feb. 26 1885 on http://web.jjay.cuny.edu/-jobrien.

[3]   H Spenser Wilkinson, *Thirty-Five Years, 1874–1909*, Constable, London, 1933, p. 106.

[4]   Ibid., p. 110.

[5]   Ibid., p. 113.

[6]   See A Egmont Hake, (ed.), *The Journals of Major-General C G Gordon*, Kegan Paul, Trench, London, 1885, pp. 453–454.

[7]   Ibid., p. 452.

[8]   Ibid, see pp. 519–521.

[9]   See the discussion in Ferris (note 14, chapter 3), pp. 20–27.

[10]   John Hughes-Wilson, *The Puppet Masters*, Casssell, London, 2004, pp. 246–247.

[11]   See Jacques Kayser, *The Dreyfus Affair*, Heinemann, London, 1931, pp. 36–38.

[12]   E J Hobsbawm, *Industry and Empire*, Penguin, 1969, p. 149.

9

Kitchener and Baden-Powell

In the period of 20 years between the battle of Tel-El-Kebir and the end of the Boer War in 1902, several military men dominated the scene in terms of the Empire, and in various ways. Some were in part diplomats and governors; some were officers turned police detectives, but at the heart of the army and its campaigns there was the charismatic figure of Herbert Kitchener. From his march to Khartoum through to his appearance on the Great War recruiting poster with its 'Your country needs you' appeal, Kitchener was the kind of leader who attracted attention in everything he did. Some thought of him as cold, emotionally bland and intellectually narrow. But he had a profoundly interesting personality under the harsh exterior. He is significant in this history largely because of his placing of intelligence within his field operations with real aplomb and insight.

Positioned with him here is Robert Baden-Powell, known as 'Stephe' to his close friends and family, a man whose place in the story of military intelligence is undisputedly great and influential. From his first work in India, then his experience in the Matabele

War up to his renown win in South Africa, he comes across as a figure in military history who can hardly be ignored. In his book – *Aids to Scouting* (1899) – written after his experience in India commanding the Fifth Dragoon Guards, he adds a new dimension to the entire concept of what military intelligence is about. Unfortunately, in his later account of his intelligence work – *My Adventures as a Spy* – there are trademark embellishments and dramatizations which extend the facts to some extent. Nevertheless, it is still a fascinating document. Baden-Powell was born in 1857 and Kitchener in 1850. What they shared was a vision of achievement and fame. Both were driven personalities. Baden-Powell, with the energetic support of his mother, was desperate for celebrity and fame. He pushed for assignments and tasks in any sphere which might have led to something more high-ranking and noteworthy. He dreamed of battles and acts of courage. When first put to the test in Africa, he undoubtedly showed qualities of courage and initiative, though there was a sense of romance and tall story-telling deep within him.

Kitchener was a strategist and a man with a presence in a battlefield. When events were developing in the process of a confrontation, he would appear just at the right time.

He was an expert – in what we might call today – the logistics of managing men, supplies and communications. More than anything else, it could be argued, he inspired men; he glowed with confidence, with the assurance that comes from good planning and research. From Wolseley he had learned that the key to success was the time allocated to find the right man for the job. When journalist G W Steevens went to the Sudan expedition in 1898, working on what would become the best-selling – *With Kitchener to Khartoum* (1898) – he wrote that the great General should be a national treasure, or in the words of the time, something that should be displayed at a national exhibition:

But it so happens that he has turned himself to the management of war in the Sudan, and he is the complete and only master of that art. Beginning life in the Royal Engineers... he early turned to the study of the Levant. He was one of Beaconsfield's military vice-consuls in Asia Minor; he was subsequently director of the Palestine Exploration Fund... The ripe harvest of fifteen years is that he knows everything that is to be learned of his subject... He came at the right hour. He was the right man.[1]

Steevens wrote of Kitchener as 'The Sudan Machine' and that was partly responsible for the hagiography that tended to gather the writings of the man. But when he started out he was an intelligence officer with Wolseley and that is what formed much of his military attitudes.

Speaking of the focus of interest in Kitchener's life with reference to the present history, was his mission to Khartoum in 1896 with his expeditionary force that was in action for the first time. The Mahdi had died and the Khedive was now in opposition. True to form, Kitchener assembled his 'team'. The intelligence was under the command of Reginald Wingate, with Rudolf Slatin as his deputy. Wingate, nick-named 'The White Knight' as he had all kinds of equipment with him, was to be the centre of a spy network and Slatin's long experience of the country and the people would also come to play a large part in this work. Wingate was born in Renfrewshire in 1861; he was the cousin of Orde Wingate's father. His military career began with a rank of Second Lieutenant in the Royal Artillery in 1880. Wingate who learned Arabic during his stay in Aden became the most appropriate person to take charge in Egypt when the time arrived. Near the close of Gordon's rule in Egypt, Wingate was given the role of aide-de-camp to Sir Evelyn Wood, *sirdar* of the Egyptian Army (*sirdar* being a Persian word that came into common usage in the Middle East in that sense).

Wingate first took the primary role of commanding the intelligence arm of the army in 1889, and then his priority was to keep updated information flowing from the Sudan. It was Wingate who first wrote about Slatin's imprisonment under the Mahdi, and he explained the phenomenon of Mahdism from the standpoint of one who had been living among the cultural and social elements of that rising. Wingate was – in the words of one historian – 'A small, terrier-like man with boundless energy and equally boundless inquisitiveness'. He first met Slatin after his imprisonment at a time when the Austrians had just arrived. Moreover, Wingate was also responsible for debriefing the man who was to become his most effective and useful spymaster. Wingate's patience and preoccupation with efficiency and minute knowledge were to become fundamental to the success of the network across that vast land. What Wingate had basically done was to gather a massive bank of information about the Mahdists, which in turn, became the heart of his success. Besides, it was truly remarkable that he could position agents in areas of vital importance, choosing the best men for each strategic place.

Perhaps, the most commendable of all Wingate's early actions that preceded his southward march was the rescue of a Roman Catholic priest – Father Joseph Ohrwalder and some nuns who were accompanying him. This was naturally a significant piece of 'spin' for the army as it meant that someone had been able to penetrate the heart of Mahdist territory. Wingate was quite well-informed about the ideology of the Mahdists, as well as of the topography of their land and social interactions, that he published *Mahdism and the Egyptian Sudan* in 1892.

Now both Wingate and Slatin faced the Khedive Abdallahi. When Slatin first arrived he was looked upon with suspicion and with a sense of awe. Here was a man who had been kept imprisoned within the enemy's central caucus of men in power. His letter explaining why he had proclaimed himself a Muslim to Gordon was not generally known, and some even thought that he deserved contempt for such an action. But with Khartoum as the objective and Kitchener keen to use the full communication systems available to him, Wingate knew that there was a major role for Slatin to play. After all, here was a man who Wingate knew had a considerable knowledge of the enemy - even the Khedive himself.

What Slatin had to impart was something very important indeed: the fact was that within the enemy there existed a fair amount of division. In the period following Mahdi's death, the appointment of Abdallahi had been a focus for dissent and resentment. The reason behind the dissent was that the new Khedive, unlike the Mahdi and his family, did not belong to the elite. In fact, he was a nomad and was perceived to be someone who was not well educated.

What Slatin and Wingate came to understand was that the followers of Abdallahi were Baggara nomads, and that class of men were loose canon, likely to follow their own ways rather than be a part of any great fighting machine. Much of the regulation of their affairs was controlled by traditional custom rather than the order of a leader. Where then, Wingate asked himself, was the evidence of these fighters' loyalty to the Khedive? That point was going to be an Achilles Heel in the coming battles. The combination of Wingate's acumen in gaining and sifting information, Slatin's insider knowledge and the tactics of Kitchener, things were looking promising as the expedition was being planned.

However, returning to Slatin, it must be remembered that he had gained immense sympathy during his reception in the British camp. Gordon, as we have seen, felt a certain degree of contempt for him and never rated his abilities fairly. Now, there he was with the reputation of having espoused Islam while in captivity - a very unBritish behaviour. Neither did he come across the part nor did he belong to an age when protocol and appearance counted for a great deal in the armed forces as elsewhere. When he appeared with the Frontier Force, Slatin did not exactly win friends quickly. He looked seedy, short and unkempt. But there is a story of his walking into the mess and whispering to an officer that he was Slatin (his name was widely known of course), an officer of the

Sixtieth Rifles, a man who was senior aide-de-camp – Jimmy Watson – bought him a beer and made sure that his guest drank it. That was a sure test that the man was really not a Muslim.

The first objective of the expedition was to assemble the right men for each task, just as the intelligence staff had been hand-picked, similarly, the essential camels for use in the journey would be handled by Kitchener's brother Walter, sent for from India, and an engineer called Girouard was brought in to repair the train line, which had been dismantled after the failure to sort out the rescue of Gordon some years ago.

The columns then began their trek into the Sudan; the train was in action and gunboats were moving on the Nile. The first of a sequence of battles was to be fought, leading to the triumph of Omdurman, when the intelligence officers would have their real talents put to full use. As they travelled, the spies would arrive and report. Steevens, the journalist, was on hand to observe as the battle of Atbara was nearing:

> The intelligence department only half believes the native stories. The native has no words for distance and number but 'near' and 'far' and 'few' and 'many'. 'Near' may be anything within twenty miles and 'many' ranges from a hundred to a hundred thousand...[2]

But Steevens had also noticed what Wingate had achieved. He wrote that 'Nothing is his from Colonel Wingate, whether in Cairo or at the court of Menelek, or on the shores of Lake Chad' and 'Whatever there was to know, Colonel Wingate surely knew it, for he makes it his business to know everything'.

On one occasion Steevens saw Wingate in action, using his Arabic and also his skills as a communicator. The journalist wrote: 'Any day from dawn to dark you might see half-clothed black men squatting before Colonel Wingate. Some were fairly fat; some were bags of bones. But all stated with one consent that they were hungry, and having received refreshments felt that they could do no less than tell Colonel Wingate such tidings as they conceived he would like to hear...'[3] This reveals the truth of Wolseley's comments about the unreliability of local intelligence, but it also shows that information given in these circumstances could have been quite certainly verified if the officer in liaison with the natives knew the factual basis of the land in which things happened – and of course, that his Arabic as well as his judgement of men and their speech were up to the mark.

It was Omdurman that asserted the testimony to success of this intelligence work. A few weeks before the battle, Kitchener had seen his last detachments of men arrive: he had a total of around 20,000 men by the time the Grenadier Guards arrived on cattle trucks. He was to have Maxim guns, of course, confirming the poet Hilaire Belloc's couplet: 'Whatever happens we have got/The Maxim gun, and they have not'. This fearsome weapon had been invented by Hiram Maxim, an American who was out to make money and who had been told by the advisers that to strike it rich he should invent something that would help the Europeans 'cut each other's throats with greater facility'. He came up with a belt-fed machine gun that could fire 600 rounds in a minute. It was first used just three years before the Khartoum expedition, in the 1893 Matabele War (where Baden-Powell was conspicuous).

The Maxim gun was to play a major role in Omdurman, but Kitchener also possessed newly-equipped gunboats and indeed, in sharp contrast, the Twenty-first Lancers. After having attempted all kinds of approaches just to be a part of the war, the young Winston Churchill who was rebuffed by Kitchener, finally managed to use powerful influences to get himself associated with this cavalry regiment. This development made it quite evident that Churchill was to come face-to-face with Kitchener soon after the main action.

Kitchener may have had technology and modernity built into his preparations, but there was also the point that he still had to take thousands of men across a massive desert. The engineer who planned the route was also a water-diviner, and somehow that typifies the *sirdar's* approach: there was always something trusting, instinctive, added into his calculations. At Omdurman, he actually risked his life several times as the British entered the city and routed pockets of resistance.

There had been a battle at Atbara some months before this and Kitchener had rested his troops effectively. Now, Kitchener possessed a large force along with the required technology – a huge step forward in the military sphere made possible by the emergence of railways. Gunboats were constructed keeping in mind the new armours and weapons. Omdurman was close to Khartoum, just a little to the north on the western bank of the river. Next to that was the area of Karari, where the open combat in the action was to take place. On 1 September, the army camped at El Egeiga on the Nile. The men built a protective banking – a *zariba*. What he had in mind was an advance, not a digging-in, as most enemy forces would expect, because Kitchener was hugely outnumbered (though he had no idea at the time just how much it was the case). Recent history has revealed that such was the case at the famous Rorke's Drift against the Zulus.

The day before the action, the heliograph communicated that a large force of Dervish was on its way to meet the British. The *sirdar* organized his positions. His army was predominantly Egyptian and Sudanese; he placed his British to the left and brought his men out in a broad arc. This was going to be the result of his tactics: an army with much inferior numbers facing a mass of men 50, 000 strong, but with artillery and Maxim guns. The spies had made it clear that Kitchener intended to attack at night, and the ruse worked because that information prompted the enemy to go on the offensive first.

Here we have different accounts of how this was done. One story is that it was entirely the work of Slatin, and this does seem to be the case, because in a biography of Osman Digna, who led one of the Dervish armies, and written by H C Jackson, we have this account:

At this point Slatin Pasha, who was on the staff of the Intelligence Department, gained his reward for ten years captivity... He suggested that the best way to prevent the Dervishes from launching a night attack was to give them the impression that their stronghold would be assaulted that night... Slatin took a few of these [spies] aside and told them as a deadly secret that the British meant to attack Omdurman during the night... and that they should go at once and warn their families....[4]

Of course, the spies informed their own leaders and the news spread through the whole Dervish camp. The Khalifa decided to move first, and he trusted the rumours. Of the massive force of men who offered their morning prayers on the dawn of 2 September, 10, 000 were to die in the battle.

Later in life, Slatin certainly enjoyed writing about the Sudan and eventually, he came to be regarded as an authority on that episode of recent history. In 1899, for instance, he wrote an account of the campaign for *The Anglo-Saxon Review* and in this essay he wrote only one paragraph on Omdurman, and in this he simply gave objective facts, concluding that, 'This was the outward and visible sign that it was these two powers [English and Egyptian] in conjunction had defeated the enemy and taken possession of the country'. The essay was hardly a defensive indulgence in telling the world what a hero he had been. Slatin wrote in the capacity of a formal expert, and not by any means as a man who had shifted to the dangerous worlds of espionage and imprisonment.

Reginald Wingate edited the text of Jackson's book and wrote an introduction; he must have known that Slatin was named as quoted above. The Khalifa did not begin a guerrilla campaign; he sat and waited, with no more strategy than a direct attack, a brave confrontation against a powerful firepower. The Mahdist front extended for five miles, and although Kitchener was not aware of the full extent of other forces further back, there were still around 20,000 men behind, some waiting in a *khor* (a dry riverbed) and these would later inflict the worst casualties on the British as they surprised the Twenty-first Lancers. But the main positions of the battle itself were that the British were in their *zariba* by the Nile, with Gebel Surgham to their left and the Kerreri Heights to the right. In the plains – between these – Ali Wad Helu attacked. There were gunboats on each side of the British position; Kitchener also had his Camel Corps, with Walter in charge, and these were in the southern parts of the Kerreri Heights. The most visible and therefore, vulnerable of all Kitchener's army was Broadwood's cavalry. The *sirdar* had to use his communications systems well to cover Broadwood.

But the day itself was a slaughter; in the centre of Kitchener's deployment was Maxwell, and Macdonald, who was for many the real hero of the day, was foremost on the right. It was a case of rapid-fire at a densely-packed advance. To some, it must have been anachronistic – the kind of battle one might have expected in the mid-eighteenth century when blocks of infantry advanced against cannon. There was terrible loss of life. However, Macdonald along with his 3, 000 Sudanese men encountered an opposition force comprising 17, 000 men and indeed they had a tough time dealing with the situation. He reported that his guns and Maxims had saved the day: 'Their advance was very rapid and determined and though they appeared to be mowed down by the artillery and Maxims they pressed on'.[5]

The principal design on Kitchener's part was to march into Khartoum, in spite of the fact that there was still a force to his rear; but he kept to that plan, trusting Macdonald to win the rearguard action. That was the case, but it may not have worked out that way – it was a calculated risk. The fact was that Kitchener had learned from Wolseley the art of the use of climate in this theatre of war. Wolseley had won Tel-El-Kebir by an attack at dawn, with troops fresh and cool. Though Kitchener's men did not have to move very much (except for the Lancers) and had also been in possession of superior firepower, it was essentially the fact that the crucial factor was the hour at which the battle had begun. The *sirdar* had not wanted an attack at night from Abdellahi; the Khalifa may well have won had he done that, with the British still in the *zariba*.

The verdict was, for many, that Omdurman was 'noble, but it is not war' (first said about the charge of the Light Brigade and now reversed to pay compliment to the noble enemy). As Michael Asher wrote: 'Whole families, whole clans of tribesmen were swept away like chaff. Men fell, their bodies torn and shattered. The warriors closed the gaps and stormed forward shoulder to shoulder towards the fearsome dragon of fire'.[6]

It had been a victory won by a combination of good intelligence work and the powers of an extremely talented leader in the battle. As for Rudolf Slatin and Reginald Wingate, they went on to other things. Slatin certainly did not retire; he came back to the Sudan in 1900 leading a group working for the Sudan Territories Exploration Syndicate. They were looking for gold and found nothing: something that may be taken as a strong metaphor, in some quarters. By September 1900, Slatin became the Inspector General of the Sudan; but he did renew links with his family and his native land, visiting Austria every summer. He was destined to move in high places, still, however: he could have worked for the Turks or the Germans, but would not work in any capacity against the British. His last work was for the Red Cross and he refused the post of Ambassador in London, for Austria. Rudolf Slatin died in 1932, after one last visit to the Sudan as a guest of the government.

Reginald Wingate became Governor General of the Sudan and stayed there for 17 years. This period witnessed the abolition of the slave trade and of raiding inland for slaves. The country was prepared for a new existence as a modern state. Wingate was even involved in the development of the Gezira irrigation plan. In 1916, Wingate took control in Darfur. But he was to have problems again when there was an Arab revolt in Hejaz in which he supported Sharif Hussain. Wingate extended his skills from intelligence operations to quartermaster and diplomat. He made a special trip to Paris to argue that the European powers should talk to an Egyptian delegation. But the case was that Lord Curzon refused this; the consequences were anarchical. Wingate had not been listened to. This is understandable when we recall Curzon's basic attitude to imperialism. As one of his biographers noted: 'His attitude towards the common people was that of a benevolent patrician. He did not even believe that Englishmen, let alone Scotsmen, Welsh and Irish... and other lesser breeds, had earned the right to equality with those who had spent their lives and their brains in learning to rule them'.[7]

Wingate became a General but moved out of the foreground; he became a company Director, Commandant of the Royal Artillery and a Governor of the Gordon College in Khartoum, which had been Kitchener's dream from the start, and which had been founded after huge amounts of money were put his way on his triumphant return home. Wingate died in Dunbar on 28 January 1953.

The best tribute to this remarkable, able and inspirational man was by Lord Cromer in 1916, who said that, 'It is to my mind the most remarkable compliment that could possibly be paid to British rule that the Sudan should have remained quiet: and this is mainly due to your wise government'.[8] In terms of the control of spies in active operations, he and Slatin had the insight to know when to ground and retrain the men in their network of agents; key men in that capacity who might be double agents were restrained and watched. Cavalry patrols were active in keeping Arab reconnaissance in the dark as well, whenever Kitchener had something important in the planning stage. That practical side to Wingate was the reason for his success.

When we compare Kitchener to Baden-Powell as leaders, one outstanding feature comes to mind, and this explains much of their difference. Kitchener, it was often remarked, only addressed any words to his men if he was giving an order, whereas Baden-Powell was the kind of officer who would have a Sergeant knitting him socks. Focusing back on Baden-Powell, he came across as someone who relished every aspect of army life. Further, he also saw the army functioning organically with all secondary elements appropriately fitting in along with the people involved. Kitchener saw things more in terms of utilitarian perspective. When he had to move a large army across a desert he conceived of the right logistics for the terrain, climate and distances. The intelligence arm of his campaign integrated smoothly as part of that 'machine'. Baden-Powell would not have disagreed with that, but he was attracted to the actual physical, hands-on approach of knowledge of the enemy in all forms of information.

The concept of 'scouting' as a term that would cover several of the skills and habits long engendered automatically by life in the wild outbacks of the Empire matched perfectly with the kinds of war sites he was to work in, from jungle to veldt. 'Spying' – for Baden-Powell – was a word that covered not only observation and covert activity but a set of fine transferable skills which could be taught and integrated into other army-friendly habits and states of mind.

Baden-Powell made a brief appearance in this phase of history However, his achievements will be analysed in greater details in the subsequent chapter. It is necessary now to trace his involvement in field-intelligence in the years before the Boer War. Powell who began his military career after leaving Charterhouse, went on to become a gazetted Second Lieutenant when he joined the Thirteenth Hussars in India. From the beginning, he specialized in scouting and reconnaissance, becoming early on a theorist and an innovator; this was something that stemmed from his childhood interest in woodcraft. He was promoted to the rank of Captain in 1883 and when the Hussars moved to Natal to support Sir Charles Warren in Bechuanaland, he got the opportunity to indulge in some real espionage, resorting to disguise, surveying the Drakensburg passes.

In this adventure the dramatic side to his nature can be observed; he loved amateur theatricals and for this secret trip he adopted a disguise, growing a beard and wore shabby clothes. The fact is that this was one of his manoeuvres to be noticed as a man who could be useful in the intelligence work in South Africa. He wrote a book, *Reconnaissance and Scouting* (1884) and he made sure that the Quartermaster General (a position with importance in the intelligence hierarchy) knew about it.

There was an element of farce in the trip, as he pretended to be a journalist writing a feature on the Boer territory with the avowed aim of producing something for the immigrants to the country. He must have been well observed and perhaps, even seen as a harmless eccentric, but the truth was that he did produce some maps of those regions of the Transvaal. Later, however, he went on insisting that had the high command in the Boer War used his maps, things would have been quite different. It has to be recalled here that Baden-Powell was a careerist at a time when soldiers were expected to find a war to participate in and to make a name, otherwise they were waiting to fill dead men's shoes. His mother was his most energetic supporter. When his book was published, she proved her worth as a public relations expert, sending flyers to 10,000 officers extolling the virtues of her son's book.

In the late 1880s, before his first major involvements in war, he also made hunting trips and used these as opportunities to accrue material for the other element in his spying – field-intelligence in the form of the supporting skills of bushcraft. In 1885 this took the form of a safari, going inland from Mozambique and travelling by sun and landmarks, as he wrote later. His principal biographer – Tim Jeal – makes it clear once again that the great man was enjoying the material as good copy for a yarn. After all, he wrote as a freelance as well and got his works published in magazines such as *The Graphic*.

Both his hard work and persistence paid off eventually, as he had made it clear to the senior officers that he was confident of his innovations in the training of cavalry; he was noticed by the hero – Wolseley – who asked Powell to make a trip to Aldershot and implement his ideas on that topic. He did impress, but it was merely a taste of achievement; his big break came when his uncle – Henry Smyth – was needed in Africa and Baden-Powell had to accompany him as aide-de-camp. This led to another landmark in his education as a scout and intelligence *guru*: experience with the Zulus.

There had been a veritable revolution in the Transvaal since the days of Isandlwana; gold was being mined there and after the Conference of Berlin, Germany subsequently possessed a territory – German South-West Africa – which was followed by an annexation of a land that eventually became the Tanganyika territory. Even though Baden-Powell during his stay in Cape Town could have remained satiated by indulging himself in theatricals and sports like polo, he was still longing for action. However, the opportune moment arrived when trouble started brewing amongst the Zulus again, this time in a place where General Smyth was in charge of policing the area with the help of a mixed army – a combination of British and indigenous men. The focus of rebellion was Cetshwayo's son, Dinuzulu, and at the time the great scout John Dunn was a powerful figure in controlling a large area of Zululand. Baden-Powell was about to learn from a master. Of course, Dunn had Zulus worked with him, therefore, Baden-Powell's intimate interaction with these people gradually made him appreciate their culture, their songs and their communal skills. Just before Baden-Powell's involvement, the battle of Eshowe had been yet another slaughter of men at the barrels of European weapons.

Smyth and Dunn combined to march, intending to meet the rest of Dinazulu's army. But this was crumbling from the centre, and when Baden-Powell and his Inniskilling Dragoons detachment of scouts arrived at a kraal, and found it was deserted. The Zulus had escaped and the blame lay at the feet of Sir Arthur Havelock, who had, in the opinion of Smyth, failed to communicate properly. With the occurrence of an incident, Baden-Powell came to be unexpectedly exposed for the wrong reasons. As he and his Zulu scouts followed a murdering band of Dinazulu's rebels, after a massacre, the killers were trapped in a cave and although Baden-Powell gave orders to spare them his scouts disobeyed his orders and massacred them. Fortunately for Baden-Powell, Wolseley was quite in favour of that outcome, for general reasons, linked to a comprehensive repression of crime policy.

For Baden-Powell, then, the years up to the 1890s were becoming a series of piecemeal and unsatisfactory short-lived shards of experience. Nothing was coming together for him in intelligence work. But then, something much more interesting happened: a chance to explore a part of the vast continent of Africa which in turn gave him a brilliant opportunity to add the last essential element to his resume. He had already proved himself in surveying, scouting, field-intelligence and map-making. Now, he was to chart some unknown land. The key figure here was a man called Frederick Selous, who had been working with Cecil Rhodes to gain and control the land then settled by the Matabele and Mashona. For Baden-Powell, it was a meeting with a man who could have stepped out of the dashing adventures in cheap ripping yarns; Selous was, in fact, the basis for Allan Quartermain in Rider Haggard's novel – *King Solomon's Mines*. What was wanted by Britain was information about the Zambezi River and its navigability. Wider issues impinged on this, elements such as the German territory nearby and the possibilities of Boer involvement in any trouble. But as with most of Baden-Powell's adventures at the time, the plan was diverted to something else and he ended up writing a report on Swaziland. But failure though this episode was in some ways, he was well prepared for what came his way in 1890, when he had become a spy in the true sense of the term.

In case of both Germany and France, their colonial expansion was always present in the background. Only eight years after this Swaziland exploit, *The Times* reported that the German colonies in Africa and in the South Seas came to a massive total of 1, 024, 262 square miles, and the area was five times the area of continental Germany. It noted that, 'Over this territory are distributed 5,125 Germans... one German to every five square kilometres'. France had colonies in North Africa, of course, and Baden-Powell was supposedly active in Algeria as well. If indeed he was active as a spy in that area, as he writes in his memoirs, then he did so under his own direction with his own aims, despite the fact that the War Office did reimburse him for the trip. This venture, which took place in Biskra, Algeria, provided some of the best materials that informed the modern reader about what a spy did in such circumstances. It is likely that he detoured to Algeria on his way home from work in Malta. Assessing Baden-Powell as a spy is difficult, as the extent of his glamourizing of that experience is not really known. But the Algerian adventure was ostensibly about gathering details of a new field gun. As Tim Jeal states clearly that the adventure here was about doing a sketch of the gun. Besides, he also added that any extra information that he might have come across was through sheer observation and enquiry. He had been hunting wild boar with French officers not long before this, and this provides an interesting contrast when we look at the two accounts – one in his diary and one in *My Adventures as a Spy*.

The latter work, written undoubtedly to embellish the experience and to entertain in a *Boys' Own* manner, works by mystique: 'I was sent to find particulars... On arrival in the colony I found that a battery of new guns was carrying out experiments at a distant point along the railway... The timetable, however, showed that the ordinary day train stopped there for half an hour.' But in his diary he refers to 'wild boar': 'I had to wade across three strips of the river. Made my sketch – wandered back in time to get coffee... Only one thing marred my pleasure – and that was that I was unable to get some information I wanted, though I had tried one or two people – viz whether there were any wild boar in the neighbourhood'.[9] Was the phrase 'wild boar' a coded reference to other intelligence information? Certainly when he wrote the account it seemed as if he was under a threat from some soldiers who had noticed him using binoculars. He may have had an exciting close shave in the enterprise, or he may have been quite normally perceived as a traveller.

Even more strange is the account he gives of methods employed while 'butterfly-hunting' in Dalmatia. Here, he writes of his exploit in assuming the role of an entomologist while actually looking at fortifications. It appeared that he had come across reality in Bosnia at a time when he had gone drawing fortifications in the Straits of Messina. In his account, he even wrote about capturing spies and even went into detail about catching some in Malta in 1891. Regarding this particular incident, he wrote that he had stopped two strangers in Valetta when they were taking photographs of an area called the French Creek.

All this means that in a combination of sheer baloney and romancing of facts Baden-Powell was entranced by the writer's need to enhance the role of a spy into the realms of the male romances of the time as written by Rider Haggard and William Le Queux. His long memoir – *My Adventures as a Spy* – was published when humanity in general was taking a profound interest in spy stories from anywhere in the world. For instance, the temperance magazine – *The British Workman* – carried a feature in its 1906 issue on 'The Death of Two Japanese Spies' and the event was reported in the fashion of a high drama as in the popular narratives for young men and readers of thrillers:

I have obtained from a Russian naval officer, who has just returned from Harbin, the following unpublished details of the death of two Japanese spies who were captured by Cossacks in the act of blowing up a ridge on the Manchurian railway... The officer was invalided home... and arrived just as the two Japanese were arrested, caught red-handed and executed.[10]

But before his participation in the Boer War, the one episode in which we see the nature of Baden-Powell's real contribution to intelligence work is in the Matabele campaign of 1896. A murderous insurrection had taken place there, with the targets being mainly white settlers; as a Staff Officer, Baden-Powell now really made his mark leading the scouting that was to locate the positions of the native forces in the Matopos. There had been one expedition – notably by an army led by Colonel Plumer – against these fearsome fighters in their native terrain. Baden-Powell, as Staff Officer to Sir Frederick Carrington, began as office-worker and administrator, but an emergency arose in which he had to lead a cavalry force against a huge body of Matabele. He did well; only four of the British forces were killed, as opposed to 200 Matabele. The victory meant that the war would now have to be carried to the Matopo Hills where the remaining Matabele were prepared to fight in guerrilla warfare.

There could not have been a better opportunity for Baden-Powell to put into practice his long-engendered reconnaissance methods. As Plumer's army set off for Matopo, he had Baden-Powell in charge of the force as guide. The situation was one in which the enemy had dispersed, placing themselves in pockets of resistance, wherever a particular chief had his men dug in, or in many cases, in caves within the rock-fissures of the country. Baden-Powell's real achievement was in placing and leading intelligence-gathering detachments into this country. Though success was limited, it was a learning experience. There was a desperate need to start talking to the Matabele chiefs and to find a way to start negotiations. Baden-Powell, in the course of his scouting, was working with Jan Grootboom when they came across a captured woman who was a relative of a principal Chief – M'zilikatze. The woman, after being helped by Baden-Powell, started the desired communication with the Chief. The following meeting sorted out many of the grievances of the rebels. Baden-Powell reported the matter to Grootboom later.

Powell made things very clear about what Grootboom symbolized and also how the work against Matabele could be undertaken:

> Jan Grootboom was a Zulu by birth, but having lived much with white men, as a hunter and guide, he had taken well to wearing ordinary clothes and spoke English perfectly well: but within him he had all the pluck and cunning of his race. For scouting against the Matabele it was never wise to take a large party since it would be sure to attract attention, whereas by going with one man such as Grootboom, one was able to penetrate their lines and to lie hid almost among them...[11]

Baden-Powell had won a good reputation as a leader as well as a reconnaissance man. However much he might have exaggerated about what he had learned from Grootboom and his type, it cannot be denied that what he was nurturing was another dimension to the work of field-intelligence. It was a matter of fine detail, much as had been common practice of scouts in the American West and indeed Baden-Powell had also learned from a man called Burnham who had toured with Buffalo Bill in 1887. In a lecture that Baden-Powell gave after the campaign, he spoke of this fine detail of observation, as in his account of what he deduced from a leaf on a tracking expedition:

> But that leaf meant a good deal; it belonged to a tree that did not grow in this neighbourhood... It was damp and smelled of Kaffir beer. From these two signs then, the footprints and the beery leaf, we were able to read a good deal...[12]

After the Matabele experience, Baden-Powell was appointed to the command of the Fifth Dragoon Guards, who were at that time stationed in India. In 1899, he published his book – *Aids to Scouting* – in which he wrote at greater length on the subjects of reconnaissance work and close-contact scouting in the field. He had earned promotion for scouting work earlier in the Ashanti campaign of 1895 but now he had become almost a legend, defined perhaps by his numerous nicknames such as the one the Ashanti gave him - 'Kantankye - he of the big hat'.

He had called the Matabele War 'a joyous adventure' and there he won another nick-name - 'Impeesa - he who never sleeps'. The restlessness of the Matabele is easily explained today - they had been exploited by what one writer calls 'a typically Rhodesian combination of fraud and force' as Cecil Rhodes had his eyes on the country. Baden-Powell found that the people and the situation were right for the application of his scouting methods. The work in small units - as described in My Adventures as a Spy - with Grootboom in mind, was prominent in the text as well. Grootboom had said of Baden-Powell, by way of compliment: 'If the Matabele want to shoot him, they must go after him and catch him out where he hides'. On one occasion, they almost did shoot him. But he showed no fear, just a temper that such a thing could happen. It was a strange experience fighting in the Matabele territory in such a wild and barren place, but it was a successful mixture of 'ripping yarn' and actual life-threatening situations that made the man begin to understand the real nature of war and where scouting fits in with that. It is quite evident, therefore, that not all of Baden-Powell was rhetoric and bluster, he knew his trade fairly well and the knowledge was to flourish later.

Notes and References:

1   Steevens (see note 17, chapter 4), p. 46.
2   Ibid., pp. 114-115.
3   Ibid., pp. 64-65.
4   H C Jackson, *Osman Digna*, Methuen, London, 1903, p. 155.
5   John Pollock, *Kitchener*, Constable, London, 1988, p. 133.
6   Michael Asher, *Khartoum*, Penguin, London, 2006, p. 382.
7   Leonard Mosley, *Curzon*, Longmans, London, 1962, pp. 31-32.
8   M R D Foot, *Secret Lives*, OUP, Oxford, 2002, p. 197.

9   See Baden Powell, 'My Adventures as a Spy' in *Fifty Amazing Secret Service Dramas*, Odhams Press, London, 1930, p. 191; and Tim Jeal, *Baden-Powell*, Hutchinson, London, 1986, pp. 149–150.

10   See *The British Workman*, 1914, p. 14.

11   Baden-Powell (see note 9 above), p. 183.

12   Ibid., p. 188.

10

The Boer War: Sir John Ardagh and Others

In the Boer War of 1899-1902 there were mercenaries and volunteers as well as the official fighting men of the opposing armies. Many Russians went to fight for the Boers, and one of them -Yevgeny Augustus - wrote in his diary an account of what happened to a captured spy; he was badly beaten and the men led by Lucas Meyer treated him abysmally, as was always the way with spies. This one was a Kaffir who had been caught in a nearby kraal. Assistant General Kock took over:

'This is not the first time that we have caught Kaffir spies', Kock explained to the Russians. 'They deliver the most exact data about our positions to the British. These rogues have almost established postal communication between Buller and White for a handful of gold'. 'Shoot him'. He said casually to the Boers. The African was shot instantly on the spot, rather to the Russians' embarrassment.[1]

In this way, we can learn a great deal about several aspects of the Boer War. First, Kock told the volunteers that his father and two brothers had been killed by the British. He was out for vengeance. It was a dirty, ruthless and desperate war with high loss of life. It was also a war in which such duties as intelligence were partly the business of a mixed range of characters of all kinds and backgrounds; the army was using traditional methods of allowing the locals the knife-edge of risk, of course. The episode also hints at just how important the war became as a focus of all kinds of discontentment and imperial rivalry. There were plenty of Germans in Africa by this time, as we have noted; there were also still a number of other locations throughout the British Empire which were still highly volatile. In some ways, the Boer War was to introduce new strategies and attitudes of mind in the British high command, and intelligence work constituted a vital part of that.

It was destined to be a violent, difficult war in all respects; the phases of the conflict were first a direct series of battles with Sir Redvers Buller being the principal military leader for Britain. Gold mining had transformed the Transvaal and a massive influx of foreigners (Uitlanders) had settled there. Repression followed, with the Boer head – Kruger – enforcing police control. Undoubtedly, the abundance of gold made the Boers wealthy enough to accumulate huge stocks of weaponry. By 1900, the Boers had won a series of victories and they held several defensive positions. Besides, after Buller was replaced by Lord Roberts, 50, 000 troops were stationed in Transvaal. But Buller at Spion Kop won a victory with heavy losses and besieged towns were gradually relieved. This led to a retreat by the Boers, who fought a guerrilla campaign in the last phase. They moved north into Natal.

South Africa had been the scene of a long-standing conflict; in 1880-1 there had been a small war in which the Dutch Boers had won at Majuba Hill. Britain had no real worries about giving independence to the insignificant states of Transvaal and the Orange

Free State at that time, but after the gold rush, things were quite different. By 1898, it was clear that the Boers' power could be a genuine threat to British supremacy in that part of the Empire. Of course, there was support from Germany for the Boers, and Germany made sure that it openly congratulated the Boers after they crushed the strange and wrong-headed Jameson Raid in which the Rhodes-backed Dr Jameson (2 January 1895) led a small army into the Transvaal ostensibly to stage a coup. The result was that by 1899 the Boers were becoming a formidable military force.

The turning point came in around May-June 1900 after Mafeking was relieved, Roberts went into Johannesburg and the Orange Free State was annexed. In October that year the Transvaal was annexed. It was from that point that the British intelligence involvement was to be particularly important. It was a lesson to be learned, as was the case with all major aspects of that war. As the Boer 'commandos' started their sabotage and skirmishing campaigns, they were fated to be up against Kitchener and his ruthlessly efficient tactics of defensive positions, internment camps and liaison with Colonel Henderson and with Lord Roberts in intelligence work. The scouting and reconnaissance work that went on was destined to be chaotic and dangerous. As Craig Wilcox has said: 'Mounted scouts combed the countryside and quasi-military intelligence officers ran spy-rings to track down resisters'. There were atrocities, such as the episode in which Harry Morant of an irregular band of volunteers called the Bushveldt Carabineers were involved in the killings of unarmed men.

The significance of the intelligence section in this bloody and frustrating war begins, however, with the work of Sir John Ardagh. There had been massive preparations for the war. Roberts had been active in large-scale manoeuvres in Ireland and there had been endless diplomatic negotiations. But when war was inevitable, it fell to Ardagh – as head of the Intelligence Branch – to prepare a report on the potential enemy and on all military factors. Ardagh made it clear to Lord Lansdowne – the Secretary of State for War – that there would be a need for a force of 200, 000 men to take on the Boer Army. Winston Churchill, at that time preparing himself for work as a war correspondent for the *Morning Post*, noted that 'Mr George Wyndham, Under-Secretary of State, alone seemed to appreciate the difficulties and magnitude of the task. The Boers, he said, were thoroughly prepared and acting on definite plans'. It transpired that the enemy would have a new Maxim model of the fearsome machine gun.

Ardagh had done a thorough job. His background made him an ideal man to lead the new Intelligence Branch. He was born in 1840 and educated at Trinity College, Dublin, followed by the Military Academy at Woolwich. He was commissioned into the Royal Engineers at the age of 19 and thereafter, some way or the other he remained associated with intelligence duties. After travelling with Sir William Jervois on a mission to Nova Scotia in 1869, he was appointed to the staff at the War Office. He became a key man in the European information-gathering and this in turn helped him to gain diplomatic positions, particularly at the Berlin Congress. Most of his work was based in a domestic and administrative context, but he did work with Wolseley as an engineer in the Alexandria campaign of 1882. It was he who organized the railway systems in the phase of the Egyptian activities culminating in Tel-El-Kebir.

In 1887, he was recalled to the War Office where he was instrumental in organizing the Mobilization Division alongside the Intelligence Branch. The new ideologies were seeping slowly into the consciousness of the hierarchy at the War Office and the impact of Prussian military structures was beginning to have an effect. *The Times* recalled later exactly what the importance of this work on mobilization was: '...it will be remembered that one of the few satisfactory features of the beginning of the South African War was that the mobilization of the troops was accomplished without a hitch. For this the good foundation laid by Sir John in 1887 was partly responsible' (September 1905).

Ardagh was always to be found where there was open discussion of innovation and efficiency. A typical example is the Durr light lamp. In 1895, a lamp invented by a German engineer - Ludwig Durr - was given some night-time trials. The idea was that this instrument would shed light when there was no gas or electric source. Ardagh directed that a reservoir be filled with petrol as the Durr lamp burned. The lamp worked well and as *The Times* commented: 'In the embarkation or disembarkation of troops and the loading or unloading of store ships or transport wagons at night it would be of the greatest possible service'. Ardagh was the man who ultimately wrote reports for the War Office. This small example tells us so much about the man: his meticulous attention to detail and his utter reliability in a position of responsibility. It astonishes us today that his estimations regarding the Boer War were very likely correct.

For six years Ardagh served in India as a private secretary to Lord Lansdowne and then moved, after a brief time in the School of Engineering, into the work he is always associated with - being Director of the Military Intelligence Branch (1896-1901). He had only just settled into that responsibility when the war in South Africa became imminent. He knew that his main priority was to prepare information relevant to the Transvaal; he had a small staff and very poor resources, but Ardagh's report - *Military Notes on the Dutch Republics of South Africa* - was produced. Later, this document became the subject of some controversy and opinions were divided, but it is apparent that the facts in that report were astoundingly accurate. His advice that almost a quarter of a million men would be needed was almost certainly not taken seriously; there was the usual underestimation of the enemy. After all, they were thought to be essentially farmers, not soldiers. It was a fatal error of judgement.

In fact, in a short letter to *The Times* in November 1899, a certain 'P S C (an anonymous writer) wrote:

> Sir, some doubt has been expressed as to the accuracy of the information possessed by the Intelligence Department of the War Office with regard to the Transvaal armaments. I have reason to know, and on the most unimpeachable authority, that in the report rendered by Sir John Ardagh... on the armed strength of the Boers, the number of their guns given, with their character and calibre, corresponds exactly with our recently ascertained knowledge of what the enemy has put into the field. Moreover, as to the numerical strength the Intelligence Department's estimate was rather over than under the totals said to be now arrayed against us.[2]

The equivalent German staff in intelligence at the time was around 250; Ardagh had 20 men under him. It was observed at the time that in the Transvaal £90,000 was spent every year on financing the corresponding office to Ardagh's, whereas Ardagh himself had a budget of £20,000. Nevertheless, the new Chief of the Intelligence Branch was consulted by the Foreign Office and the Colonial Office for assistance in a range of matters. Ardagh, however, did not keep his mouth shut on matters relating to resources. He clearly fought a battle with the hierarchy. When he gave evidence before the War Commission he expressed the problems he had encountered in trying to explain why intelligence work needed more staff and finance. He always showed wholehearted commitment to every task he was entrusted with. Ardagh was always attached to any scheme generated by the new department and indeed, as all staff involved in espionage has to do, he had a wider remit than field-intelligence and in fact, as was learned after the war, he even had agents particularly linked to diplomacy, something that had been the case since the beginnings of the Empire. This had become more difficult as time went on, and particularly in the case of reliable maps when war should arise.

He needed a network of agents *in situ* in South Africa, but had none. One of the foremost historians of the Boer War makes it clear what Ardagh's problem was in this respect:

> But Ardagh was a shy, cautious man, known for his alarming silences. Moreover, Ardagh had been given only a shoestring budget for the Intelligence department – £20, 000 to cover the whole world. He had no professional intelligence agents in either the Free State or the Transvaal. So his forecasts were hesitant or conflicting. Where they were to prove accurate – and to favour Wolseley – it was easy for Lansdowne to brush them aside.[3]

It is quite evident from the above that views with regard to Ardagh's achievements vary to a great extent. Nevertheless, the central question was how the military thinkers anticipated the action of the Boers. It was essential to know not merely what the Boer strength was but whether or not they had the capabilities to conduct a conventional land war or whether they would be raiders. Ardagh considered that the latter was the most likely. His report had a thesis related to this at the heart of its assessment. First, he thought that the two states would join together (and they did); they would mean that they had almost 40, 000 fighting men. He also reckoned that they would have Mauser guns and 'Long Toms' of no more than 16. The kernel of the thinking behind all this was that the Boers would raid.

The assumption underlying the report was that the organizational powers of the Boer leaders would be limited and that they had no experience of warfare to compare with the generals who would be leading the British forces. The artillery they possessed were thought to be inferior to the British Armstrongs and practical topics, such as these, made sense at the time in the perspective of previous engagements. But one entrenched attitude was a line of thought that added to the miscalculations, not so much as those written by Ardagh but by the military minds who extended their initial thinking: that was the reliance on the established reputation of the British imperial armies. This led to the certainty that the Boers would not be able to stage an invasion and that indeed the British could take the offensive and defeat the enemy in the field, forcing them into raiding tactics. With these thoughts in mind, Buller aspired for a 'forward policy' – an offensive to capitalize on these perceived features of British superiority. It was assumed that one sizeable confrontation would put paid to the 'farmers'. It is not difficult to see, with hindsight, the difficulty of Ardagh's situation. He had been given a major responsibility and his natural sense and caution then restricted him to the estimations and assumptions based on the limited information he could gather with his resources.

One of Ardagh's more interesting achievements came in this way and it also illustrates the spy's best friend – sheer serendipity. We know this tale of the acquisition of Transvaal maps because an account was written by the famous military historian Brigadier General J E Edmonds in 1922. His account was from the standpoint of a man who was actually Ardagh's agent in this minor triumph. His story was that in December 1899, the British minister in Berne – Sir Francis St John – noticed a large-scale map on a wall in an antechamber of the federal building there. It was a map of the Transvaal and the creator of this very useful item was an inhabitant of Zurich, so the diplomat noted the name, and then contacted him. Sir Henry Angst – a senior diplomat – saw to it that sufficient knowledge was gained about other copies of the maps. It was discovered that 3, 000 of them could be bought for £3, 000. Edmonds then completes the saga: 'Sir Francis St John communicated with London and a high officer of the Foreign Office brought his telegram to the old Intelligence Offices at 18, Queen Anne's Gate. Sir John Ardagh instructed me to go to the War Office in Pall Mall, see the permanent Under-Secretary, Sir Ralph Knox, and stay there until I got the authority for the money'. Edmonds obtained what he wanted and travelled to Berne immediately. He was taken by Angst to Winterthur where the maps were all packed and ready for movement. He notes that 'The production of the proof-sheet settled the matter. I took as many maps as I could carry back with me, arriving in England on Christmas Eve. Mr Angst dispatched the cases of maps to my private address, where they arrived safely'. In other words, although one box of maps had already been transported to South Africa before all this had occurred, but fortunately Ardagh had accidentally discovered this box and Ardagh had obtained copies of the same because of a chance sighting by a man walking through a room involved in other business.

What begins to emerge subsequently when we look at the military intelligence of the Boer War in the early stages and in the pre-war days is a series of actions all disparate, some linked to mere opportunity and chance; in the actual mainstream information, with Ardagh at the centre, there is a mix of system, caution and theoretical thinking that is uneven in its results. But as there was no network of agents in place, it became clear that the actual field-operations of spies was going to be (as can be seen in the shooting of the 'Kaffir spy') the use of native personnel along with anyone else (military or civilian) who could be included in specific ad hoc actions. Of course, for the most perilous and frustrating phase of the war, the guerrilla war from 1900-2 with Kitchener in pursuit and a method of gradual and patient blockading in progress, spy activity was certain to be dangerous, adventurous and pragmatic. Hence we have, for instance, a proliferation of correspondence between officers concerning piecemeal information, handled as it comes along. For example, a telegram sent by a staff at Colonel Ian Hamilton's field force in July 1900 to the Director of Military Intelligence about estimates and disposition of Boer forces, notably commando forces at Boekenhoutskloof and communicating worries about the standard of ability among the officers working under Colonel Hickman. In other words, the larger picture is difficult to perceive. It is useful to recall in this context that a powerful influence on the views that led to the Boer War decisions happened to be the 1888 Stanhope Memorandum. This document laid down the policy of sending two corps into the Empire after the reserve was mobilized. With massive basic concerns such as troop mobilization at the heart of plans, intelligence took a backseat.

The issue of cartography – as highlighted by the story narrated by Edmonds – was important. The existing maps were unsatisfactory because, according so some estimates, the acquisition of maps through survey work would have required massive amounts of investment and years of survey work. Major E H Hills, who was in charge of cartography in 1902, reported to the Elgin Commission that it was a question of lack of money but also of a long-standing neglect of mapping in several areas of strategic importance. For instance, Baden-Powell had conducted survey work in both Cyprus as well as Palestine; such duties in marginal areas had been considered to be tasks for junior officers who needed some experience as extensions to their general training.

In all matters of spycraft, the Boer War attracts special interest since it was used for both innovation and experiment. The Playfair Cipher, for instance, was first used in that war, secretly taken up by the War Office along with many other things. This was a system of coding in which pairs of letters in a plain text are replaced by another sequence of paired-letters. This is entirely typical of the marginalization of espionage, placed in situations in which success is less important than experimentation. After all, from the beginning, the War Office had done some bewildering things in terms of using intelligence in that war; in July 1899, as Christopher Andrew has explained, ten men with experience of field-intelligence were sent to South Africa. Their role was to gather information and then, at a later date, they were to assemble and collate these findings. But as Tammy Proctor writes: 'By November, 1899 several of the original ten male officers were unavailable, having been besieged in settlements such as Mafeking and Kimberley'. It was only after Lord Roberts took command that the well-organized field-intelligence corps was put in place, with 132 officers and a massive body of agents. It was at that point, when communication became the key issue to combat the commando raiders and the dispersed enemy, that other ancillary aspects of intelligence were employed, such as signalling and cables, pigeon post and press censorship.

It was clear by the end of the war in 1902 that the army needed a revisionary study and some radical changes from inside. When Sir William Robertson was based at the War Office from 1902-7, he was once again assigned to intelligence duties. His work was to exist as part of the changes brought about by the 1903 War Office Reorganization Committee, led by Lord Fisher and Sir George Sydenham Clarke. Their proposals were that the aim of the War Office must be to prepare the military forces of the state for war, and that there should be a Defence Committee in the Cabinet. They also made an Army Council which was developed from the template of the Board of Admiralty. All actions of primary importance should be made to the Crown by the First Lord, as with the Admiralty. The Intelligence Department was to be amalgamated with the General Staff. One of the members of the Army Council was supposed to have undertaken the responsibility for intelligence; William Robertson was a major player in this new scheme of things.

Robertson was given the task of controlling intelligence in all foreign countries, collecting and preparing details of all main aspects of that work, embracing such topics as geography, resources and armed forces in a range of locations; he also had to liaise with military attachés and work closely with the Director of Military Operations. There were three subdivisions of the new intelligence section: (i) strategic and colonial defence, (ii) foreign and India; and (iii) executive and telegraphy/special duties. In the new Directorate of Military Operations there were 43 staff members and they were led by Major General J M Grierson.

We can learn something of the changes that took place by summarizing what Robertson did with his time. He was mainly concerned with work relating to Russia and France. As generally believed, there was a shift in the centre of power in Central Asia when Russia gained more influence in the region. Therefore, it became extremely essential to build closer ties with Russia, at least on the diplomatic front. Robertson concentrated on the study of what role intelligence and diplomacy could play in the fundamental situation of being a state with an army ready for war at any time.

What had happened after the lessons of the Boer War was that Britain had become a more forthright military state; militarism was something that was expressed in a variety of ways and the concepts of espionage or of field-intelligence were notions that were to be changed and transmuted in many ways as more profound aspects of the *Zeitgeist* found expression. With reference, particularly to the growth of the intelligence initiatives in the establishment, the war against the Boers made it clear that there had never been a master-plan regarding responses to emergency situations within the Empire. Furthermore, the significance of the contributions made by an Intelligence Department became clearer. One expression of the lesson learned was put strongly by one historian: 'It was not until December 1899, some months after the war had begun, that any thought was given to the question of security intelligence; then a new section under Major Edmonds was created, H section'.[4] This was a wholly new conception, and Edmonds was vastly experienced in all kinds of organizational leadership and indeed in covert work (note his work over the Kruger maps). H section was, in fact, the forerunner of MI5. Security intelligence was something new; this was where Robertson fitted in well, along with other experienced men. What was new was that this was a more intellectual, comprehensive view of intelligence in war and in national security.

One comment at the time about this reform was that 'The days when the War Office was fit for a gentleman came to an end with the Boer War'. Obviously, the man to be consulted regarding staffing the new structures of command was Lord Roberts. In 1899, before the emergence of the later version of the control of the intelligence work at the War Office, the key person was the Director General of Mobilization and Intelligence, and on Robert's advice that post went to Sir William Nicholson. An Order of Council of 1901 made it clear that Nicholson's first duty was to prepare and maintain detailed plans for the defence of the Empire. Nicholson's energetic application to that task paved the way for the successes later, when that first plan was improved, it also took note of liaison with other organizations. Classic theorists such as Clausewitz once again endorsed compulsory reading, though opinions came to be divided on his suggestion. E A Altham, mentioned in Robertson's memoirs, was a deeply influential figure here and the team as a whole had a leader who was prepared to fight to obtain more finance. The staff was becoming aware, as the shortcomings of the intelligence influence in the Transvaal became more known, that Britain's Directorate in that regard were under-financed.

Nicholson began his series of requests for more money and resources in 1901 when he consulted the Treasury on the topic of the size of his domain. He wanted eight more officers for a start and the salaries required for that amounted to over £4,000. This request was modified later, but the next ploy to use against the man with the money - Hicks Beach - was that Germany was well in advance of Britain in this matter. In the end, the support of Lord Roberts proved to be essential when, in 1902, Nicholson asked for a more ambitious increment - the development of his department into a team with 11 more officers, thereby, enhancing the cost even more. This shook the top brass to the core, so much so that they set up a committee to report on exactly what this Intelligence Division was all about.

What was happening was that there was a clash of opinion: some thought that intelligence work in the field was always dependent on specific circumstances and therefore no blueprint could cover every eventuality; others considered that if a commander in the field put together his own plan for how intelligence should integrate or even operate within his scheme of things, then that would be too whimsical and individual, not relating to any grand plan. It was a confrontation between practical men (some of the advisers fresh from the war in South Africa and therefore, not exactly open to theoretical discussions) and officers with a more abstract, comprehensive frame of mind. But in March 1903, a decision was arrived at whereby Nicholson's department was allotted three additional officers and four civilians, along with a great deal of official language in which directions were given as to the use and application of resources. Nicholson made it clear that he still thought the higher echelons of power had not understood the concept behind the linking of intelligence and mobilization: 'Unless matters of this nature are carefully studied at the War Office in peacetime it is extremely improbable that a right decision will be given under high pressure...'

In other words, it was an issue of forethought and preparation, together with a perception that all arms of military might should be integrated. It was the Prussian lesson of 1870 – the matter which still lay on the table waiting for definite action to be taken rather than settling the issue through mere talk. To make matters worse, after the Boer War the notion of having a Director General of Military Training was revived. So, once again there was going to be dissension and crossovers of influence. Much of Nicholson's work came to little due to arguments and jealousies within these corridors of power, and even the King interfered at times. The seat of this confusion and dissent was the wounded pride at the failures in South Africa and of course, the status and prestige of Lord Roberts was a factor there. The result was that, by the time Robertson was involved in 1902 and up to 1907, he and other fellow officers were carrying on regardless of these machinations at the highest level.

In practical terms though, it meant that by 1902 nothing constructive had yet happened to give a permanent footing to any new status and size of the Intelligence Department. Committee followed committee and discussion followed discussion; only when eventually a document was produced called *Field Service Regulations Part II* – created by Rawlinson, Lieutenant Colonel Wilson and Hildyard – was something definite achieved: the manual would be the basis of mobilization when that actually happened, and there was at least a measure of understanding as to what part intelligence staff would play in that.

Regarding the Boer War, then, intelligence in terms of the more office-based, paperwork kind of knowledge – as exhibited by Ardagh in his report – was often seen as something superfluous and hence its low regard in many quarters. It is generally believed that when Redvers Buller was given a copy of the report, he swiftly returned the document with a comment that he was already familiar with the happenings that he was supposed to know. But several important and powerful people were learning that intelligence reports on both security and on enemy assessments were going to matter more and more. One of them was Churchill. It was often held that Churchill – after having heard the news that Austria (and its Empire) had given an ultimatum to Serbia following the assassination of Franz Ferdinand – immediately compiled a list of items for consideration, with the aim of preparations for war. Nevertheless, the main focus in this case too happened to be the new War Office. The list contained the term 'K espionage', which in turn indicated that while compiling the list Churchill kept in mind Vernon Kell – who has been discussed in the following chapter.

But Churchill, ever since his own youthful adventures as a spy/observer in Cuba and with the Lancers in the Sudan, had been more aware than most of the pitiful state of British intelligence and the community that sort of network normally depends on. Since returning from South Africa, he had given talks on the subject.

One of his key references to the Boer War, specifically to Spion Kop, was a fight that made an excellent case study in this respect. British forces were crushed there, and one main reason for that was the lack of maps. The battle took place on 23-24 January 1900. The essence of that defeat was that Spion Kop ('Lookout Hill') was occupied by a small force of infantry under the command of General Edward Woodgate but having done so, they found themselves under merciless fire from several quarters. The troops were totally exposed for a long time and casualties were very high. Churchill himself was present that day, and wrote later:

> One thing was quite clear – unless good and efficient cover could be made during the night, and unless guns could be dragged to the summit of the hill to match the Boer artillery, the infantry could not, perhaps would not, endure another day. The human machine will not stand certain strains for long...[5]

Woodgate, who was killed, was succeeded by Colonel Thorneycroft and he retreated from the position. Buller lost the fight and the statistics make grim reading: 300 men dead and a 1,000 wounded. In addition, 200 were captured.In some places the corpses lay piled three levels deep. The central fact of the misery of the whole experience was that riflemen had been firing down at a vulnerable position. That was something very rarely encountered before that date. It was one more example of how failings in battle in the history of the Empire were often down to underestimation of the enemy or to inadequate attention given to prior knowledge. The basic fact that British troops were 'playing away from home' – as at Isandlwana – was seldom noted and acted on in terms of using intelligence in all forms. We can see with hindsight that simple cartography would have been the answer in this case.

Churchill, along with many other individuals, was clear on the need for a revision of the whole structure of intelligence work, but that was only the official, establishment side of the business. The fact is that other states had advanced into the realms of far more sophisticated organization of espionage and had placed military intelligence much higher on their agenda. In Churchill's case, one example of how easy it was to undertake any kind of subversion or spying in Britain was the siege of Sidney Street. In 1911, when Churchill was Home Secretary, a gang of Latvian immigrants broke into a jeweller's shop on Houndsditch. They took shelter in Stepney in order to save themselves from pursuit and capture. Here, two of them barricaded themselves in 100 Sidney Street. The area was cordoned off and surrounded. The detective force was out, along with Churchill himself, and there was a gunfight, leading to the deaths of two officers. What caused extraordinary interest after the men were found dead in the gutted-out building was that the identities of these men were discovered. They happened to be left-wing extremists, either Bolsheviks or Anarchists. They had not merely been burglars, and the most embarrassing element in the response to this attack had been that the police armaments were woefully inadequate and therefore, Churchill had had to call out a Maxim gun and a force of Scots Guards along with a detachment from the Royal Engineers from Chatham.

For the past 20 years and more there had been an increasing influx of political refugees into the East End. Naturally, some of these would have links with the Russian Secret Service. Scotland Yard had been trying to cope with the Fenian bombers at the same time as they were considering responses to the anarchist threats. The turning point in this development of the Yard's responsibilities came with the appointment of William Melville, who was brought in to lead the Special Branch after John Littlechild resigned in 1893. It was Melville who was to learn more than most about Sidney Reilly (Sigmund Rosenblum) – the double agent. More importantly, for the future of espionage – as Britain was to learn about it – was the efficiency of Melville's network of agents and informers. Earlier in his career, Melville had been in charge of 'counter-refugee operations'. When he resigned in 1903, he became more involved with the understanding of the émigré intelligence network. The Special Branch made a high priority of the need to infiltrate the refugee communities and agents were recruited by Melville and his team. Some came forward to offer to be informers, of course. It could be lucrative; others were approached by detectives after surveillance. Reilly/Rosenblum became one of these Special Branch informers.

What was starting to happen was going to be of immense value to the new Intelligence Branch within the army, and a liaison was inevitable. Reilly settled into the London community and worked under the guise of a small businessman. In the street directory for 1896 he was listed as 'Rosenblum and Co. Consultant Chemists'. Melville was the man who helped his agent take on a new identity; the chief modern biographer of Reilly has found out that Melville had ancestors called Reilly (he was an Irishman) and that is how his spy's assumed name originated from. In 1899, a passport was issued for one named S G Reilly who started some kind of a 'business' for his new spymaster. Japan and Russia were at the time fighting over Manchuria, and we know that Reilly was present there. It is astounding to note that here was a man acting for Melville on the domestic front within the émigré community. Reilly – a man with Russian origins – was almost certainly taking on other duties abroad, and at the very moment when the Great Game was in decline, destined to end officially in 1907 after a treaty was arranged on the far Eastern Question.

The basic fact at the centre of this was that, with the new developments in field and security intelligence taking place at the War Office, as was confirmed by a note in the War Office Military Intelligence Records for 1903: 'The first four officers were sent to Japan as language students'. Of course, a double agent like Reilly had particular value: he traced an Englishman called Horace Collins who was spying for Russia.

In 1997, when materials relating to Melville were released by the Public Record Office, suppositions were confirmed. William Melville had been employed by the War Office from 1 December 1903. He was working in a category of personnel referred to as 'shadowing staff' who observed and wrote reports on specific people under suspicion. He was in that role at least until 1909. In 1901, Melville had investigated an American, and again had also reported on alleged German spies, notably in Epping; between 1905 and 1907 Melville filed several such reports and he learned a great deal from that about the need for liaison. He suggested the organic working of three organizations together: (i) the police, (ii) the post office; and (iii) the coast guard.

Melville's career represents that important development of staff working across previously preserved boundaries. The lessons of the Boer War and of the later phases of the Great Game and the advance of Russia into Manchuria had taught the War Office that such changes were essential. In fact, one case study in Melville's career illustrates this: what has become known as the D'Arcy affair. D'Arcy had managed to gain oil concessions in Persia and was doing the same negotiations in Turkey for similar rights in Mesopotamia. He was trying to sell the rights to the powerful Rothschild family when the Admiralty found out about his dealings. Britain – who understood that very soon petrol was to substitute coal as fuel for ships – was very much supportive of D'Arcy's dealings. The Admiralty decided to back D'Arcy in the project. The Admiralty wanted to move D'Arcy away from the Rothschild influence, of course, and be the sole backers of the oil enterprise.

Speculation suggests that Melville may well have been the agent who worked on behalf of Military Intelligence (linked with the Admiralty) to bring D'Arcy into the fold. Certainly, Andrew Cook makes a convincing case for this, looking into how and why Melville left the Special Branch in 1903.

The story of Melville attracts good amount of interest because his career illustrates to a great extent what kinds of innovative plans and projects were being planned out as the new intelligence staff was gradually shifting towards a very different period, namely the twentieth century that showcased the world of diplomacy and intrigue. The Boer War too appears to be interesting in many respects in the context of field-intelligence; it is even more significant when we consider the repercussions and what 'domino effect' occurred in order to launch what was soon to become MI5. Robertson's memoirs and Churchill's work with various politicians at the time suggest that the year 1902 was a watershed in the history of British intelligence, but not so much for what was achieved quickly and dramatically: it was more so that it happened to be the first step towards the kind of complex modernity in which Melville and others were to move in the 'new age' of double agents and this in turn, initiated a closer network between the 'backroom' intellects of espionage and the men in the field.

Notes and References:

1   Apollon Davidson and Irina Filatova, *The Russians and the Anglo Boer War*, Human And Rousseau, Capetown, 1998, p. 29.

2   *The Times*, 10 November 1899.

3   *The Times* obituary, 1920.

4   Richard Deacon, *British Secret Service*, Grafton, London, 1992, p. 224.

5   Thomas Pakenham, *The Boer War*, Abacus, London, 1994, p. 304.

11

The Foundations of MI5

It is difficult to avoid sharing in Sir William Robertson's sense of new beginning in his memoirs covering the first years of the new century when he writes of the new Intelligence Branch. To his mind, the organization was to be in the hands of the great military men who had finally triumphed in South Africa and who had been dealing with the affair in Chitral and with the last throes of trouble in the Sudan, men like Lord Roberts and Kitchener of Khartoum. But, in fact, there were influences bearing on the renewal of intelligence organization and theory from much more universal sources.

This was due to radical changes in the balance of power and in the rise of the German Empire. The origins of what was to become first the Special Intelligence Bureau and later MI5 are in a meting of a subcommittee of the Committee of Imperial Defence; Captain Vernon Kell of the South Staffordshire Regiment was on that panel and he was one of many who heard a comment that day about a German spy in England. The man - who related the tale of a spy called Steinhauer - was of the opinion that the spy menace could not be combated since there was a shortage of men available who could perform such tasks on the domestic arena. It seems almost a piece of bumbling amateurism now, but a short discussion led to the suggested formation of a special unit to do what would be later called counter-espionage. Since the turn of the century, a war with Germany seemed more and more likely, and the Committee together with the Cabinet, was aware that adaptations were going to be necessary. At that point no one was really aware that Germany – via Admiral von Tirpitz and the German Admiralty – was accelerating the level and effectiveness of a German spy network, far more determinedly than desultory talk about Steinhauer might have suggested. Moreover, when the plan was approved it was agreed that the concept of counter-espionage unit should exist in England, it was soon realized that no one had considered what kind of personnel would do such a thing.

A profound influence on this indecision and uncertainty about espionage was the nature of the military mindset in the imperial phase. The wars of the Empire, both large and small, had been in the hands of men who conceived of soldiering and battle as aspects of brave and honourable behaviour: a code of courage and army operations inextricably bound up with the concept of gentlemanly attitudes and respect for conservative values. Therefore, in that context, the idea of spying on enemy dockyards or gun emplacements was something outside the lines of thought of many; Germany had inherited the same values, entrench in Prussian militarism, and both countries also had to cope with the nature of counter-espionage. The notion of military intelligence in the field was a very different ball game altogether: it could be integrated into general army structures and absorbed without being seen as anything new and innovative; after all Wolseley had proved that it was all a matter of having a staff who could ascertain information about the enemy and about the terrain involved in the theatre of war.

But there had been so much literature and so much media coverage of the work done by the spies that it was being accepted as a legitimate line of work for a soldier. Captain Kell was observed at that meeting as a likely candidate to lead the new Branch. After the decision was approved the two senior men in intelligence at the meeting – General Sir Fraser Davies and Colonel James Edmonds – turned their attention to Kell. Edmonds said: 'What about you, Kell? And from that moment it was left to Kell to take a few days to think it over. He was accustomed to changes of responsibility and indeed to location in his army career because his skill as a linguist and diplomat had made such moves possible. But this was totally different and he mentioned some objections: mainly his lack of experience in that and administration within the government structures. The result was that the panel still thought he would be suitable and he was given some time to consider.

The doyen of military theory, Edmonds, described the nature of the new post. It would be secret and its actions would be covert. Although such work would entail a complete volte-face in his military career, even to the point of being in plain clothes, it attracted him and he made the decision to accept, yet not after his wife and family had expressed support. It was soon in process, beginning with an office within the bureaucratic corridors of government and directed to liaise with Scotland Yard. The Yard had had its Special Branch (originally the Special Irish Branch during the Fenian troubles) since 1888 and had become increasingly cosmopolitan. They had been watching Lenin and Trotsky, for instance, since their arrival in London just after 1900, and Herbert Finch – a superbly efficient linguist – had proved that espionage was possible in a dramatic way by hiding in a cupboard to listen to the Russian émigrés and their discussions.

There was Kell, with no staff and a strong suggestion that he should work with the Yard, initially merely gathering any information he considered to be useful either at present or in the future, with Germany and German connections topping his list. Although Kell had the good fortune to work with the highly experienced Melville, the latter failed to realize this at that juncture. Nevertheless, Melville was to play a crucial part of that new world of pre-war preparations and military revolution that was to be energized partly by the Official Secrets Act of 1911 and also by the Agadir Crisis of 1909. But for the time being, Kell's immediate concerns were to have some help, particularly in the clerical line.

Kell was working closely with Major General Ewart – the then Director of Military Operations – as his line manager; Kell's demand for help was reluctantly listened to and he was given a secretary, with the reminder that there was a limited budget behind his activities. But by 1910 everything had changed; with the support of Major General Henry Wilson, Kell was seen as someone of increasing usefulness and importance, and therefore, cash began to come his way. His hard work had paid off. He was given more staff – first Captain Stanley Clark and then, others including Melville who had been permanently drafted in from the Yard. The new department's priority was to be defined and also understood. Their roles and responsibilities had to be disseminated throughout all the arms of the services and diplomacy so that the establishment would become aware of their existence. Kell's men personally met and opened discussions with the staff in various departments including the police and the ancillary services. Even such bodies as the coast guard and the port authorities would be important in what was to come.

After the expansion of the department and the increase in staff, a pattern of work began to emerge and that was to become exactly what readers of spy stories would have expected: officers detailed to trail and observe suspects, and at any place in the land where reports had been made. Spying really was becoming undercover and impinging on traditional detective skills. Part work done against Anarchists and Fenians was proving to be very useful.

It is important at this juncture to understand something of Vernon Kell, the man who was at the centre of what was to become MI5. He was born in Great Yarmouth in 1873 and his father was a distinguished soldier who had seen service in the Zulu wars. Since Kell's mother was the daughter of a Polish count, Kell partly had Polish blood running through his veins, and that fact, together with his private education given before he entered Sandhurst, probably explains why he was such a proficient linguist. He enlisted in the South Staffordshire Regiment (his father's) and his language skills and his exceptional abilities in the more diplomatic duties of soldiering took him to postings in Russia and in China, where he played his part in the Boxer Rebellion reprisals. His early years in a cosmopolitan milieu clearly became a profound asset as he grew older.

Back in England, with his appointment as a Staff Captain in the War Office, his destined career as a spymaster became possible. He had always had an element of restlessness and terrific ambition; when in Shanghai (and newly married) he had served with Colonel Dorward in Tientsin and in that campaign Kell had been mentioned in despatches. During the Boxer troubles, one aspect of his character came out well: there was a rumour that the besieged troops in Peking had given in and the resistance had failed; Kell refused to give in to the pressure of sending any reports to that effect, and eventually his strategy proved to be correct since the rumour turned out to be absolutely bogus. Obviously, his talents attracted senior staff and he was assigned to General Lorne Campbell's staff in Tientsin as an intelligence officer.

Another valuable learning experience for young Kell was during an episode when he was posted to the remote Shanhaikuan in northern China, close to the Russian border. Here he came to understand the importance of Manchuria to those two Great Powers; he was in close contact with a Russian officer called Ignatieff and spent time usefully making notes on the nature of the Russian presence there. This was followed by some time in Moscow, and he added Russian to his language repertoire. When a serious illness struck him his travels ended and he was assigned the office job; but his time travelling the world was to prove invaluable in his intelligence work at home.

As Kell established himself and his team in the War Office, developments in the German espionage activities across Europe and in particular in the context of ascertaining the real power and condition of the famous Royal Navy, statute law was changing with regard to protecting Britain's military establishment. The Official Secrets Act in 1889 highlighted an entirely new attitude to intelligence theory. Under that law, espionage was a version of high treason and it stated that 'a foreigner convicted of espionage was liable to the same penalties as a native-born subject'. Much of the substance of that Act influenced the attitudes of the subcommittee on invasion – a group which had met no less than 27 times between 1907 and 1908. What always appeared to be the basic reassurance of such groups was that British naval supremacy was beyond dispute and led to fears in the enemies of the land over the seas.

But in Royal Navy manoeuvres in 1908, there was a disturbing slowness and inefficiency with which the Territorial men had responded to a pretended German invasion. Naturally, this was all grist to the mill for those who considered a potential German threat of invasion to be something they could not possibly combat. This made the high command realize that the state had to be familiar with the developments in Germany with regard to espionage. What was happening was that a section of the War Office with responsibility to know about Germany stated that there was an element of truth in the media panics about potential invasion. All this helped to initiate the beginnings of Kell's group. Therefore, even before Kell's new office and staff got to work, there had been a movement to strengthen the intelligence network, such as it was. The turning point was arguably with the appointment of Edmonds as Director of MO5 – the first core personnel of what would become the true intelligence arm of the War Office.

At this juncture it is useful to recall that the role played by the Admiralty came to be fruitful, and the naval experience too constantly came handy in these early preparations. After all, the dockyards and naval technology had always been a priority for foreign powers. Now that Tirpitz and the other members of the German high command had decided that England was their real enemy, as opposed to France or Russia, the Royal Navy was their prime target in terms of gathering valuable information regarding any future conflict. Prior to 1909, Edmonds – after much cooperation with the navy – noted several acts of attempted espionage, notably 48 cases in 1908 and 24 in the first three months of 1909.

Admiral Alexander – the Director of Naval Intelligence – was a member of the committee that appointed Kell. Knowledge of the German equivalent group was beginning to percolate into the consciousness of the men in power. At the centre of this was a group of dignitaries who were clearly trying to accelerate the move towards the creation of an intelligence community that would rival that of Germany. Their arguments were strengthened by world events, such as the assassination of Sir William Curzon-Wylie – aide-de-camp to Lord Morley, the Secretary of State for India – by a Punjabi student in Kensington. The pressure group included Winston Churchill, Lord Haldane and Ewart himself – Kell's superior and supporter. David Stafford has described Ewart as:

A veteran of Tel-El-Kebir, Omdurman and the Boer War, since 1906 he had been in charge of strategic planning and intelligence. A sociable and well- connected Scot, he enjoyed a close relationship with Haldane and they frequently dined together... Ewart was obsessed with espionage, both lamenting the lack of British spies abroad and deploring the presence of German spies in Britain. For much of the previous six months he had been laying plans for a new organisation...[1]

That is, the group around the Committee for Imperial Defence had been waiting for the right time and the right man to come along, and in Kell they found the leader they needed.

Churchill himself had been well aware of the need for the reform of intelligence within the army, certainly since the Boer War. He had been clamouring for reform before the end of that conflict; in 1901 he had written that 'The whole Intelligence Service is starved for want of both money and brains'. In the House of Commons he confronted the estimates made by Sir John Broderick – the Secretary of State for War – on the costs of army reform and he spelled out the advantages of reforming the Intelligence Branch. Lord Haldane's cousin – Aylmer – told Churchill that Germany had over 200 intelligence officers whereas England had around 20. The pressure group needed a spokesman and it certainly had one in Churchill, who spoke of the need for 'an army of elasticity, so that comparatively small regular units in time of peace might be expanded into a great and powerful army in time of war'. He believed that to facilitate such an occurrence, what was needed was 'an efficient and well-staffed Intelligence Department'.

When it came to a diplomatic incident such as the Agadir Crisis of 1911, other aspects of intelligence work became apparent. After visiting London in May 1911, the Kaiser Wilhelm II stated that he intended to step in and claim a place in Morocco for Germany, responding to a revolt in Morocco in which tribesmen had forced the French troops to move in and protect Tangiers. The Kaiser sent a gunboat in Morocco since Germany thought that the time was appropriate to annex a part of the former. Britain issued a challenge to that, embodied in a speech by Lloyd George in which he said: '...if a situation were to be forced upon us, in which peace could only be preserved by the surrender of the great and benevolent position Britain has won... peace at that price would be intolerable for a great country like ours to endure...'[2]

What this generated – despite Germany's withdrawal from confrontation – was the creation of a mindset in the German naval command regarding future conflicts, and in this endeavour espionage happened to be the first step for preparation. The Kaiser supported a statement by his Admiral von Heringen that a clash with Britain would be welcome and German intelligence adapted to work that would support this long-term aim. The man in charge – Tapken – started to plan actions that would lead to the Royal Navy being watched and monitored from close range, from within the land of Britain, with major ports as the first espionage target.

In England, the writers of books on espionage were playing their part in the coming acceleration of intelligence organization. Erskine Childers's novel – *The Riddle of the Sands* (1903) – concerns two yachtsmen who, while in the North Sea, accidentally came across naval war preparations at a place called Borkum: Childers envisaged a major plan of invasion, launched across the sea from Holland. Articles with titles such as 'The Drama of the Missing Spy' and 'Secrets of the French Foreign Office' were everywhere in the popular press and of course, the Dreyfus affair of 1894, followed by Emile Zola's famous essay 'J'Accuse' in 1898 opened up a whole new rage for literature about spies and traitors in the popular media.

It was widely known that that British sea power was still burgeoning, particularly when the development of the *Dreadnought* is considered. Earl Cawdor, formerly a major industrialist, became First Lord of the Admiralty in 1905. Despite not having retained his position as First Lord for long, both Cawdor and 'Jacky' Fisher had had a stunning impact on the navy. Fisher suggested to Cawdor that the whole fleet should be redeployed. Cawdor relished the thought of being responsible for such an achievement and however large the task, they both warmed to it. The main fleets were repositioned, with the Mediterranean Fleet based in Malta and the Channel Fleet at a range of home ports. As the Atlantic Fleet was to be in Gibraltar, there was a clear indication to Germany that

Britain was determined to retain a tight grip on key strategic positions for any confrontations that might occur, and the positioning of the fleets was in line with Napoleonic history – a fact the Germans would have been well aware of.

Then Fisher set to work to create the *Dreadnought* – a new kind of battleship. The design for this advanced warship was done by Vittorio Cumberti who described and explained the potential of this innovation in sea power, as if it were a creative as well as a warlike dream. In the standard work of *Jane's Fighting Ships* for 1903 the template is there; clearly Fisher and Cawdor thought it was worth the investment. The accepted view was that turbine engines just would not work with very large ships; whatever the points argued by all interested parties, the central fact that turbines would have to be sued always existed, a definite factor should plans go ahead. So ambitious was Fisher that he not only wanted the new ship to the specifications he planned, but he also wanted the ship to be completely ready within a year – something thought impossible by many. But the first trials took place by the end of 1906. Results were impressive, in gun capabilities as well as in speed. The *Dreadnought* was made with the massive size of 17,900 tons; it could also fire huge shells of 850 pounds. The building of this new ship was a direct challenge to Germany. Could she equal that? She was certainly going to try, even widening the Kiel Canal, as the current state of the Germany corridor to the North Sea was that it was not wide enough to accommodate something with the dimensions of a *Dreadnought*.

Of course, there was a lobby for peace, and so a restraining arm was applied, to the extent that Fisher and Cawdor saw that the plans for building a series of *Dreadnought* ships were shelved for the time being. It was an indication that Britain was not warmongering. A cynical view would be that all the Great Powers were playing for time, and that not only would more time give some space for building vehicles (and 'ironclads') and ships, but would also allow for the real contributions of intelligence activity to show through. There was the usual game of 'diplomatic chess' in which each government made promises not to build more murderous engines of war if the other would do likewise. But certainly, the navy became the centre stage interest; it was playing a vital role in the gradual militarism encroaching on all sides in British life and culture. The social historian – Anne Summers – has shown how this process happened and just to what extent the navy, by means of the Navy League, was prominent in these developments. The Navy League was founded in 1895 and its main objective was to press for an increase in the sheer manpower and strength of the Royal Navy. By 1914, the League had 100, 000 members. Summers' research on the increasing militarism of the country leads to the presentation of huge figures of reservists and volunteers, and lends credence to Churchill's theory of fewer professional soldiers but with an Intelligence Section to apply logistics. Summers has calculated the daunting arithmetical perspectives on the forces of the Empire at the end of the nineteenth century:

> The British suppression of an uprising of armed and mounted farmers required a war of three years, an expenditure of over £222 million and the deployment of 450, 000 imperial troops. As the Empire had only about 250,000 men in training, the numerical deficiencies had to be met by virtually denuding the defences of the Empire and by seconding the volunteer hosts of Great Britain... [3]

These figures help the modern reader to understand why militarism accelerated and went so deeply into the consciousness in Britain in the last decade of the Victorian years and into the pre-Great War years too. It partly explains the attention given to naval matters also, as the notion of home defence became more urgent as it was observed that Cardwell's earlier reforms, which gave each regiment a home as well as an Imperial force, were gradually becoming ineffective with the expansion of the Empire.

In the pre-Great War years, not even the huge power of Russia, embracing almost a half of the globe, had an efficient intelligence system linked to its work in maintaining and policing the Empire stretching across far Asia. The army there had a section called the Military-Academic Committee, reporting directly to the War Minister. But, in the war on the Manchurian front the intelligence measures failed. There was no real knowledge of Japan nor of the militaristic philosophies and traditions of that state; according to David Schimmelpennick van der Oye, the failure was explained in terms of communication and a paucity of knowledge, something Britain at the time would have understood, licking its wounds after the debacle in South Africa:

> Despite its existence, intelligence was carried out neither systematically nor thoroughly. Aside from despatching quartermaster section subalterns and recruiting the occasional 'confidential', the committee did little to gauge enemy intentions and capabilities.[4]

With this broader background in mind, the cultural and military climate around Vernon Kell begins to explain why the first steps in establishing his work and his responsibilities were so tentative. With hindsight, historians can see why it was inevitable that his work would be so hugely important in that uneasy Edwardian decade before war on a European scale became assured. Kell had no inheritance of previous working methods or indeed of consolidated records: he had to create these from scratch.

In this respect the early alliances and cooperations were vital; he did have one Special Branch colleague – Patrick Quinn – a Superintendent. This collaboration cannot be underestimated. With Quinn to assist, Kell began to understand exactly how the criminal underworld worked and what networks were set-up. The obvious parallels between 'espionage' and 'standard detective work' became clear. Naturally, there would be some characters under observation who may well have been involved in espionage but there was no clear offence for which the Special Branch could approach them. It was out of these hard lessons that Kell began to see what was needed and he wrote copious reports for his superior - Ewart - outlining these difficulties, but on the positive side, the difficulties were only ways to open up quite optimistic developments. Basically, the world of information-gathering had been too long open to the exploitation of what should have been secure locations by 'gentlemen' and scientists, merely wandering around taking notes. The 1889 Official Secrets Act was toothless in respect of acting on that kind of activity.

What was being learned in the dark and secret world of Bolshevism and Anarchism was also open to a revisionary inspection. Joseph Conrad's novel - *The Secret Agent* (1907) - dealt with the undercover world of terrorism, and the villain - Verloc, - operated his nefarious business from the cover of a London shop. The novel instructed readers on the new phenomenon amongst the spy - someone so mundane and seedy that he was even capable of slipping unobtrusively into the everyday affairs of life: he could be the man in the doctor's waiting room or the man sitting opposite to you on the omnibus. The character Vladimir looks at Verloc and thinks: 'This was then the famous and trusty secret agent, so secret that he was never designated otherwise but by the symbol of a triangle in the late baron Stott-Wartenheim's official, semi-official and confidential correspondence...'[5]

A significant step forward in Kell's work came after he learned of something that had happened in 1907. Quinn told Kell about a German naval officer of senior rank who had gone for a haircut in a German barber-shop in London. Quinn was sure that the barber was a spy - a certain Karl Ernst. To take this up, as Kell wanted to do, would entail looking at Ernst's mail, and for that a go-ahead was needed from the Postmaster General. It was just the beginning of a new departure for British espionage. What happened was that a cache of letters was collected, signed by 'Fraulein Reimers' from Potsdam. The correspondent turned out to be a major figure in German intelligence – Steinauer – known to the British Foreign Section. This mail interception was extended across the land and it brought incredible results. For instance a German officer named Helm – who was living with an English girl in Portsmouth – was captured while in the process of drawing fortifications. Hannah Woodhouse, his live-in partner, who had previously dated Helm's friend became suspicious of Helm's activities and had eventually, informed the local army at the Royal Marines barracks. Although, the officers failed to take any prompt action, two officers spotted Helm sketching. Subsequently, Helm was arrested and Kell's counter-espionage bureau was informed about the incident.

Here we have a useful insight into Kell and his work. Helm was tried before the famous Rufus Isaacs (Lord Mansfield) but really there was no evidence of espionage. He was bound to pay over £250. But Kell was busy through this enquiry, even contacting Miss Wodehouse and looking at Helm's luggage; he then sat in the courtroom during the hearing, in disguise, and even tracked Helm and a friend on the train journey to London, in an effort to overhear their conversation.

Kell comes across as an individual who had learned police detective measures, and specifically in that aspect of detective work that had to cope with the networks of criminals in gangland within cities. He had had to learn to fade into the background when necessary and also to talk and put on a performance too, when that had to be done. But whatever the case with Helm, it was a frightening episode, very much like a section in a current dramatic spy tale, even to the extent that poor Woodhouse had a threatening letter beginning with the words: 'Dare go into the witness box against Lieutenant Helm and you will be marked down for extermination'.[6]

In her autobiography – Stella Rimington – former Director General of MI5, summarizes the turning point in Kell's reign that led to MI5 – his stunningly successful work against the German espionage system in Britain:

> One of Kell's helpers was travelling one day on a train in Scotland when quite by chance he heard two men in the same compartment talking in German, a language he understood. One was telling the other about a letter he received from Potsdam asking questions about the British preparations for war... The letter gave addresses in Potsdam to which Holstein was supposed to send his information...[7]

As Rimington adds: 'No intelligence system worth its salt would make such a mistake in tradecraft nowadays...' Kell got to work, and by the outbreak of war, the Germans were brought in. On the day war was declared, 21 key spies were arrested and tried. Some were hanged. Thomas Pierrepoint, for instance, hanged Robert Rosenthal on 15 July 1915. Coded telegrams were sent by Rosenthal to his spymaster in Holland. Rosenthal then did what so many spies have done since: he thought that naming a spy in Britain might save his neck, even writing to Lord Kitchener might help spill the information. Indeed, he named a man called Melton Feder. But he was hanged – the only spy to be hanged as others faced the firing squads.

Vernon Kell's primary achievement was that he had established the modus operandi of internal security operations. In his time in office, he had to concentrate on tracking spies, preventing their entry to Britain and in fact, to apply detective methods to find them once they were present. He also defined counter-espionage. There have been criticisms of him, and these have been well expressed by Nigel West in his book on MI5: '...a widely held assumption is connected with this: that old Sir Vernon Kell was quite unsuited to head a counter-intelligence organisation, and that his methods were, to put it bluntly, quaint'. West's defence is that Kell was old-fashioned and paternal, but as he puts it: 'MI5 was never accused of behaving like the Gestapo'.[8]

The momentous date of Monday, 23 August 1909, when the Special Intelligence Bureau came into being, will always be the birth of what everyone calls MI5. Kell was to remain at the helm until 1940, and he died just two years later. It is difficult to underestimate Churchill's part in that creation. He was also fighting for similar changes in the context of the navy. As he wrote in 1911: 'The lack of secrecy which prevails in this country with regard to naval matters, and the levity with which disclosures are regarded, appear to me to amount to a very considerable national evil'.[9] He had backed Kell in the matter of making warrants easier and quicker to obtain when there was a spy in sight about to be arrested. He was aware of the fact that Kell's work in intercepting mails procured major results – and also brought in significant implications for future undercover work. Kell even gave the Home Office a form for alien registration, and Churchill also saw the immense value of that.

By the time the first spy arrests took place, Kell's department had expanded considerably. By then he had the essential backup of clerical assistance and also a more significant recognition and respect from peers. Even the scaremongers who had been advocating all kinds of national defence measures involving volunteers and police had to admit that the secret services were giving results. Even Lord Roberts, who had been working with the novelist William Le Queux on hypothetical measures to cope with German invasion, had to admit that a new age in intelligence had arrived. The only problem then, as Churchill had seen, was to bring naval intelligence in line. Sir George Aston – in his memoirs – includes some reflections on naval intelligence at the end of Victoria's reign and he has plenty of anecdotes about the rather lax attitudes in this respect, such as this: 'An Admiralty messenger got into serious trouble. One of their Lordships went out to luncheon, leaving a drawer of his writing-table not quite closed There was an attachment which rang a bell in the next room, which was occupied by a private secretary, if the drawer was opened. Directly after the Admiral left his room, the bell rang, and the private secretary came in and found the messenger at the drawer'.[10] On a more general level, Aston makes it clear that there was no real comparison with Kell's work even at the point when war broke out, but then limitations could be expected, as naval intelligence is a concept that has to have applications across vast areas of the world, and Aston's notes about the navy in 1914 knowing nothing about German wireless stations in the Pacific have to be accepted with some healthy scepticism.

The overall picture of intelligence work before Kell arrived, and before the office led by Ewart was really in full swing, is that Britain was caught between differing conceptions of what home security meant as well as what exactly should happen in communication between field-intelligence and theoretical texts written by men such as Sir John Ardagh. The military theorists could see what was needed, but in the 1890s, the gap between the theorists and the practical soldiers in the field was immense. When criticisms of the intelligence information used in the Boer War were all over the daily newspapers, it was very hard for anyone in the high command to take up a stance regarding the failures of that war with any real objectivity. Churchill had been in amongst it all and he had seen the nature of the new tactics of winning battles by means of what Steevens – the journalist – had called 'Machine warfare' led by the Kitcheners of the army. He could see just how entrenched the attitudes in the officer class regarding the reliance on traditional values and priorities were. To create a new Intelligence Department took vision and courage; it also meant that new breeds of officers would be required: men who would happily see military efficiency as something that could work alongside such august and civilian institutions as the post office. Fortunately for Britain, the top brass in the Metropolitan Police since its creation in 1829, had been military men. In fact, the very first Commissioner – Sir Charles Rowan – had fought with Wellington at Waterloo.

The new world of espionage in the twentieth century was to be, as Kell soon learned, a milieu in which a soldier was quite likely to need some acting skills and an ability to wear plain clothes as to gallop on a horse. Fights had become quite evident with the enemies, who were strolling on the streets of London, and Kell had found the tactics to combat the enemy.

Of course, at the heart of Kell's first successful operation there was mail interception: an infringement of liberty. But at that very moment when he was developing such activities, the Official Secrets Act of 1911 and its effects was drawing out interesting debate in the general populace on that score. Everyday events were changing minds: notably in the stories of the lives and adventures of real spies. One writer in *The Times* described a spy of the distant past in this way: 'Karl Ludwig Schulmeister, whom the Germans called Napoleon's *Hauptspion* (top spy) who was indefatigable in procuring, at great personal risk, useful military information. Perhaps he is not the only specialist in this line of military activity...' The last few words say a great deal: the implication is that, in 1910 when that letter was written, spying was thought of as a military activity and the previous masters in the art were gradually being considered heroic rather than despicable.

As Kell carried on with his work during the Great War, the Directorate of Military Intelligence began to employ women. At first it was a case of using them as typists, but as time went on, this massive arm of intelligence work, with a staff of 6,000 by 1918, used women for all kinds of work. MI5 itself employed many women. Kell had four women on his staff when war broke out; but by the end of the war, women were working overseas as well as in London, being most numerous though, in H Branch – the section in control of records.

In the field, there were women working in intelligence networks in occupied territories, notably for the organization in Belgium known as *La Dame Blanche*. At the War Office, Captain Henry

Landau held the pivotal control and was the liaison man working with the Belgian people. Women began work as couriers and observers amongst other roles and of course, everyone knew that if caught they would face a firing squad. Field-intelligence was just as dangerous as it had been for the Kaffir spies in the Boer War, but at least communications had become more sophisticated by 1914. Cryptography was becoming more advanced and technology was influencing the work of agents as never before.

As Tammy Proctor has said, with regard to women's work in Belgium, in this respect: 'In a larger sense, wartime intelligence networks such as *La Dame Blanche* helped define the twentieth century development of the concepts of espionage, resistance, clandestine activities and military intelligence'.[11]

But as these general changes were taking place and Whitehall was becoming excited by the prospect of an internal warfare done invisibly and with high drama as well as tedious police work, the press and media, along with literature and film were advancing the cause of the spy as international man of mystery. The media had to handle mundane tales such as that of the Swede Olsson caught on Grimsby docks talking too freely about his ship-watching, but on the other hand, they had characters like Helm and Steinhauer who really were 'the enemy within'. Espionage – as soon as Vernon Kell walked into his new office and surveyed his shelves and filing cabinets – was here to stay. The drama and adventure was sure to happen as codes and writing in invisible ink began to be part of the trappings of the work done by the profession.

The final chapter in this history concerns that drama and literature, all bound up with the 'Spymania' and mythology of the secret agent in Edwardian and Wartime Britain. But we cannot move on without noting the revolution that had taken place, not simply for espionage but for Scotland Yard and the Criminal Investigation Department (CID) because in that fateful collaboration between Kell and Quinn there were the beginnings of a relationship of course, but something more: a sense that rationalization of expertise and resources in as many policing contexts as possible was the way forward. It was the kind of attitude that led to the formation of such outfits as the Flying Squad and in the 1960s – the Regional Crime Squads.

Whether that spirit actually eroded much of the bastions of conservatism in the war machine is another question, and open to debate, but Churchill was fighting that corner.

Notes and References:

[1] David Stafford, *Churchill and Secret Service*, John Murray, London, 1997, pp. 28–29.

[2] Thomas Boghardt, *Spies of the Kaiser*, Palgrave, London, 2006, pp. 51–52.

[3] Anne Summers, 'Militarism in Britain before the Great War' in *History Workshop Journal*, Autumn, 1976, pp. 104–124.

[4] David Schimmelpennick van der Oye, 'Russian Militarism on the Manchurian Front 1904–05' in *Intelligence and National Security*, vol. 11, no. 1, January 1996, pp. 23–24.

[5] Joseph Conrad, *The Secret Agent*, Penguin, London, 2000, p. 63.

[6] Boghardt (see note 2 above), pp. 50–51.

[7] Stella Rimington, *Open Secret*, Hutchinson, London, 2001, p. 85.

[8] Nigel West, *MI5*, Grafton, London, 1987, p. 192.

[9] See Stafford (note 1 above), pp. 28–29.

[10] Aston (note 3, chapter 5), p. 40.

[11] Tammy Proctor, *Female Intelligence*, New York University Press, New York, 2003, p. 96.

12

Spy Mania

In 1917, writer D H Lawrence was staying in Zennor, Cornwall, with his German wife, Frieda. They stayed for a time at the Tinner's Arms and then rented a house in Higher Tregerthen. There was a good deal of suspicion from the locals: here were a couple, staying by the sea on an isolated stretch of coastline, and the woman was a German. Rumours began to circulate that the couple were signalling to German submarines. Stories abounded, including rumours that there were smoke signals from their chimney or that there was a supply of petrol for the submarines below the adjacent cliffs; people thought they heard German songs being sung in the house. After all – they reasoned – the route for the Atlantic convoys was close by. The couple were stopped and searched as they carried shopping home. They were not the only temporary residents in the area, and others, like Lawrence, had been rejected for conscription or had somehow avoided it.

In his letters, Lawrence wrote that he was 'innocent even of pacifist activities, let alone spying of any sort, as the rabbits of the field outside'.[1] It all led to a military exclusion order and they had to leave. Had the locals known that Frieda was actually Frieda von Richthofen – a relative of the Red Baron fighter pilot – this might have brewed even more trouble. This episode in Lawrence's tempestuous life was a template example of the 'spy fever' that swept the country during and before the Great War. Perhaps, the most typical example of this irrational paranoia was the accusation that Frieda was signalling by using clothes on her washing-line. The mass media were largely to blame for this, and they built on the fears already in existence in literature. As far back as 1871, Colonel G T Chesney had written *The Battle of Dorking*, in which there is an imagined Franco-Russian invasion of England. The novel created all kinds of spin-off stories and sales were huge – 80, 000 copies were sold. Then in 1906, William Le Queux published *The Invasion of 1910*. This novel offered something new: the account which spoke of just a few years ahead, and by the Germans, the nation with the new Empire vying for supremacy with England. The shock comes from the mundane domesticity of the setting, as in this passage in which there is a report of the advance in Suffolk:

> In a moment the superintendent had taken the operator's eat, adjusted the Ear-piece, and was in conversation with Ipswich. A second later he was Speaking with the man who had actually witnessed the cutting of the trunk- line while he was thus engaged an operator at the farther end of the switchboard suddenly gave vent to a cry of surprise and disbelief. 'What do you say, Beccles? Repeat it,' he asked excitedly. Then a moment Later he shouted aloud, 'Beccles says that German soldiers, hundreds of Them, are pouring into the place![2]

A play called *An Englishman's Home* ran for over a year and was also filmed in 1914. The enemy – though not referred to as Germans – wore spiked helmets, and so the reference was obvious. Early spy films involved the Royal Navy, partly due to the furore over the building (or shelving) of the *Dreadnoughts*.

Despite his involvement in espionage in an amateur way, Le Queux appeared to be particularly interesting. Besides, he also made a number of statements on the potential threat from Europe on Britain's domestic security, though often he was considered to be a propagator of myths. He even claimed to have contacts in Berlin and that he had been supplied with a list of British traitors there. He wrote that there was a secret group in Germany called the Hidden Hand. Though he had no proof, he insisted that the traitors on the list included very prominent people in Britain, including politicians and writers. What he did achieve that turned out to be a serious matter having significant repercussions was his strategy to team up with the distinguished soldier - Lord Roberts - to organize a make-believe invasion. With the help of the *Daily Mail* they turned the affair into a fiasco that generated universal fears of the vulnerability of English shores and defences to attack and invade. It was a classic example of the journalistic coup of creating a terrifying 'might be' situation in order to make the government act, as in recent times when a journalist might board a train with a mysterious parcel and not be stopped and searched by anyone.

Le Queux went his own way in his romantic and playful world of spying; this sort of activity at home in England was mainly of the provocative variety, such as imagining German arsenals and spies in disguise as ordinary workmen. But what surely did happen was that his warnings and fabrications did catch the attention of Edmonds, and via him, to the Committee for Imperial Defence.

There were certainly German agents in England, and they were here to buy information, make sketches from observation, write reports, study communication systems and particularly, to ascertain the true nature of British naval power. Naturally, there were spies in the field as well, and the propaganda machine made it clear what was happening to them. A typical story - printed in the popular press – was that of a tale narrated by an American Ambulance Field Service volunteer:

> Early one morning a soldier appeared in a trench... he started chatting with some passing poilus [soldiers in the French infantry]. He told them he was inspecting the lines and they showed him around their trenches... He wandered around the woods with his new-found friends, who showed him the positions of many guns. As night came on, he... left his friends and went to the trenches... he told the sentry he had orders to inspect the barbed wire... The man never returned... there is little doubt that he was a German spy.[3]

Magazines such as *The British Magazine* showed graphic photographs of German spies being executed by firing squads or lying by a roadside, dead and tied to a stake.

Before the outbreak of the war though, Kell's arrest of the hairdresser – Karl Ernst – in 1911, was the start of a remarkable operation against the spies, and that the success explains the mania. Reports of Ernst's spy network were everywhere and were of course, subject to exaggeration. The reports came to editors in fragments and with a sense of high drama, such as a man seen messing with a telephone cable in Dover or the story that the Officer Training Corps at Berkhamsted were called out to block the road as a German armoured car advanced on London. Some views on these stories are, understandably, that they were intentional, and indeed the work of the intelligence men. After all, this was the time when intelligence work was taking up the Wolseley notions of ruses, tricks and deceptions. The expert writer on these matters was Arthur Ponsonby, whose book of 1928 – *Falsehood in War* – summarized the Great War deliberate lies, such as these, mentioned by a contemporary reviewer: 'They include many atrocity stories, such as that of the nurse with her breast cut off; the Belgian baby without hands; the crucified Canadian soldier – and most famous of all, the corpse factory in which the Germans were said to process their dead in order to extract from them materials for munitions'.[4]

An insight into what was happening but with no involvement of the Intelligence Department comes from a memory by Sir Basil Thomson – head of the CID in 1913; he recalled his meeting with one of the staff of the Intelligence Branch and wrote the following in that context:

> While I was talking to him it grew dark and there was a sudden peal of thunder like an explosion. He said, quite gravely, 'A Zepp!' That was the state of mind we were all in. That same night my telephone became agitated; it reported the blowing up of a culvert near Aldershot and of a railway bridge in Kent. I had scarcely repeated the information to the proper authority when the bell rang again to tell me that both reports were the figments of some jumpy reserve patrol.[5]

But the fact is that there was indeed a network of German spies, and solid research by Thomas Boghardt has increased our understanding of how this worked, and indeed how it was stopped. Boghardt has shown that the *Admiralstab* in Germany were not very successful in accessing and using the large number of Germans already living in Britain at the time. In 1911, there were 56, 000 such people. But not many of those were sympathetic to the *Kaiserreich*. Widenmann – the naval attaché in London – pointed out what amounted to a large percentage of these being acculturated English, many being integrated into communities clustered around established industry (as in Bradford for instance, a city with a long-established German population).

The German intelligence network therefore, had to look elsewhere for recruits. The foremost spies in the ring – Schultz, Grosse, Graves and Hentschel – as Boghardt notes, were actually criminals. For instance, Grosse being in prison at the time was brought into espionage work. A summary of what Max Schultz did and what obstacles he encountered will illustrate the nature of the challenge for Germany during that period. Basically, he was a disaster. A pattern of work was for the spy to become friendly with a woman, often a secretary or a typist. Schultz was released from an asylum to engage him in the work of spying, a fact that suggests desperation. He had a housekeeper and accidentally shot her while high at a party. Parties were regular affairs on his houseboat. He was notably unhinged in most respects, and after trying to suborn a solicitor to the cause of espionage, he was watched by the police, day and night. All this happened in Plymouth, where he was sent in 1911.

The network was controlled by 'N' – the code name for the *Admiralstab* Director – Arthur Tapken, and he must have been bitterly disappointed in this particular agent. Kell and his team were never worried about him, and eventually when he was tried, he received only a short sentence after which he left for England.

In spite of all the efforts of 'N', the espionage net was never successful. One of the clearest cases that prove why there was such failure was that of Armgaard Graves. Again, he was something of a rogue and an adventurer who had lived a criminal existence across the world before being recruited by 'N'. After having settled in Edinburgh, he followed his brief to report on warships off the coast of Scotland. The Royal Navy was beginning to use a new variety of gunpowder, and finding out about that was a special part of his brief. But as the mail of other agents was being intercepted, he was soon identified. When his room in Edinburgh was searched all kinds of incriminating evidence was found, including a code. The way in which *The Times* reported on this is very instructive regarding the incredibly minute details known about the suspect. He pleaded 'Not Guilty' but the evidence was solid, such as this account by the reporter on the spy's possessions when searched:

> At the time of his arrest Graves had in his possession a history of the Forth Bridge, showing Rosyth naval base and the surrounding district. The police found among his possessions a note-book and a pocket-book, one of which contained two documents in German fastened

together, a number of phials filled with deadly poison, a hypodermic syringe, and needles, a book of maps of Scotland...[6]

There was a stack of evidence against him and plenty of witnesses who recalled conversations and the types of enquiries he had been making. The German controllers must have begun to see at that point where they were going wrong, but the fact was that they just could not adapt to any other approaches. Nor could they come up with other means of communication within their agents. But then, they struck lucky and came across George Parrott. Working under the directions from an agent named Hentschel, Parrott - who had been in the navy since 1887 - was a spy for monetary gain. He was indeed an excellent source for Germany, as he was based at Sheerness and had served well for several years, being highly thought of. He earned £260 a year and his payments from Hentschel were usually around £10. Parrott stole a large number of books giving details of guns and armoury.

Even after his split with Hentschel (who left Europe altogether eventually) Parrott was actively seduced by the Germans to carry on with his espionage work. But he was discovered and trailed to Belgium, by Melville - the ex-CID man. Matters were beginning to move into the area of spy fiction at this time, as in this adventure, Melville was also being watched - by Steinauer, who could not act to save Parrott when he was stopped and arrested. At his trial - the eminent judge Travers Humphries - expressed the opinions of such a man very well: 'When we turn to the case of a man who spies for the enemy, who gives (or more likely sells) naval or military secrets of his country, one is apt to think of him as the most degraded creature alive'. We can gauge how closely he had been watched, and exactly how much the counter-espionage men knew about him, from Humphries' details:

There he was arrested in November as he came to receive one of his letters.. His rooms were then searched and some thirty-five pounds in gold were seized together with the return half of a railway ticket from Grimsby Docks to London of a type issued to passengers coming from Hamburg by sea. The letter... contained numerous questions as to the dispositions of the Home Fleet, the speed with which reserves could be called up etc...[7]

The great Mr Justice Darling thought that Parrott had 'succumbed to the wiles of a woman' and that was apparently true, but the cash was the initial inducement.

This pre-war espionage operation by the *Admiralstab* was based on an initially confused notion on the part of the German high command about which navy would be the biggest threat in the immediate future, as other nations were potential enemies, notably France and Russia. But some things were settled and Tirpitz took over, the focus was on London and on the major ports. As there was no clear line of thought with reference to the Royal Navy as a potential target, a certain amount of blurred thinking behind the espionage measures always existed. The first plan was simple: to use the German naval attaché in London as the underpinning communication channel and to have men planted in most major ports, all systems working by telegram. But there were several flaws, mainly that if ever the attaché had to be elsewhere, nothing could be done, so if that absence coincided with something of great military importance, nothing could be done from the ports.

The attaché was Widenmann and he was both reluctant and somewhat dilatory. There were usually excuses when the *Admiralstab* tried to set communication in motion. Eventually, the controller gave in and decided to work with individuals, and there lies the heart of the following failure. Arguably, the most successful agent was Gustav Steinhauer, a man who certainly felt pride in his achievements. He later wrote his memoirs under the title, *The Kaiser's Master Spy: The Story as Told by Himself* (1930), which was regarded as a book of arrogance and fascination.

In a wider cultural context, the spy mania of the pre-war and war years did create much of the narrative substance and the fictional conventions of the spy stories of the period, and these linked well with the male romance of such writers as Rider Haggard and G A Henty. It was in many of the spy legends that these narratives had their beginnings. One of the most powerful was the myth of the hidden German gun placements in London. A massively influential book at the time was *German Spies in London* (1915). A statement recorded in the book says the following: 'Why they have even failed to see that tennis courts in country houses occupied by the Germans were really gun platforms'. The beginnings of this can possibly be traced to a journalist who had written about such a development arising in France at a time when the Germans were bombarding the area of Mauberge.

A typical rumour in this context was that it was coming from Little Waltham where, according to the vicar: 'Miss Gold says that in Little Waltham the populace have discovered another German fort: 'Cranhams' was owned by Herr Wager, who is now said to be an Austrian... The villagers say that at Cranham... there is a concrete floor for the emplacement of heavy guns...'[8]

The impact of both – the spy mania and of the more publicly disseminated accounts of espionage 'behind enemy lines' spawned a new genre of fiction and film. Well into the 1920s, the new mass media publications such as the Odhams Press anthologies gathered tales of derring-do behind enemy lines; the profession of spy was becoming not only sensationally fascinating but quite respectable, something to textualize by the side of the new detective stories.

But central to the paranoia about spies was the real possibility of invasion. The reasons behind this are principally related to the German Navy. It is important to grasp the fact that such a thing as a navy was a very new concept in Germany. Since Bismarck's unification of the German states in 1870, there had been a long and difficult fight by notable individuals to establish a navy that would be confident in confronting the Royal Navy. In the latter half of the nineteenth century, the tiny German fleet had actually been trained and supplied by Britain, though on a very small scale. It was a case of Britain, with its massive fleets across the Empire – looking upon Germany as a minuscule operation – something almost childlike; so the attitudes were those of a schoolmaster.

The Prussian cast of mind with regard to the military front was always fixed on land armies. Prussia and its new accretions from other states in the new Germany were of the opinion that it could easily defeat Britain on land. The elder statesmen, including the aged Bismarck who was in his eighties when Tirpitz started his campaign for a proper navy, would have to be persuaded.

Tirpitz – a great admirer of the Royal Navy and of most aspects of English life and culture – actually visited Bismarck and convinced him to back his plan for battleships, albeit with qualifications. The entrenched attitudes to sea power in Germany were focused on the notion of using cruisers and later torpedo boats, instead of investing huge amounts of money on a fleet of battleships. Most military men thought that it was pointless trying to take on Britain with battleships: they preferred the idea of attacking a fleet with torpedo boats or cruisers and relying on speed. Tirpitz was convinced, particularly as the German Empire grew and the threat from France and Russia declined, that a battleship fleet was essential to security. When in 1897, the Royal Navy at a review displayed 165 warships that extended over 30 miles, it caused a certain amount of alarm in the German high command as its efforts had been directed towards resisting Tirpitz. When he pushed his Navy Bill and persuaded the Kaiser to support him he was beginning to win in his struggle for a German Navy.

Tirpitz had his Navy Bill ratified in 1898; there were to be 38 battleships and a building programme of 17 years was planned. Partly, what had won the day for the Admiral was his 'risk theory' – that a huge Empire such as Britain's would require considerably large emplacements of the Royal Navy across the world and so, there would never be a force on the domestic front too large for the German Navy to tackle if any attack on the German harbours was ever to take place. Another factor in ideas of defence was that the two chief ports were placed – one in the Baltic and the other on the North Sea, so as to multiply the problem for any aggressive fleet who wished to attack Germany.

All this explains why there was a growing fear of a German presence in the North Sea that had never been there previously. But there was also something else bearing on the need for German espionage in Britain to be taken seriously: there had been a major scare before, and not so long ago, in 1882. In that year, the fear was based on a French assault, and by means of a Channel Tunnel. For decades, the notion of 'Splendid isolation' had been a basic belief of the imperialists. But with the possibility of a tunnel across that crucially significant 21 miles of North Sea, apprehensions grew. The Channel Tunnel Company had been formed after a plan conceived in parliament and a bill in process; its offices in London came under siege. There was a widespread opposition to the idea of a tunnel, with a petition signed by such celebrities as Lord Tennyson and Cardinal Newman. Naturally, in the popular press there was a conception of a spy – a French spy, usually disguised as a waiter. When the opposition was joined by the great Sir Garnet Wolseley, there was a profound impact on the whole idea. He expressed the view that a few thousand armed men, travelling through the tunnel in disguise, could easily become a platform for a seriously dangerous invasion of England.

Regarding the possibility of a German invasion, one of the most influential factors from the world of literature was Erskine Childers' novel, *The Riddle of the Sands* (1903), published just two years after Kipling's *Kim*. The contrast is significant: Kim treats the Great Game in a manner exactly in keeping with that phrase: it is a narrative of spycraft entirely concerned with the element of intelligence tied to battle and empire and in a world of gentlemen-officers. Whereas Childers gives his readers an image of espionage linked to the inexorable advance of a civilization next door to Britain. The two main characters sailing in the North Sea come across fictional examples of Tirpitz's fleet: referring to Germany, Childers' character Davies says: 'We aren't ready for her; we don't look her way. We have no naval base in the North Sea and no North Sea fleet...'[9]

A strong presence in Childers' novel is the theme of England's complacency. The references to the rather tired and effete nation that was once young, aggressive, thrusting forward to conquest is present in the novel as a dispiriting version of contemporary Empire. The fears about the protection of the homeland are present throughout – entirely in keeping with a world in which the Navy League and the societies of riflemen flourished. The militaristic culture of Britain at the time, from the boys' brigades to the regiments of volunteers, is easily understood as a reaction to those fears Childers describes.

Summing up the spy mania of the Edwardian years, it has to be said that our understanding comes from the nature of the wars Britain fought throughout the nineteenth century. They were distant ones. That simple fact explains so much, as the very idea of an enemy on the doorstep was terrifying in contrast to the previous concept of war – one in which regiments were seen off from the quayside at Portsmouth on their way to the Crimea, South Africa or India. It had been prevalent for a long period that one war followed another and the movements of troops happened to meet particular emergencies. Most were small-scale combats involving the normal groupings of imperial infantry, artillery and various deployments of cavalry. Intelligence had always been integral to those movements, either included with artillery or left to the control of the Adjutant-General. Gradually, ever since 1873, intelligence work had attained a newer dimension and hence, needed to be understood separately, with its own specialisms and responsibilities. The Fenian bombings at the very heart of the Empire had shown that something new was needed, something as ruthless and efficient as the potential enemies could be.

Therefore, when the new century began and there had already been talk of spies infiltrating the land, a common view of such a threat was that it could be handled in traditional ways, but with intelligence personnel involved. Sir George Aston summed up the attitudes clearly:

Their idea was that Germans, spies and others, needed leaders, and that they were helpless without them. That they liked working 'according to plan', according to the letter of a plan... No matter how big a swarm of German spies there might be in England, Scotland, Wales or Ireland in pre-war days, they would look for guidance to certain leaders... and if the leaders were taken away the followers would be helpless...[10]

Aston in his memoirs was keen to show that the amateurism in the image of the British was in fact a virtue, and that luck was on the British side because they had an enormous capacity for hard work. His connection of the intelligence success story and what he calls the 'John Bull legends' falls in well with the successes of Vernon Kell and his team. They may have had their insight into the spy ring because of a fortuitously overheard conversation on a train, whatever might have been the implication, such an incident occurred because of the presence of the British undaunted spirit too.

It has to be said that the spy network was indeed beaten because of hard work. In fact, it cannot be denied that the established methods of the comparatively new CID men were at the heart of the success. Police work against Anarchists and Communists was notably successful, as in one typical account of Special Branch men from 1909 involving two robbers who were Latvian immigrants. The men – Hefeld and Lepidus – were armed when they robbed a rubber factory in Tottenham High Road; there was a police station opposite the scene of crime. The robbers waited for a car to arrive in which two men were carrying the wages of the company's workers. A pursuit followed, including gunfights, and the two fugitives were so desperate that one shot himself in the head before he could be caught and the other did the same later, while under siege. However, the point that was conveyed through the above incident was that the detectives were working against gangs of Anarchists and the chase involved local as well as Metropolitan officers. In other words, normal detective practice was already in prevalence for Kell to master the art. Liaison between different parts of the country was well established by that time; in fact, decades before, in a famous case in which several detectives were corrupted by a forgery gang, regional undercover work had tracked down the culprits, and also interception of mail had been conducted. Kell was learning from the experts.

By 1909 when Kell needed such help, the detective branch had become skilled in such basic strategies as disguise, using informers, infiltration and in fact, some basic forensic science such as fingerprinting. They had also learned how to work with other organizations and how to use local knowledge. All this would become vital in the work against the German spies in the ports. The spy – Olsson – in Grimsby, for instance, was noticed and then 'tapped' – he must have been trailed and traced with a high degree of sophistication. The port of Grimsby was accustomed to military presence at that time for other reasons, mainly a major strike and confrontation in 1903 in which a very heavy police and army presence was required. Some of Kell's other 'clients' had been to that port as a matter of course. Common sense would have told MI5 that the Humber Estuary, with both Hull and Grimsby as prime targets, was the logical place for members of a spy network to be placed – Childers territory.

In the end, the German espionage ring was beaten by traditional solid police work, but Kell had a dash of genius. What he must have been surprised by, however, was the element of novelty and enterprise shown by the enemy as the intelligence team had to cope with different initiatives as the war came on. For instance, Tammy Proctor has shown that there was a female presence in espionage during that time, though only a handful. Colonel Edmonds had something to say on this matter: 'The use of women in procuring intelligence for Germany is very considerable, and extends from ladies... down to professional *horizontales*...'[11] Proctor makes it clear that most of the women detained for espionage were not born in England and many were interned without a trial. A large number of these were deported at the end of the war; British women who might be suspected were usually simply trailed and monitored or even sent to a convent as a substitute for prison. Again, interception of mail was the usual method of tracking these women down.

Throughout the course of the Great War, only 30 people were formally charged with spying, but beyond this there was a massive number of individuals who had been blacklisted; on the MI5 lists there was an astoundingly high number of 27, 000 files and many more individuals monitored, ranging from observations and 'blacklisting' for ideological unsoundness to mere intellectual expression of such things as pro-German feelings, writings or social-cultural pursuits. It has to be recalled that in the course of the war, on the home front, there had been savage riots, such as the violence in Liverpool after the sinking of the *Lusitania* in 1915, and the disorder in Deptford in which 15, 000 people roamed around the streets looking for German shops and restaurants to destroy. In the latter case, it took hundreds of police and men from the Army Service Corps to bring the trouble to an end.

Spy mania then, in terms of its widespread media-generated myths and legends, played a part in the perceptions of Kell's work and indeed, of the work done by all the professions involved in national security. But it also highlighted the depth of social paranoia beneath the pre-war patina of home security and middle class progress. The age of the proliferation of the new city commuters and the suburbs was also the age of amateur militarism and of insecurity. One thinks of those thousands of people holidaying in Skegness ('so bracing') who must have been looking out to the sea, imagining a fleet of German warships across that tranquil water.

Writing in 1956, Douglas Browne assessed the liaison at the time of the Great War between Special Branch and intelligence: 'The value of the work of the work of Special Branch in connection with espionage caused it, towards the end of the war, to be so closely associated with Military Intelligence that it was virtually seconded from the CID; and in 1919 the experiment was tried of detaching it altogether. It became a separate department under an Assistant Commissioner who was styled Director of Intelligence'.

This did not last long, but there is one notable case in which this joint work has been illustrated, and it runs parallel with Kell's operations. This was nothing less than an attempt of the life of Prime Minister, David Lloyd George. In the shady world of counter-espionage there existed two characters, one of whom was assigned the task of murdering Llyod George in Walton Heath while playing golf. The means of murdering the great man was to fire a dart tipped with curare. The people who attempted this murder could well have been characters in a popular novel of espionage, though they were in fact conscientious objectors who mixed with a bad crowd.

The great lawyer F E Smith (later Lord Birkenhead) has given the fullest account of the events and of the trial of the villains. What is particularly interesting is the detection of the would-be assassins. It was a case of mail interception yet again, and the family involved – the Wheeldons – were resisting the Military Services Act and so were under slight suspicion of dissent and on a blacklist. But as there was a noticeable Communist activity, some hid their Communism under the pacifist surface. In terms of the undercover work done, the hero of the day was Alec Gordon, a man who was an 'inquiry agent' and who pretended to be a conscientious objector escaping some kind of trouble. His brief was to become intimate with Mrs Wheeldon and her family in Derby. She was a widow, and one of her daughters was married to a key player in the story – Alfred Mason. They were living in Southampton at that time.

Gordon's suspicions about certain discussions among the Wheeldons led to a more senior officer being called in to help: Herbert Booth, who was clerk to a barrister, Mr Purcell. During Christmas in the year 1917, Booth was in Derby and his fellow officer created an interest in Booth from the Wheeldons by giving him the cover of being a member of a subversive group called International Workers of the World. They were duped and Booth inveigled his way into their confidence. Booth even said openly that his group were sympathetic to the German cause. The Wheeldons had acted as friends and confidants to a number of other objectors and political dissidents on the run, and hence they were becoming well-known. They soon began to talk about their scheme to assassinate the Prime Minister.

Booth started the process of bringing an interception of their mails and somewhat naively, it was discovered that they were writing to the relatives in Southampton using a code that could have been from a *Boys' Own* comic: the code was worked out from this sentence: 'We'll hang Lloyd George on a sour apple tree'. The coded texts were about getting hold of curare and strychnine. But so well did Booth deliver his performance that, well in the confidence of Mrs Wheeldon, she confessed to an act of sabotage done earlier. Then came the details of the assassination attempt – 'to get Lloyd George with an air gun' as she put it, the parcel containing three phials of poison was taken, with one phial in particular having a highly lethal dose of strychnine in it; the curare was outstandingly nasty as a means of taking life – put on a wound or any broken skin, it causes instant death.

F E Smith led the prosecution when the gang was on trial at the Old Bailey on charges of conspiring to murder and inciting Booth to commit murder. Mrs Wheeldon was sentenced to ten years penal servitude; her daughter was given five years of the same and her husband, Mason, seven years. As Smith concluded in his account: 'What they wanted was to inflict punishment on people who would not do what the prisoners thought they ought to do....'[12]

The real interest of the case, however, for the story of intelligence work is that it provides a very early example of a type of infiltration of terrorists from within the very fibre of the domestic order. Ridiculous as the plan to ambush Lloyd George might have seemed, had it happened, it would have no doubt been compared with the Phoenix Park murders, but with a more famous and important victim. The point of the story is that it illustrates Browne's note about the CID and Special Branch coming together, and what is missing is an in-depth account of Booth and his extremely impressive undercover work.

Subsequently by the end of the Great War espionage was in the hands of the War Office, and the latter had also come to possess allies in all the major public services; what had happened was that a integration had taken place: military, naval and civil forces had come together and for the first time it was becoming possible to have a large number of specialist professionals who could operate on both the domestic and the imperial or European fronts.

Notes and References:

[1]   See John Worthen, *D H Lawrence* online, www.nottingham.ac.uk/mss, Chapter 4.

[2]   James Hayward, *Myths and Legends of the First World War*, Sutton, Stroud, 2005, p. 26.

[3]   See www.greatwardifferent.com. The letter is a personal memory from the front by Leslie Bulwell.

[4]   *Peace News*, 23 December 1949, p. 4.

[5]   Hayward (see note 2 above), p. 5.

[6]   *The Times*, 12 June 1913.

[7]   Sir Travers Humphreys, *A Book of Trials*, Pan, London, 1956, p. 97.

[8]   See Hayward (note 5 above), p. 12.

9 Quoted in Robert K Massie, *Dreadnought*, Pimlico, London, 2004, p. 634.

10 See Aston (see note 10, chapter 11), p. 62.

11 See Proctor (note 11, chapter 11), p. 44.

12 Birkenhead, Second Lord, F E: *The Life of F. E. Smith: the First Earl of Birkenhead*, Eyre and Spottiswoode, London, 1960, p. 130.

13

Epilogue

As Peter Hopkirk wrote in *The Great Game*, Britain and Russia found themselves fighting as allies in 1914. He wrote: 'For the first time, instead of glowering at one another across the mountains and the deserts of innermost Asia, Sepoy and Cossack fought together'. Indeed, as Britain was looking for spies on the domestic front and a new secret service mentality was engendered, even the notion of military field-intelligence was beginning to change. The world of immediate concern to the likes of Churchill, Kell and Haldane was one of increasing specialization and of technology applied to espionage. Gradually, as the long nineteenth century came to a close in the last peaceful summer of 1914, all the signs of alliance with France and enmity towards Germany were coming together in what was destined to be a new kind of war, on a scale previously unimagined.

The role of espionage in that war was to be quite marginal in some ways, nevertheless, MI5 was there, increasingly claiming a major role in that new world. The idea of the Great Game was bound to recede into the realm of imperial adventure. In fact, one could argue that even in the major events of the Raj years, such as the Afghan wars, the Mutiny and the wars in Chitral and on the North West Frontier, there had always been something that emanated from a heady mix of paranoia and Realpolitik. The distant machinations of British diplomacy, sending individuals into war zones or even buffer zones in order to maintain a flow of military information, still very much existed and something which was to continue in the future, but it gradually lost its sense of being part of a context of adventure and of personal heroism and endeavour. Sir Francis Younghusband, who led an expedition into Tibet in the first years of the new century, has come to represent that former high adventure in the Great Game; and since then, the lengthy and large-scale conflict that was a milieu somewhere between the fictional narrative of *Kim* and the real deeds of officers who actually did give their lives for high diplomacy and Russophobia has declined to a considerable extent.

Yet, in the area of the popular media that Game persists. In the *Flashman* novels of George Macdonald Fraser for instance, the element of gentlemanly play and risk has been isolated as the stuff of self-conscious military fiction. Hollywood may have mostly ignored that material, but the myth of imperial military enterprise and courage never disappears; its stories are being revisited regularly in the popular magazines of military history.

In terms of what the early twenty-first century sees as espionage, the theatre on which the likes of Conolly, Sykes and Younghusband acted has faded into a partially-understood time when all kinds of bias and denigration of ethnic groups were non-existent as social concepts of the 'whites' and the 'others'. That is, the modern media-driven world of meta-narrative sees the British Empire as something of a curiosity, and consequently the deeds of derring-do by the brave and often eccentric officers engaged in military intelligence in some distant desert or mountain range appear to be anachronistic oddities.

However, in the main spine of the narrative history of how the Great Game and the beginnings of work by Special Branch staff at home led to the more recent notion of the spy, the Victorian years have much to teach us today. Mainly, those lessons are about how individuals eventually play a part in the bigger picture. A writer was once asked if she wrote about political ideas. She replied that she wrote about people, and that ultimately people made the political ideas, so it came down to the same thing in the end. Arguably, the same line of thought applies to the work of strong personalities such as Baden-Powell and Wolseley. Their intuitions as well as their obsessions led to new ways of thinking about field-intelligence, and in strange but powerful ways, these ideas had an impact on the more central ideologies of their time.

Military intelligence in both the field and at home, in transparent, obvious activity and in covert operations, has always been a force in the story of the British Army and indeed of the police force; I hope that this introductory history has opened up questions about how the Empire worked and to what extent it relies on mainly the marginal figures who insisted on following their own rules in life and eventually, played a significant role in establishing the secret services as we read about at present. Gentlemanly amateurs have often been principal players in the theatre of British history, and never more so than in the Great Game in which Britain, Russia and a cluster of other states made gambits, both offensive and defensive for a century or more.

There had been countless other achievements along the way: if streamlining military intelligence had always been the main concern, since the harsh learning experiences of the height of the Empire, then the dawn of mechanized warfare had expanded military thinking in all possible ways. Individuals such as Steevens, with the knowledge of hindsight, appear to have been thinking ahead of their time, but a massive lumbering creature like the army of the Victorian Empire could not change direction without affecting a whole mass of secondary creatures following closely. Part of that was the ever-increasing civil service and the diplomatic service; so as time went on, all these elements mixed inextricably and the change only tended to happen on an ad hoc basis until new thinking truly permeated the old ways of looking at both domestic security and maintenance of armies across the globe.

In fact, as things turned out, many of the best insights into military structure and ideas came from amateurs, and that was in a sense, the basis of Victorian advance. It was an age of amateurs – gentlemen with classical educations who tended to cultivate passionate involvement with theories, courting momentary success and rather limited esteem among their peers at the heart of the officer's life. As was seen in the flourishing of clubs and societies in the Raj, was the implied understanding that if needed, any acquired knowledge could be turned to a military purpose. That was exactly the type of ideology that allowed Baden-Powell and many lesser lights of his cast of mind to flourish. That trend created parodies and satire as it had its ludicrous aspect (such as Baden-Powell's love of pig-sticking) but the bachelors – Kipling wrote about – tied to imperial ideals, saw their small place in the larger meta-narrative of Victoria's reign as something always potentially significant, something more than honours, medals and memoirs in the mess. Intelligence work – in all its manifestations – developed a crucially important place in that scheme of things.

There is a narrative at the very end of the period covered here, and it is a sick coda with a dark presentiment of things to come. In the Irish War of Independence – Michael Collins – organized a squad of men to systematically murder the agents of G Division based in Dublin Castle. Nancy O'Brien, who had security clearance to work in the Castle, actually worked with the secret coded messages which were in use there. A photograph exists of nine agents from that British counter-intelligence group, known as the 'Cairo Gang'. Something in those poses and swaggers tells us of a war to come, a combat deeply embedded in the kinds of mental war games destined to mark the years of Hitler, Stalin and the later Cold War.

The faces staring out from the photograph appear to challenge everything. Some smoke nonchalantly; others have a suspicious glare. All were marked men and none of them smiled, standing with their hats pulled low over their brows. We might say, following Yeats's great line about the Easter Rising, 'A terrible beauty is born' but that particular variety was 'born to blush unseen'. That would be either in dark corners or in well guarded offices.

If we had to look for phases of development in the way in which military intelligence changed between the 1830s and the Great War, it would make some sense to delineate the following periods.

First, two decades in which the notion of spying on the enemy was almost purposefully in contradistinction to methods on the continent. Yet, paradoxically, on the domestic front, the *agents provocateurs* in action against the Luddites and Chartists were aggressively successful. From the first scares on the part of the establishment – coming to a head in the 1799-1800 Combination Acts, through to Peterloo in 1819, to the action against sedition in the 1830s – the government saw a worthwhile place for covert action against any kind of dissent.

In that first phase there was a very clear line in the morality between subversion when in action against such enemies as the thugs in India and against the activists at home. In the field, the lessons were learned often through the work of individuals and the corporate mentality was slow to emerge.

The second phase really begins with the failures of the Crimean War. In spite of the successes of Cattley's network, which was excellent 'behind the lines' the close relationship of military intelligence in the field of battle and the quartermaster's areas of responsibility, the strategy did not match up to the practice. Until around the mid-1870s the Great Game in Asia and the beginnings of more confident organization in what was then the Levant was still piecemeal, depending on often pragmatic decisions and the whims of people in high diplomatic positions.

After the establishment of the Intelligence Branch and the first Fenian bombings at home it is possible to make out definite moves towards matching the enemy – 'tit for tat', that is, nurturing networks and agents who were more loosely aligned to the army and Scotland Yard. This meant that towards the end of the nineteenth century we have the kind of character such as the Russian – Yevno Azev – as described by Paul Dowswell and Fergus Fleming: '... he was happy to betray and destroy anyone who crossed his path. Unlike many spies, who are motivated by strong moral or political convictions, Azev cared for only one thing – money'.[1]

In the twentieth century, within that Edwardian supposed 'long summer' before the terrible Armageddon of the trenches, there was paranoia. Xenophobia mixed with militarism to create a social and cultural representation of the spy as a man with a secret identity, lurking in shadows and writing in code: a force of amorality, nothing at all to do with figures such as Percy Sykes or James Abbot. It seems strange to express this conclusion in terms of innocence, but in a perverse way, an innocence was lost in the world of military intelligence as well as in so much else in British life when the crushing desperation needed to win the war with the Boers, followed by fears of World War, penetrated the national consciousness.

Notes and References:

[1]   Paul Dowswell and Fergus Fleming, *True Spy Stories*, Usborne, London, 2002, p. 23.

Chronology of Main Events: From the Great Game to MI5

1831	Arthur Conolly, who coined the term 'the Great Game' returns from a year's dangerous travel in the NorthWest Frontier of India.
1833-5	Alexander Burnes makes his first great expeditions into the Indian frontier through Afghanistan.
1837	The Russian officer, Vitkevich, arrives in Kabul.
1839-42	William Sleeman actively pursues the Thuggee killers. He remains a Political Resident in Gwalior from 1843-5.
1841	Alexander Burnes is killed, after he had 'cut to pieces' six of his enemies.
1842	The terrible retreat from Kabul of Elphinestone's army. Death of Conolly.
1842	Richard Burton joins the Indian Army.
1852	Wilhelm Stieber poses as an agent in Paris.
1854-6	The Crimean War.
1857	The Indian Mutiny.
1858	Creation of the Indian Army. The army of the East India Company transferred to the Crown.
1858-63	Stieber reorganizes the Russian secret service.

1860	The Committee on Military Organization under Sir James Graham formed: the Commander-in-Chief made secondary to the Secretary of State; Horse Guards and the War Office merged under the same roof.
1860	Russell of *The Times* publishes his Indian diary.
1863	The death of Dost Mohammed.
1864	Sir John Lawrence is appointed the Governor General of India.
1867	The Clerkenwell explosion kills 13 people. Secret Service Department created to protect London against Fenian bombings.
1867	Army Reserve Act.
1868	International Telegraph Convention.
1869	Thomas Beach appointed Assistant Adjutant-General of the Fenians.
1870	Unification of Germany – Bismarck in power.
1870	Kitchener joins the Royal Engineers.
1872	The Cardwell reforms: regimental organization is restructured based on linked battalions – one serving at home and one abroad.
1873–4	Wolseley wins in the Ashanti War.
1873	Khiva is occupied by the Russian forces.
1874	Opening of Suez Canal.
1875	Fred Burnaby makes his *Ride to Khiva*.
1878	The Treaty of the Congress of Berlin signed by Britain, along with all major European powers.
1879	The defence of Rorke's Drift in Zululand.
1880	Baden-Powell at Maiwand. Starts taking interest in tracking.
1880–1	The first Boer War: Battle of Majuba Hill, 27 February.
1882	Wolseley in Egypt, Tel-El-Kebir. Arabi Pasha defeated.
1884	Baden-Powell publishes *Reconnaissance and Scouting*.
1884–5	The Berlin Conference: outlines the partition of Africa.

1885	The death of Charles Gordon (Gordon of Khartoum). A relief force failed to arrive in time to rescue him.
1887	James Monro takes over the 'Secret Department' in London. The Special Branch of the Metropolitan Police is created.
1887	The Imperial Federation League is founded.
1887	Charles Stewart Parnell accused of involvement in violence in rural Ireland, but after the discovery of a forgery, he is cleared.
1888	Conference on the free navigation of the Suez Canal.
1893	Major Henri le Caron's memoirs, *Twenty-Five Years in the Secret Service* published. His real identity of Thomas Beach becomes known soon afterwards.
1888	Baden-Powell as aide-de-camp to Sir Henry Smyth.
1888	Sydenham Memorandum.
1893	Percy Sykes sets off for Persia.
1895	The Jameson Raid.
1897	Baden-Powell on active service, scouting against the Matabele.
1897	Churchill and Bindon Blood at the Malakand Pass, Chitral.
1898	The Battle of Omdurman. Rudolf Slatin plays a major role as deputy to Reginald Wingate; Winston Churchill takes part as a member of the Fourth Hussars.
1898	Sir John Ardagh in charge of the Intelligence Branch.
1898	Lord Curzon becomes the Viceroy of India.
1899	Beginning of the Boer War. Wingate becomes Governor of the Sudan.
1899	Elgin Committee.
1900	Siege of Mafeking.
1900	Roberts sent to command in South Africa.
1900	Balloons used for scouting in South Africa.
1901	Rudyard Kipling's novel – *Kim* – published.

1900–2	Sidney Reilly (and his wife) almost certainly in London.
1900–5	Spenser Wilkinson writes on army reform.
1902	May, the last Boers surrender.
1903	Erskine Childers' *The Riddle of the Sand* published.
1903	War Office Reorganization Committee appointed. Intelligence Department merged into the General Staff.
1904	The Entente Cordial between Britain and France: a mutual agreement concerning assistance of a military nature, if required.
1904	Roger Casement influenced by the principles of the Gaelic League.
1905	The end of the 'forward policy' of the Tsarist regime: a peace treaty signed at Portsmouth, Virginia. Japan and Russia agree to evacuate Manchuria.
1907	Joseph Conrad's *The Secret Agent* published.
1907	Germany rejects any agreement concerning disarmament.
1909	Vernon Kell at work in the new Secret Service Bureau.
1909	An intelligence subcommittee called Committee of Imperial Defence is formed: James Edmonds suggests the formation of a secret office to combat the threat of German espionage.
1911	Official Secrets Act.
1914	Aliens Restriction Act.
1915	Sinking of the *Lusitania*, 7 May. Large-scale anti-alien riots in England.
1915	The writer, Somerset Maugham recruited into the Intelligence Department and is posted to Geneva.
1916	D H Lawrence and Frieda settle in Zennor, Cornwall. They were investigated as potential spies and finally ordered to leave in October 1917.

Bibliography and Sources

Note

Clearly, the following lists have to be selective and they represent only a fraction of the literature encompassing this subject. Most of the important manuscript sources I have taken through the previous work by writers who have completed monographs on their particular interests. Otherwise, there are a few of my own, taken up after conversations with specialists or sometimes looked at by chance, after the researcher's common experience of sheer serendipity. But there was never any need in a general history such as this to enquire closely into primary sources in some of the principal areas of investigation, as these questions have already been asked and answered. In most cases where primary sources have been important for the understanding of the course of events, they have been summarized by previous historians. I am indebted to the specialists who have made certain phases in the history of military intelligence very much their own field, and also, for different reasons, I pay my respects to the writers who have shown the way in how to write the meta-narrative of a time and also how to integrate the events on the battlefield or in a city street to the universal *Weltanschauung* of the time in question.

Anyone trying to bring together these elements of military history, national ideological changes and personal memoirs in the area of military intelligence will always owe a massive debt to the doyen - Peter Hopkirk. His readings and reflections always lead successive writers to the key central narratives of this theme.

There is an overlapping narrative also of police history, and in that sphere, the chroniclers of Scotland Yard and the CID have been an important source.

1.   Mss sources

Chelmsford Papers, National Army Museum, King's College, London, Liddell Hart Centre for Military Archives.
Hamilton Papers, OIOC records W6971, IOR l/MIL/15/1-4.
Mss notes from Col. Connillan, University of Hull.
Papers of Sir Alexander Bruce Tulloch, Gwent Record Office GB 0218 D460.
Pearson Papers, National Army Museum, London.
War Office Papers in the Public Record Office.

2.   Contemporary sources

Books

Aston, Sir George, *Secret Service*, Faber and Faber, London, 1930.
Briggs, Sir John Henry, *Naval Administrations 1827–1892*, Sampson Low, Marston and Company, London, 1897.
Burnaby, Frederick, *A Ride to Khiva*, edited and introduced by Hopkirk, Peter, OUP, Oxford, 1997.
Churchill, Winston, *My Early Life*, Collins, London, 1930.
Clausewitz, Carl von, *On War*, edited by Griffith, Tom, Wordsworth, London, 1832.
Duke, Joshua, *Recollections of the Kabul Campaign*, W H Allen, London, 1883.
Earl of Birkenhead, *Famous Trials*, Hutchinson, London, 1930.
Everitt, Nicholas, *British Secret Service During the Great War*, Hutchinson London, 1920.
Forbes, Archibald et al., *Battles of the Nineteenth Century*, Cassell, London, 1902.

Gordon, Major General C G, *The Journals*, Kegan Paul and Trench, London, 1885.

Hackford, F W, *The Life of Lord Kitchener*, Collins, London, 1902.

Humphries, Sir Travers, *A Book of Trials*, Pan, London, 1956.

Jackson, H C, *Osman Digna*, edited by Wingate, Reginald, Methuen, London, 1910.

Kingslake, Alexander, *Eothen*, Nelson, London, 1930.

Kipling, Rudyard, *Kim*, Cassell's Magazine, London, 1901.

Kipling, Rudyard, *Plain Tales from the Hills*, Thacker, Calcutta, 1889.

Le Caron, Major Henri, *Twenty-Five Years in The Secret Service*, Heinemann, London, 1893.

Le Queux, William, *The Invasion of 1910*, Eveleigh Nash, London, 1906.

McDonagh, Michael, *In London During the Great War*, Eyre and Spottiswoode, London, 1935.

Robertson, Sir William, *From Private to Field-Marshall*, Constable, London, 1921.

Russell, William Howard, *My Diary in India*, Routledge Warne, London, 1860.

Russell, William Howard, *Despatches from the Crimea*, edited by Bentley, Nicolas, Panther, London, 1970.

Steevens, G W, *With Kitchener to Khartoum*, Blackwood, Edinburgh, 1898.

Temple, Sir Richard, *Lord Lawrence*, Macmillan, London, 1889.

Trotter, Captain Lionel, *The Life of John Nicholson*, Nelson, London, 1904.

White, Arnold, *The Hidden Hand*, Grant Richards, London, 1917.

Wilkinson, H Spenser, *Thirty-Five Years 1874–1909*, Constable, London, 1933.

3. Secondary Sources

Books

(a) Reference

Beales, Derek, *From Castlereagh to Gladstone 1815–1885*, Nelson, London, 1969.

Browne, Douglas G, *The Rise of Scotland Yard*, Harrap, London, 1956.

Cannon, John, *Oxford Dictionary of British History*, OUP, Oxford, 2001.

Holmes, Richard (ed.), *The Oxford Companion to Military History*, OUP, Oxford, 2001.

Seth, Ronald, *Encyclopaedia of Espionage*, NEL, London, 1972.

Talbot-Booth, E C, *The British Army*, Sampson Low, London, 1937.

Townson, Duncan, *The New Penguin Dictionary of Modern History 1789–1945*, Penguin, London, 1995.

(b) General

Alexander, Michael, *The True Blue: The Life and Adventures of Colonel Fred Burnaby*, Rupert Hart-Davis, London, 1957.

Allen, Charles, *Duel in the Snow*, John Murray, London, 2004.

Allen, Charles, *Soldier Sahibs*, Abacus, London, 2000.

Andrew, Christopher, *Secret Service*, Sceptre, London, 1985.

Anonymous, *Fifty Amazing Secret Service Dramas*, Odhams Press, London, 1920.

Arthur, Max, *Symbol of Courage: The Men behind the Medal*, Pan, London, 2004.

Asher, Michael, *Khartoum: The Ultimate Imperial Adventure*, Penguin, London, 2005.

Barnett, Correlli, *Britain and Her Army*, Cassell, London, 1970.

Bassford, Christopher, *Clausewitz in English: The Reception of Clausewitz in Britain and America 1815–1945*, OUP, New York, 1994.

Baxter, Ian A, *Baxter's Guide: Biographical Sources in the India Office Records*, British Library, London, 2004.

Bayly, C A, *Indian Society and the Making of the British Empire*, CUP, Cambridge, 1988.

Boar, Roger & Blundell, Nigel, *Spies and Spymasters*, Octopus, London, 1984.

Boghardt, Thomas, *Spies of the Kaiser: German Covert Operations in Great Britain during the First World War Era*, Palgrave, Basingstoke, 2004.

Brendon, Piers, *Eminent Edwardians*, Penguin, London, 1979.

Brighton, Terry, *Hell Riders*, Penguin, London, 2005.

Campbell, Christie, *Fenian Fire: The British Government Plot to Assassinate Queen Victoria*, HarperCollins, London, 2002.

Charques, Richard, *The Twilight of Imperial Russia*, OUP, Oxford, 1958.

Cook, Andrew, *Ace of Spies: The True Story of Sidney Reilly*, Tempus, 2002.

Coulson, Major Thomas, *Mata Hari: Courtesan and Spy*, Hutchinson, London, 1939.

Cromb, James, *The Highland Brigade: Its Battles and its Heroes*, Eneas Mackay, Stirling, 1902.

Dash, Mike, *Thug: The True Story of India's Murderous Cult*, Granta, London, 2005.

David, Saul, *The Indian Mutiny*, Penguin, London, 2002.

David, Saul, *Military Blunders*, Robinson, London, 1997.

David, Saul, *Zulu: The Heroism and Tragedy of the Zulu War of 1879*, Penguin, London, 2005.

Davidson, Apollon & Filatova, Irina, *The Russians and the Anglo-Boer War*, Human and Rousseau, Cape Town, 1998.

Deacon, Richard, *British Secret Service*, Grafton, London, 1991.

Deacon, Richard, *A History of the Russian Secret Service*, Grafton, London, 1987.

Dowswell, Paul & Fleming, Fergus, *True Spy Stories*, Usborne, London, 2002.

Duckers, Peter, *The British-Indian Army 1860–1894*, Shire, Princes Risborough, 2003.

Edwardes, Michael, *Raj*, Pan, London, 1967.

Ferris, John Robert, *Intelligence and Strategy: Selected Essays*, Routledge, London, 2005.

Fishlock, Trevor, *Conquerors of Time*, John Murray, London, 2004.

Foot, M D R, *Secret Lives*, OUP, Oxford, 2002.

Fremont-Barnes, Gregory, *The Boer War 1899-1902*, Osprey, London, 2003.

French, Patrick, *Younghusband: The Last Great Imperial Adventurer*, Harper, 2004.

French, Yvonne, *News from the Past*, Gollancz, London, 1960.

Gall, Lothar, *Bismarck: The White Revolutionary*, Unwin Hyman, London, 1986.

Gooch, John, *The Plans of War: The General Staff and British Military Strategy 1900-1916*, Routledge, London, 1974.

Greaves, Adrian, *Rorke's Drift*, Cassell, London, 2002.

Haldane, Lord Richard, *Autobiography*, Hodder and Stoughton, London, 1929.

Hamilton, C I, *Anglo-French Naval Rivalry 1840-1870*, OUP, Oxford, 1993.

Harris, Stephen M, *British Military Intelligence in the Crimean War 1854-1856*, Frank Cass, London, 1999.

Haswell, Jock, *The British Army: A Concise History*, Thames and Hudson, 1975.

Hattersley, Roy, *The Edwardians*, Abacus, London, 2004.

Haythornthwaite, Philip J, *The Armies of Wellington*, Brockhampton Press, London, 1998.

Hayward, James, *Myths and Legends of the First World War*, Sutton, Stroud, 2002.

Herman, Michael, *Intelligence Power in Peace and War*, Royal Institute Of International Affairs, CUP, Cambridge, 2000.

Hernon, Ian, *Britain's Forgotten Wars: Colonial Campaigns of the 19th century*, Sutton, Stroud, 2003.

Holmes, Richard, *Sahib: The British Soldier in India*, HarperCollins, London, 2005.

Hopkirk, Peter, *The Great Game*, OUP, Oxford, 1977.

Hopkirk, Peter, *Foreign Devils on the Silk Road*, OUP, Oxford, 1980.

Hopkirk, Peter, *Quest for Kim: In search of Kipling's Great Game*, John Murray, London, 1996.

Hovell, Mark, *The Chartist Movement*, Manchester University Press, 1943.

Ind, Colonel Allison, *A History of Modern Espionage*, Hodder and Stoughton, London, 1963.

James, Lawrence, *Raj: The Making of British India*, Little Brown, London, 1997.

Jeal, Tim, *Baden-Powell*, Pimlico, London, 1991.

Jenkins, Roy, *Churchill*, Pan Books, London, 2001.

Johnson, Robert, *Spying for Empire: The Great Game in Central and South Asia, 1757-1947*, Greenhill Books, London, 2006.

Kayser, Jacques, *The Dreyfus Affair*, Heinemann, London, 1931.

Keay, John, *The Great Arc*, HarperCollins, London, 2000.

Keay, John, *The Honourable Company*, HarperCollins, London, 1993.

Keegan, John, *Intelligence in War: Knowledge of the Enemy from Napoleon to Al-Qaeda*, Pimlico, London, 2004.

Knight, Ian, *The National Army Museum Book of the Zulu War*, Pan Grand Strategy Series, London, 2003.

Laband, J P C (ed.), *Lord Chelmsford's Zululand Campaign 1878-1879*, Sutton, Stroud, 1994.

Laffin, John, *Tommy Atkins: The Story of the English Soldier*, Sutton, Stroud, 2004.

Lee, Stephen J, *Aspects of European History 1789-1980*, Methuen, London, 1982.

Lehmann, Joseph, *All Sir Garnet: A Life of Field-Marshall Lord Wolseley*, Jonathan Cape, 1964.

Marwick, Arthur, *The Deluge: British Society and the First World War*, Little Brown, Boston, 1960.

Madeira, Victor, 'No Wishful Thinking Allowed': Secret Service Committee and Intelligence Reform in Great Britain, 1919-23', *Intelligence and National Security*, Vol. 18, No. 1, Spring 2003, pp. 1-20.

Massie, Robert K, *Dreadnought: Britain, Germany and the Coming of the Great War*, Pimlico, London, 2004.

Morris, Donald R, *The Washing of the Spears*, Cape, London, 1965.

Morris, Jan, *Heaven's Command: An Imperial Progress*, Faber, London, 1998.

Moss, Alan and Skinner, Keith, *The Scotland Yard Files*, The National Archives, London, 2006.

Nasson, Bill, *Britannia's Empire*, Tempus, Stroud, 2004.

Nutting, Anthony, *Gordon: Martyr and Misfit*, Constable, 1966.

O'Brion, Leon, *Fenian Fever: An Anglo-American Dilemma*, Chatto and Windus, London, 1971.

Pakenham, Thomas, *The Boer War*, Abacus, London, 1992.

Panayi, Panikos, *The Enemy in Our Midst: Germans in Britain during the First World War*, Berg, Oxford, 1991.

Pollock, John, *Kitchener*, Constable, London, 1998.

Ponsonby, Arthur, *Falsehood in Wartime*, Allen and Unwin, London, 1928.

Porter, A N, *Atlas of British Overseas Expansion*, Routledge, 1991.

Preston, Adrian (ed.), *In Relief of Gordon: Lord Wolseley's Campaign Journal Of the Khartoum Relief Expedition 1884–5*, Hutchinson, London, 1967.

Punch Library, *Mr Punch on the Warpath*, Educational Book Co., London, 1909.

Proctor, Tammy M, *Female Intelligence: Women and Espionage in the First World War*, New York University Press, New York, 2003.

Rayner, Ed & Stapley, Ron, *Debunking History*, Sutton, Stroud, 2002.

Richelson, Jeffrey T, *A Century of Spies: Intelligence in the Twentieth Century*, OUP, Oxford, 1995.

Rimington, Stella, *Open Secret*, Hutchinson, London, 2001.

Royle, Trevor, *Crimea: The Great Crimean War 1854–1856*, Abacus, London, 2003.

Royle, Trevor, *War Report: The War Correspondent's View of Battle from the Crimea to the Falklands*, Mainstream Publishing, Worcester, 1987.

Singh, Simon, *The Code Book: The Secret History of Codes and Code-breaking*, Fourth Estate, London, 2000.

Spear, Percival, *A History of India Volume 2*, Penguin, London, 1965.

Stafford, David, *Churchill and the Secret Service*, John Murray, London, 1997.

Steiner, Zara S, *The Foreign Office and Foreign Policy*, CUP, New York, 1969.

Stevenson, David, *1914–1918: The History of the First World War*, Penguin, London, 2005.

Stewart, Jules, *Spying for the Raj: The Pundits and the Mapping of the Himalaya*, Sutton, Stroud, 2006.

Sweetman, John, *The Crimean War*, Osprey, London, 2001.

Taylor, A J P, *Essays in English History*, Penguin, London, 1976.

Taylor, Stephen, *Shaka's Children: A History of the Zulu People*, HarperCollins, London, 1995.

Teed, Peter & Clark, Michael, *Portraits and Documents: Later Nineteenth Century 1868–1919*, Hutchinson, London, 1969.

Thornton, Edward, *The History of the British Empire in India*, W H Allen, 1845.

Warwick, Peter, *The South African War*, Longman, London, 1980.

West, Nigel, *MI5*, Grafton, London, 1985.

White, R J, *Waterloo to Peterloo*, Penguin, London, 1957.

Wynn, Antony, *Persia in the Great Game – Sir Percy Sykes: Explorer, Consul, Soldier, Spy*, John Murray, London, 2003.

Young, Kenneth, *Arthur James Balfour*, G Bell, London, 1963.

Periodicals

A few of these publications have been used as general sources for background, but some of the less easily available ones include a few of the biographical materials I have drawn on, such as Current Science (the materials on George Everest and Jervis, for instance). But these are fragmentary and I have not listed them in detail.

The Atheneum, 1903.
Current Science.
The English Historical Review.
Historian: The Historical Association.
History: The Historical Association.
History Today.
History Workshop.
Intelligence and National Security, Frank Cass, London.
Irish Historical Studies.
Journal of Asian History.
Dolby, I E A (ed.), Journal of the Household Brigade, 1871.
Journal of Imperial and Commonwealth History, Routledge, London.
Journal of the Society for Army Historical Research, Spring 2006, Vol. 84, No. 337.
Military History, Leesburg, VA, USA.
Newark, Tim (ed.), Military Illustrated, London, April 2006, No. 215.
Punch.
Illustrated London News.
Social History.

Non-Book Materials

The Boer War, Eagle Rock Video, London, 2002.
South African Military History Society, Military History Journal online http:/
    rapidttp.com/milhist/vol103di.html
Codes and Ciphers in History: www.Smithsrisca.demon.co.uk
Oxford journals online: www.Oxfordjournals.org
SIB History: www.Lhooper/sib-history.htm
South Australians at War: Ned Kelly in Khaki. www.slsa.sa.gov.au/saatwar
The Times Digital Archive.

INDEX